✄ **W9-ASH-131**

PN   van Leunen, Mary-Claire.
146   A handbook for scholars.
.V36

89021621

GALVESTON COLLEGE
LEARNING RESOURCES
CENTER

DAVID GLENN HUNT
MEMORIAL LIBRARY
GALVESTON COLLEGE

GALVESTON COLLEGE

THIS IS A BORZOI BOOK
PUBLISHED BY ALFRED A. KNOPF, INC.

Copyright © 1978 by Mary-Claire van Leunen

All rights reserved under International and Pan-American Copyright Conventions. Published in the United States by Alfred A. Knopf, Inc., New York, and simultaneously in Canada by Random House of Canada Limited, Toronto. Distributed by Random House, Inc., New York.

Library of Congress Cataloging in Publication Data

van Leunen, Mary-Claire.   A handbook for scholars.

Includes index.
1. Authorship—Handbooks, manuals, etc.
I. Title.
PN146.V36   1978   808'.042   77–24436
ISBN 0–394–40904–3
ISBN 0–394–73395–9 pbk.

Manufactured in the United States of America

FIRST EDITION

Contents

A Handbook
for Scholars

Introduction

Scholarly writing is formal, accurate, and allusive. It has to be. It does not have to be wooden, finicking, and cabalistic. The idea of this book is to help you achieve the first set of characteristics without sinking into the second.

Let us not deceive ourselves. "There is no God but Allah" is a more gripping sentence than

> Mohammed (also Mahomet, Muhammad; 570?–632) asserted a doctrine of unqualified monotheism (suras 8, 22, 33–37, 89, 91, Koran).

By its very nature, scholarly prose lacks the rhetorical virtues of reckless passion. Custom and propriety hem the scholar in on every side. His obligation to his material and his obligation to his sources restrain him. He may not gloss over imperfections, smooth out irregularities, turn a blind eye to objections, no matter what good effects these temptations might offer in the way of clarity and simplicity.

On the other hand, the built-in limitations of scholarly prose are no excuse for bad writing. Bad scholarly prose results, as all bad prose does, from laziness and hurry and muddle. Good scholarly prose is probably even harder to produce than other kinds of good prose. All that means is that the scholar must work even harder at it.

This book will not tell you everything you need to know about scholarly writing. At most points it's no different from any other kind of writing. The scholar should aim at clarity and force and grace, but so should every writer. There are any number of books to help you with these aims. This book is about the mechanical problems that are specific to scholarly writing. I have tried to avoid overlap with general manuals of style except in the sections on quotation and on scholarly peculiarities. For help with punctuation, spelling, grammar, diction, style, organization, logic, and rhetoric, look elsewhere. For help with citations, quotations, footnotes, references, and reference lists you have come to the right place.

In order to focus on the points I wished to make with no distractions or irrelevancies I made up many of the examples in this book whole cloth. Others I wove together with threads of fact and fiction. Don't rush to your library for *Frontiers in Psychometrics* or *The House of Plantin* or *The Journal of Classical Philology*; they are inventions. Don't puzzle over the texts on chemistry and sociology and mathematics; they may mean nothing. I have tried to avoid plain silliness, but pastiche is a difficult art. I can only hope that real psychologists and historians, philologists and chemists, sociologists and mathematicians will enjoy any howlers and understand I meant no disrespect by them.

Two points of diction:
Throughout this book, for my own convenience, I have used "citation" as the name for the mention you make in your text of a source you are indebted to and "reference" as the name for the bibliographic item that appears in the list at the end of your text. The distinction does not exist in the language as a whole, and there is no reason for anyone else to observe it.

My expository style relies heavily on the exemplary singular, and the construction "everybody . . . his" therefore comes up frequently. This "his" is generic, not gendered. "His or her" becomes clumsy with repetition and suggests that "his" alone elsewhere is masculine, which it isn't. "Her" alone draws attention to itself and distracts from the topic at hand. "Their" solves the problem neatly but substitutes another. "Ter" is bolder than I am ready for. "One's" defeats the purpose of the construction, which is meant to be vivid and particular. "Its" is too harsh a joke. Rather than play hob with the language, we feminists might adopt the position of pitying men for being forced to share their pronouns around.

NOTE

Throughout this book, bad examples are marked with an arrowhead (▷). "Bad" often means bad in the context of the discussion, not absolutely evil.

THE TEXT

The four sections that follow take up the major mechanical issues scholars encounter in writing their texts: citation, quotation, footnotes, and a miscellany of small matters.

Problems with citation result from the scholar's unique responsibility to his sources. Essayists may pass on anybody's ideas as their own; penny-a-liners plagiarize with abandon; journalists go to jail rather than reveal the names of their informants. Not so the scholar. For him the open acknowledgment of where he got his stuff is at least a duty, and possibly a joy. You can observe the shift in each generation of undergraduates. At first they say "I think," and follow it with a mishmash of received ideas. But in a few weeks they've learned the ropes, and then you hear "Hegel thinks" and "Freud thinks" and "Aristotle thinks." We smile, but such habits are the stuff of scholarship.

Scholars and novelists share the need to quote extensively, but in different ways. I have ignored the creation of dialog and stuck to the matter of quoting from a source. In the first draft of this book, I tried to skirt the issue by sending readers to the standard guides, but I found them wanting. The conventions for quotation are outrageously complex, and someone had to spell them out.

The section on scholarly peculiarities takes up a group of questions related only by some relevance to scholarly writing. This section demonstrates the soapbox phenomenon. Given any slim excuse, 99.624 percent of all persons will sound off. Given no excuse at all, 99.608 percent of them will do so. I hope that you will have even a tenth of the pleasure in reading the section that I had in writing it.

But what about footnotes? How do footnotes come to be characteristic of scholarly prose? The rest of the world gets along without them very nicely, and they have seduced many a young scholar into writing so highly parenthetical as to be incoherent. I believe they date from the time when scholarship consisted mainly of biblical exegesis, with a little patristics and canon law thrown in. Scholars dealt with set and sacred texts, and they dealt with them reverently, pushing their own ideas off into the margins. Today, although the scholarly purview extends from cash flow to cough syrup, from color blindness to comic books, and few scholarly fields require the reverent explication of texts, the footnote habit lingers. Why? I think it's that soapbox phenomenon again. The footnote permits the scholar to say another word, just one other word, just one word more, before he has to stop.

To avoid confusion, I should mention that this book is arranged seductively, not chronologically. In real life, you do your research and collect your references first, then compile your reference list, and then write your text. There may be a good deal of backing and forthing along the way, but that's the over-all order. Here I've begun with the text because it's the goal for which the whole process is intended and because it's the most interesting part. You don't need to feel guilty about looking on your reference list as a chore; only a bibliographic maniac could care more about a list of sources than about his own ideas and his own words.

Citation

Scholarly writing is distinguished from all other kinds by its punctilious acknowledgment of sources. This acknowledgment is not just an empty form.

For the reader, citation opens the door to further information and to independent judgment. He can find more about your topic, fill in the background, catch up on what he's missed. He can also judge for himself the use you've put your sources to. Have you left a mitigating clause out of a quotation? Have you ignored the gerrymander of a data base? Have you misinterpreted a nuance? Have you misread a line? Have you failed to notice a qualification?

For the writer, these are frightening possibilities. Contrary to vulgar belief, the world of scholarship is no place for the timid. By disclosing freely and fully the origins of your thought, you may be putting a sword into your enemies' hands. If you can welcome that risk, it must be because your acuteness, your thoroughness, your scrupulosity have already, so to speak, beat the sword into a plowshare. Citation keeps you honest.

The documentary function of citation need not be carried to extremes. Young scholars have a tendency to overcite. "The variorum edition [6,19,38] cannot be used [2,12] to verify [8,28,31] this conjecture [2,8,28]." It comes out like a stutter. Still, this is a better fault than citing too little.

Citation relieves you of expository burdens in your writing. You needn't recover every piece of old territory that lies behind you before going on to the new. In theory, if your citations are honest, and your sources' citations are honest, and so on back, an assiduous reader should be able to trace every notion in your writing to its beginnings. If you abuse this evocative function of citation, your writing will become cryptic. If you keep it within sensible limits, citation can strengthen and simplify your expository line.

Citation can also strengthen your rhetoric. When you must stand alone in an opinion, so be it. But when you have allies, call them to your side by citing them. Again, you must not abuse the seconding function of citation. All too much scholarly disagreement degenerates to the level of "My advisor's bigger than your advisor." But within limits, citation can lend force to your arguments.

There is one last reason for every scholar to cite his sources. The greatest reward scholarship has to offer is the respect of one's peers. Citation is the courtesy of scholars. In the simplest way, the attribution says thank you to the source. Even a negative citation asserts that the source requires consideration. Every scholar remembers the pleasure of first finding himself cited in a stranger's work, and even the most blasé among the elders relish praise in the form of apt acknowledgments. The scholar who hopes to receive such praise will award it gladly.

For a student writing papers, it's hard to achieve the right frame of mind for citation. Your reader is no hazy construct of hopes and expectations; he's your teacher, a single, solid human being whom you know and who probably knows many of your sources at least as well as you do. In all student writing, there's an element of let's-pretend that you need in order to prepare yourself for the future. Pretend, then, that your instructor is the reader you will write for in your later life, the reader who will look to you for guidance. Write your citations for that reader.

The New Style of Citation

The chief reform this book recommends is the elimination of bibliographic information in footnotes. Content footnotes (like

the one below) still exist, but the bibliographic ones disappear.
Old style:

  ▷ Grandin's work on Lawrence[7] develops the themes of caste
     and untouchability.

---

    7. Jonathan Grandin. "Lawrence among the Philistines." *English*
    Letters XI(4):203–226, 1974.

At the back of the old-style text the bibliographic information
appeared again in an unnumbered reference list. In the new style,
the number is bracketed on the line instead of superscripted, and it
points to a numbered item on the reference list. New style:

    Grandin's work on Lawrence [12] develops the themes of
    caste and untouchability.

No bibliographic information appears at the bottom of the page.
The corresponding entry in the reference list appears only once,
no matter how many times the source is cited in the text:

    12] Jonathan Grandin.
       Lawrence among the Philistines.
       English Letters XI(4):203–226, 1974.

Embedding Citations

Doing away with bibliographic footnotes saves space, makes a
handsomer page, and avoids interrupting the reader's attention.
These are automatic benefits. A much greater benefit is possible,
but it will not come automatically. Abolishing bibliographic foot-

---

Bad examples are marked with an arrowhead (▷). I will repeat this notice
at the first bad example in each section for the benefit of the reader who
skips around. "Bad" often means bad in the context of the discussion, not
absolutely evil.

notes can help the scholar overcome some of the stylistic difficulties that footnotes encourage, but the process requires work.

Take a typical old-style citation:

▷ It has been argued[19] that the transformation of France into a cohesive state was accomplished by the Jacobins.

There's little value in merely making it new style:

▷ It has been argued [4] that the transformation of France into a cohesive state was accomplished by the Jacobins.

It's still as vague as ever. The writer who mechanically goes through his work transforming superscripted numbers into bracketed ones has missed the point. The new style is not just a tidying device. It is meant also to nudge the scholar toward making his writing more concrete and vivid. Without the excuse of a footnote below, the deficiencies of the sentence are glaring.

The primary change to make is to embed the citation—to add to the bracketed number enough information so that your reader can tell what you're talking about. Mentioning the author's name is the simplest form of embedding:

Butterfield [4] argues that the transformation of France into a cohesive state was accomplished by the Jacobins.

But again, embedding is not a mechanical process. The sentence as it now reads may be a rich, full, evocative citation in a paper on the Napoleonic period, where Butterfield is a household word; it may be utterly opaque in a paper on the modern French state or the origins of dictatorship or the effects of revolutionary democracy. Depending on the topic of the paper you are writing and the audience you hope to reach, any of the following embedded citations might be appropriate.

Herbert Butterfield [4] argues . . .

Herbert Butterfield [4], former Regius Professor at Cambridge University and an authority on modern European history, argues . . .

A modern historian, Herbert Butterfield [4], argues . . .

Butterfield argues in his little book on Napoleon [4] . . .

There is no easy formula. Take another example, starting with the old style:

▷ One student of the subject[44] identifies forms by syntax rather than morphology.

Changing this mechanically to the new style is clearly insufficient:

▷ One student of the subject [28] identifies . . .

Nor is it necessarily enough to write:

F. R. Palmer [28] identifies . . .

There are any number of ways to expand the sentence and any number of contexts in which it needs to be expanded. What are you getting at?

F. R. Palmer, writing in the distinguished Miami Linguistic Series [28], quite sensibly calls "better" a verb in the spoken sentence "You better go."

F. R. Palmer, one of Firth's more prominent epigones, outdoes even his mentor in extending the concept of predication beyond all recognition [28].

Much information and emotion was hidden behind those old-style superscripts; let it out into the open.

In general, you will find that you can improve your text by avoiding not only footnote references but the empty allusions that footnote references encouraged. The scholar has extraordinary opportunities for being compact and concise. He can rely on his audience to fill in reams of information at a mere hint. He can say "Halliday's versions of Scott" or "Watson on annuities" or "Lyman's life of Perry" or "Strassen's algorithm" and with the single phrase call up in his reader's mind whole articles and books and bodies of work, all the information in them, complicated lines of reasoning, attitudes and biases and strengths and failings.

With the opportunity for conciseness comes also an unparalleled opportunity for being obscure. The reader can take a hint and run with it, but he does need at least the hint. "It has been said" and "a scholar of the period asserts" are not enough. The scholarly writer who is too lazy or too snobbish or too insecure to spell out what he means can produce sentence after sentence, paragraph on paragraph of hot air. Then young scholars mistake the habit for "professionalism" or "playing the game" and carry it further still, as the review-of-the-literature section of almost every dissertation is at pains to demonstrate. "A specialist in the field" follows "according to some of the early researchers" and that follows "the argument has been made" with never so much as the name of a single human being in sight.

We all encounter scores of bad examples daily. Here are a few at random, with suggestions on how to improve them.

▷ The robust application[9] of Lipton's theorem unfortunately proves ineffective.[10]

Dobkin and Snyder [3] tried applying Lipton's theorem to each member of the lower-order matrices. They themselves later repudiated the results as absurd [4].

▷ Another interpretation[15] attributes a duality of purpose to Plato's characterization.

S. Ishima points out in his monograph on the Phaedrus that Plato has it both ways. He is both playful and rationalist in making Socrates pour cold water on his own words [9].

▷ A superior exposition can be found elsewhere.[22]

Hermione Mummson, who is a painter rather than a physiologist, produced a better outline of study in her book *The Human Frame* [18], which is unfortunately out of print.

In other words, scholarly writing, like all kinds of writing, improves as it becomes more concrete and less ethereal, more tangible and less abstract.

Embedding alone: If you can embed in your text all the information about a source that your reader needs, then you don't have to give him a bracketed number pointing to your reference list. For most sources, embedding alone would be unwieldy:

▷ R. M. Canter's *Game Breeding in Elizabethan England* (Routledge & Kegan Paul, 1958) describes the attempt of a Yorkshire cartel to introduce turkey-shooting to the British Isles (pages 441–452).

But there are a very few central sources for which short but thorough citations are possible. The Bible, Shakespeare, and the Greek and Latin classics have been worked over by generations of scholars, and we fall heir to their passion for numbering and counting.

John 6:41–58 so elaborates the image that even today we can feel the horror of it.

Another of his infrequent descriptions of infancy is in *The Two Gentlemen of Verona* I(2):55.

I am reminded of Catullus, who also loved and hated (*Carmina*, 85).

Embedding alone works only when you can be both complete and brief.

Brackets Alone

Now, having examined in such detail the case for embedding citations, let us consider the opposite. When do you want not to embed? When do you want simply to drop in a bracketed number and let it go at that?

Your citation is just a courtesy, a bob of the head toward the original discoverer of a result you are making use of:

Since the lower bounds approach zero magnitude [17], we can feel confident in setting our constant equal to zero as well.

You are citing too many sources to mention each one gracefully (or, as my mathematical friends say, the case of n citations where n is large):

Hugh Peters was probably the son of Thomas Dyckwoode, alias Peter or Peters [6,15,28,29,34].

You're trying to carry forward a narrative line without too much intrusion of scholarship:

Swiftly the men reloaded their guns and remounted their positions. "Bait their bluidy ayes oot," said Old Fain [3]. His companions licked their chops and fired.

You're giving so complete a summary that your reader never need look at the source. This comes up when you need the summary to round out your own exposition. It comes up when the source is difficult to get hold of or written in a foreign language. It also comes up when the source is so badly written that you summarize it to be sure your reader gets it straight.

There are three ways of forming phenanthrene—by passing the vapors of benzene and toluene, stilbene, dibenzyl, ortho-ditolyl, or coumarone through a red-hot tube; by distilling morphine with zinc dust; and (along with anthracene) by the action of sodium on ortho-brombenzyl bromide [22].

Notice in all these examples the wholehearted use of the brackets alone. What you want to avoid is half measures. Do not write

▷ Many authorities [6,15,28,29,34] agree that Hugh Peters was probably the son of Thomas Dyckwoode, alias Peter or Peters.

Do not write

> ▷ According to a research paper on the subject [22] there are three ways of forming phenanthrene.

If you have something to say about a source, spit it out; otherwise, let the bracketed numbers alone do the work. Betwixt and between lies flaccid writing.

No rule of thumb exists for when a citation is better embedded and when not. In making your decision you have to consider your material, you have to consider your source, and you have to consider your reader. What will help him understand what you mean? What will convince him to agree with you? What will interest him and give him pleasure?

Handling Bracketed Numbers

Placement: Tuck your bracketed numbers neatly inside the phrases they annotate:

> ▷ But it proved impossible to find a centrosome in some resting cells, like muscle cells, [6] and Maeton and Standish concluded that the organ might be formed anew at each cell division. [9]
>
> But it proved impossible to find a centrosome in some resting cells, like muscle cells [6], and Maeton and Standish concluded that the organ might be formed anew at each cell division [9].

On the larger question of just what to annotate, embedding your citation, saying a word or two about the source, insures against misinterpretation. Any of these is perfectly acceptable:

> Thomas Bland uses the word "plunder" in his *Annals of the Long Parliament* in talking about the Thirty Years' War [3].

Thomas Bland uses the word "plunder" in his *Annals of the Long Parliament* [3] in talking . . .

Thomas Bland uses the word "plunder" [3] in . . .

Thomas Bland [3] uses . . .

Citing with brackets alone can be trickier. You must be cautious about the possibility of accidental misattribution.

The annotation of the north mound manuscript [31] was obviously faulty.

The annotation of the north mound manuscript was obviously faulty [31].

Neither of these is necessarily wrong, but there's a world of difference between them. Embedding can save you from embarrassment:

Zeeman's annotation of the north mound manuscript was obviously faulty [31].

or Zeeman found some obvious faults in the annotation of the north mound manuscript [31].

Frequency: Try to avoid scattering your pages with bracketed numbers like buckshot. Use a bracketed number at the first mention of a source, or at the first mention after a long gap; use a bracketed number to point your reader to a specific page or passage when you must. But assume that he is of at least average intelligence, that he has a modest attention span, and that he is reading through your work in order, at least within each section, not skipping hither and thither. Young, inexperienced scholars tend to cite too much and too often. They are at their worst in comparative studies:

▷ Another tragic type is the faithful friend of the hero, like Horatio in *Hamlet* [18]; more often he is an outspoken critic of the tragic action, like Kent in *King Lear* [19] or Enobarbus in *Antony and Cleopatra* [17]. Horatio's role is supportive and reinforcing [18]. Kent and Enobarbus are more abrasive [19,17]. Hamlet and Lear each comment in their own way on the relationship [18,19].

Taking the word "another" as a clue about where this discussion falls in the exposition, we can guess that all of these bracketed numbers are unnecessary. Hypercitation is a funny and touching fault, and certainly a better one than failing to give credit where credit's due.

Clustering brackets: Group bracketed numbers whenever you can do so without causing confusion.

▷ Similar claims are made with a similar lack of conviction by Sparrowthwaite [29], Fanphman [5], and Hoolinan [18].

Similar claims are made with a similar lack of conviction by Sparrowthwaite, Fanphman, and Hoolinan [29,5,18].

Note that no spaces follow the commas that separate clustered numbers in brackets. It is a further refinement to cite your sources as they appear on your reference list (usually in alphabetical order) so that the bracketed numbers appear in numerical order:

Similar claims are made with a similar lack of conviction by Fanphman, Hoolinan, and Sparrowthwaite [5,18,29].

But it's hardly worth wasting your time on if they don't come out that way.

Embedding brackets: A bracketed number is just a pointer, not a word. Never, ever, use a bracketed number as if it were the name of an author or a work.

▷ [5] and [63] have turned their attention to less weighty matters of late.

▷ The elevated language of [19], the poetic sensibility of [7], the insight and vision of [22], the rapture of [36]—how thrilling a combination!

No brackets: When you're buying a typewriter, look for crisp, well-drawn brackets in a convenient location. But many students have no choice; they get their machines as gifts from unscholarly relatives or inherit ancient cast-iron castoffs. If you have no brackets, you may on student papers use parentheses around the numbers that point to your reference list:

        On 22 May he took command of the British
        forces occupying Germany (14).

On manuscripts to be set in type, draw the brackets in by hand:

        On 22 May he took command of the British
        forces occupying Germany [14].

Do not attempt to construct brackets out of other symbols on your typewriter. They will look dreadful, and no one will be able to make heads or tails of them.

There's nothing sacred about bracketed numbers, by the way. Superscripts would do just as well if readers didn't expect them to point to footnotes. The writer with a strong preference for superscripts may certainly use them if he informs his readers about what he's doing. It might make for a moment of awkwardness at the first occurrence:

This paper is a response to the plea Twiller issued to all Africanists in her introduction to *The Ghana Handbook*,[26]* that we start with what we sense and feel, not with what we think.

---

* The raised numbers in this paper point to the reference list at the end.

But after that there should be no difficulty. The reader will look at the reference list, see item 26, and grasp the system. It's sometimes hard, in using a book like this, to keep a sense of proportion about forms. Their only value—their *only* value—is in easing communication with your reader. When you're working hard to conform to a convention, it seems to be drawn in bold, black lines. But if you succeed, it becomes invisible for your reader precisely because it is conventional.

Pointing Citations

See: There is seldom any reason to tell your reader to "see" a source.

▷ See J. Thornton Green [27] for an explanation of several systems for transliterating Russian.

J. Thornton Green [27] explains several systems for transliterating Russian.

Any time that you can eliminate words without changing the sense or the force of a sentence, do so. "See" must of course never take a bracketed number as its object:

▷ B. P. Brown (see [1]) comments on Franklin's magpie mind.

B. P. Brown [1] comments on Franklin's magpie mind.

"Vide" is even worse than "see," being pompous as well as wordy. "Q.v." is worse yet.

Cf.: This abbreviation stands for the Latin *confer*, compare. It does not mean "see." If you're going to use it at all, reserve it for times when your source disagrees with you or arrives at your position by an entirely different line of reasoning. Even if you are an exceptionally fierce and cantankerous person, such occasions are rare; when they do occur, "cf." is seldom the best way to introduce them.

Here is a technically correct "cf.":

> Then $x_{ij} \equiv \{\Lambda_{ij} \mid 1 \leqq i \leqq j \leqq 3^n\}$, which is a contradiction. Cf. Zalcstein and Meyer [41] for the constructive proof.

In other words, the author has just completed the proof of a theorem by contradiction, and Zalcstein and Meyer have another proof of the same theorem by construction, an entirely different method. The "cf." is correct, but wordy. The author would do better to write simply

> Zalcstein and Meyer [41] give the constructive proof.

Here again is a technically correct use of the expression:

> Blessed Oliver made a good defense, but the jury convicted him of treason on absurd evidence (cf. Stratton [19]).

In other words, Stratton disagrees. Correct, but bloodless. Which version would you rather read, that one or this?

> Blessed Oliver made a good defense, but the jury convicted him of treason on absurd evidence. (Stratton, on the other hand, thinks that Blessed Oliver was guilty and the jury was quite fair, if a little enthusiastic, in having him hanged, drawn, and quartered [19].)

If you eliminate the wordy "cf." and the "cf." that is too mild, none will be left.

Reference: "Reference" is not a verb. At the least, you should correct it to "refer to."

▷ Reference Volka and James [31] for the origin of "bogus."

Refer to Volka and James [31] for the origin of "bogus."

But then "refer to" has all the flaws of "see" and should itself be eliminated from most sentences:

Volka and James [31] describe the origin of "bogus."

Ed. cit., loc. cit., op. cit., idem, ibid.: It would be a waste of time to explain the fine points of these expressions, because they should have no place in your writing. Even in the past, they were never common in text, although footnotes were riddled with them. In the new style of citation, they are extinct, and good riddance. Never should you catch yourself writing something like this:

▷ Grady, op. cit., suggests that the storax might serve as the Oriental counterpart to the linden.

If it's been some time since you gave a pointer to the Grady item on the reference list, repeat it:

Grady [8] suggests . . .

Otherwise, forget it:

Grady suggests that the storax might serve as the Oriental counterpart to the linden.

Tense in Citations

Is it "Schneider [42] says" or "Schneider [42] said"? Either. Just remember to stick by the tense you started out with, at least in the immediate vicinity.

▷ Y. Aharoni [2] gave other examples of the same motif on stamps of the period, which he dates by metallurgic development.

Y. Aharoni [2] gives other examples . . . which he dates . . .

or   Y. Aharoni [2] gave other examples . . . which he dated . . .

Citing Authors

Naming names: The first time you mention an author, call him by a name your audience can recognize. In an article on formal language theory, "Greibach" is sufficient for a first citation; in an article on current trends in mathematics, "Sheila Greibach" is a better choice. In case of uncertainty use for the first citation the full name the author uses to sign articles.

Be sure to respect his preference. You may know from private knowledge that behind the initials of "M. H. Peters" lies Mandrake Hannibal, but it's no business of yours to tell the world. Familiarity is equally out of place. "G. Kitson Clark" is the way to style the author you are citing even if he asks you to call him "Kitsy" over lunch.

With joint authors, the combination of last names is usually sufficient identification. "Hall and Lindzey" is in fact easier for a personality theorist to recognize than "Calvin S. Hall and Gardner Lindzey."

Once past the first mention, family name is sufficient unless you have the misfortune to be using two or more authors with the same family name.

Do I need to say that male and female authors are treated just alike? Apparently, since I just read an article in which C. Vann Woodward was consistently called "Woodward" and C. V. Wedgwood was consistently called "Cecily Wedgwood" or "Miss Wedgwood." A pox on false gentility.

Personal titles: The rule of thumb is that personal titles don't belong in scholarly citation. Why this should be so is hard to say.

The feeling may be something like: X's work is not worthy of citation because he holds position Y, he is worthy of holding position Y because his work is cited. Whatever its origin, this bias is so strong that citing "Professor So-and-so" or "Dr. So-and-so" is likely to be meant and taken as sarcasm. If you must mention credentials, bring them in after the name:

▷ Professor Harlan Cooke starts from a different angle [5].

Harlan Cooke, a professor of pathology at the University of Texas Medical School, starts from a different angle [5].

This feeling extends beyond academic titles and degrees to all titles. Only in writing about an institution should you call your sources by the titles they hold within that institution. Naval historians properly call their sources by their Navy rank, "Admiral So-and-so," "Lieutenant So-and-so." A student of church polity properly calls his sources by their ecclesiastical rank, "Father So-and-so, S.J.," "Archbishop So-and-so." But in using these sources for some other field, once again you dodge around their titles.

▷ Invaluable observations on dormancy and hibernation have now come to light in the diaries of Captain Edward M. Hayes, USN [16].

Invaluable observations on dormancy and hibernation have now come to light in the diaries of Edward M. Hayes, an officer in the United States Navy who was stationed in the Antarctic for eighteen months in 1935–36 [16].

Once past the first mention, family name is sufficient: Cooke, not Professor Cooke; Hayes, not Captain Hayes.

Nobles and royals are a special headache. We of humble birth are dim about sorting out their titles. How "John Emerich Edward Dalberg, Baron Acton of Aldenham" comes to be "Lord Acton" is mysterious to us. Why not "Dalberg" or "Aldenham" or "Sir John"? If you're citing such sources in their political and historical roles, you have your own knowledge, the practice of your colleagues, and the standard reference works to go by (Cokayne, Burke, and Debrett for England, the *Almanach de Gotha* for the Continent). But what in the world does the poor geometrician do

who finds himself citing a paper on oblate spheroids by "Adolf
Georg Meitmann, Schlechtgraf von Schwarzburg"? I take the
disgruntled egalitarian view that he never should have signed
himself that way to start with, culture-bound though I may be.
The gentle, conscientious geometrician who wishes to do so may
telephone the nearest German department to find out how one
styles Schlechtgrafen in the third-person singular. The geometrician
who shares my plebeian ill-temper will call the fellow "Meitmann"
and have done with it. To accommodate the reader who knows
more than I do, I'd spell out the full version on my reference list,
alphabetize it under "Meitmann" since that was what I called
him, and put a cross-reference at "Schwarzburg" and perhaps at
"Adolf" on a long list.

These strictures may be relaxed a little in talking about historical
sources. To the scholar immersed in his period, calling Samuel
Johnson "Dr. Johnson" comes naturally. Thomas More can come
out "More," "Sir Thomas," or "St. Thomas," depending on how
you think of him. But be cautious. Calling Abigail Adams "Mrs.
John Adams" is anachronistic; that version of the title wasn't yet
in use. And calling William Morris "Topsy" is likely to strike any
reader over the age of eight as cloying.

Et al.: Particularly in the sciences, collaborative research produces
papers with monstrous long strings of joint authors. In citing joint
work, name up to three authors. For four authors or more, give the
first author's name followed by the expression "et al." It stands
for the Latin *et alii* or *et aliae*, meaning "and others." Notice that
the "al." has a period after it and the "et" does not—it's treacher-
ously easy when you're writing quickly to do both the same way.
Use the expression only with the first author's name, not with
the first and second or the first, second, and third.

▷ Schultz, Eisenstat, Sherman, Lewis, Chandra, and Schreiber
   [23].

▷ Schultz, Eisenstat, Sherman, et al. [23].

▷ Schultz, Eisenstat, et al. [23].

   Schultz et al. [23].

Two papers of joint authorship with the same first author will come out looking the same:

▷ Etinham, Alworthy, Indermarch, and Spons [6] and Etinham, Abbot, Abbot, and Awhol [5].

▷ Etinham et al. [6] and Etinham et al. [5].

Etinham et al. [5,6].

Usually it's best to write in one language at a time and to search for native equivalents of foreign expressions. But for indicating joint authorship "et al." is preferable to "and others," which can too easily be taken to mean that other authors have written other papers on the topic at hand.

"& al." is just not the way it's done.

Spelling: From what I understand, spelling ability correlates with nothing—not with intelligence, not with verbal ability, not with age (after childhood), not with eye color, left-handedness, cyclothymia, blood type, structure boundedness, authoritarian impulses, sex, race, religion, national origin, or any other measure the testers can develop. Some people spell well, some people don't, and that's all there is to it. If by the time you're twelve or thirteen you don't spell well, you probably never will, and you should plan your life accordingly. I know what I'm talking about—I have already had to look up how to spell two words in this paragraph.

Spelling other people's names correctly is the most difficult task the poor speller can undertake. Undertake it he must, for the sake of his readers and his sources. The reader who goes to a card catalog to find "Philip Smith" is a long way off if the source's name is "Phillip Smithe." And as for Smithe himself, he's likely to hold it against you forever. The old newspaper joke about names is quite accurate. Print a piece that calls Simon T. Watchmere a bounder, a crook, and a drunkard, and he'll telephone to tell you there's no "t" in "Wachmere." People are irrational about their names; they know perfectly well that names are harder to spell than anything else, they may even spell other people's names incorrectly, but they expect you to get theirs right. Again, I am ashamed to say, I know what I'm talking about.

If you spell well, I envy you. If you spell poorly, here are some tricks to try: Take your bibliographic notes in block capitals. Go back and check the spelling of the names again, while you still have your source in front of you. Circle each verified spelling and write "stet" beside it. Check the spelling in your manuscript against the spelling in your notes—preferably aloud, enunciating each letter. Enlist if you can the help of a friend to check over the names once again. If you work with an editor, be frank about your difficulties. Knock on wood, keep your fingers crossed, and the best of luck to you.

Concord: Is it "Ullman and Aho [62] say" or "Ullman and Aho [62] says"? Either. The former stresses the authors, the latter stresses the work. Just don't change horses in midstream:

> ▷ Perls, Hefferline, and Goodman [35] has a tendency to ignore problems of resistance, and they are sometimes equally unrealistic in their belief that the therapist can withstand all temptation to manipulate.
>
> Perls, Hefferline, and Goodman [35] has a tendency . . . and it is sometimes equally unrealistic in its belief . . .
>
> or Perls, Hefferline, and Goodman [35] have a tendency . . . and they are sometimes equally unrealistic in their belief . . .

Citation with possessives: Form any singular possessive by adding apostrophe-"s" regardless of the root word.

> Peterson; Peterson's book.
>
> Manderewski; Manderewski's book.
>
> Minsky; Minsky's book.
>
> ▷ Charles; Charles' book.
>
> Charles; Charles's book.
>
> ▷ Patice; Patice' book.
>
> Patice; Patice's book.

▷ Labox; Labox' book.

Labox; Labox's book.

("Charles's" may be pronounced with only one final "z" sound and "Patice's" and "Labox's" with only one final "s" sound apiece by an interesting phenomenon called haplology.)

Form the possessive of an "s"-plural by adding an apostrophe. (This won't come up often.)

Sidney and Beatrice Webb; the Webbs; the Webbs' book.

Indicate joint possession by adding apostrophe-"s" to the last name in the series. Indicate multiple possession by adding apostrophe-"s" to each name in the series.

Mummson and Wilshire's books—the books they have written together.

Marriman's and Leander's books—some books by Marriman, some by Leander.

The double genitive is a correct construction required by English idiom that timid authors wrongly shy away from. Test the construction with a pronoun if you're in doubt.

▷ A book of G. Ernest Wright; a book of him.

A book of G. Ernest Wright's; a book of his.

Overlapping citations: Collapse overlapping citations when there's no particular reason for mentioning each one separately:

▷ Cannonito [3] and Cannonito and Gatterdam [4] have investigated the computability level of the word problem for various classes of groups.

Cannonito and Gatterdam [3,4] have investigated . . .

Citing characters: Attributing to an author the words of his fictional characters is sloppy scholarship, and rather hard on the author. Shakespeare is not retailing the advice on borrowing and lending he puts in Polonius's mouth; Dickens is not endorsing the solecisms he gives his lowlife characters to speak; quite the contrary. Always be sure there's no confusion in your reader's mind.

▷ "All journalists are dirty dogs," wrote Place [9].

"All journalists are dirty dogs," said Matty Small in Place's *Antics* [9], and we have reason to believe Place shared the sentiment.

Although you may sometimes see it, putting quotes around the names of fictional characters is neither necessary nor desirable:

▷ Ford Madox Ford's "Christopher Tietjens" may be the last hero in the history of the novel.

Ford Madox Ford's Christopher Tietjens may be the last hero in the history of the novel.

Citing Works

Books and non-books: In citing a work by title, you need to decide whether it's a book or a non-book. Since you usually do your research and compile your references before writing your text (I hope), I have put the long discussion of books versus non-books in the section on references (pages 164–166). Briefly, a book is a book or a journal; a fat thing bound by itself; or the equivalent in some other medium of a fat thing bound by itself. A non-book is an article or a story or a poem or a pamphlet; a thin thing or a thing that's part of something else; or the equivalent in some other medium of a thin thing or a thing that's part of something else. The long discussion goes into these distinctions in great detail. Just be sure to be consistent; don't punctuate a borderline work as a book in your text and as a non-book in your reference list.

Book titles in text: Use uppers-and-lowers punctuation (capitalize the first word, the first word after a colon, and all other words except articles and unstressed conjunctions and prepositions). Underline straight through, spaces as well as words, or use italics.

Kaman has an essay on the theater in Godfrey Halliwell's *The Arts Today* and a contribution in the memorial volume *Berlin Symphony: Portrait of an Orchestra* [6,14].

In your reference list, these titles will appear as

The Arts Today.
Berlin Symphony: Portrait of an Orchestra.

In a short, simple reference list, the underlines might be omitted, but they would never be omitted in the text.

Non-book titles in text: Use uppers-and-lowers punctuation (capitalize the first word, the first word after a colon, and all other words except articles and unstressed conjunctions and prepositions). Use quotation marks around the title.

He reaches the height of his powers in "A Drunk Man Looks at the Thistle" [17].

In your reference list, non-book titles will appear with sentence punctuation (capitalize the first word, the first word after a colon, and no other words except proper nouns and proper adjectives) and without quotation marks:

A drunk man looks at the thistle.

The layout of the reference list permits this pleasing representation, but in text both the quotation marks and the uppers-and-lowers punctuation are necessary.

If there's no way around it, use single quotes inside double quotes.

> Horn's "Threads in the Make-up of the Verb 'To Be' " [26] puts the case most convincingly.

Usually, however, a little cleverness can get you out of the situation:

> Horn's piece on the make-up of the verb "to be" [26] puts the case most convincingly.

Short titles and nicknames in text: Often in your text you'll want to use a short title for a work:

> Roseman's "Heating and Cooling in Igneous Rocks" [55] calculates the time elapsed from the outbreak of the magma to its cooling in terms of hours, not days.

Short titles never appear in your reference list:

> The effects of heating and cooling in igneous rocks of the Hassar region: A preliminary investigation.

Some works, especially journals, have nicknames you'll want to use in your text. They need neither underlines nor quotes:

> Seymour's blast at the phonics-mongers in JEEM [36] was greeted by a vast silence.

Nicknames never appear in your reference list:

> *The Journal of Elementary Educational Methods.*

Peeling off initial articles: To make your prose flow smoothly, you may want to peel off the initial article from a title you mention in your text. (Only in your text—titles on your reference list are never altered.) "The" can almost always be peeled off from the beginning of a title; "a" or "an" can be peeled off unless the title sounds like nonsense without it. Peeling off is optional with possessives:

> Prochaska's *The Functions of the Nervous System*; Funey's "An Inquiry into Metanephrosis."

or Prochaska's *Functions of the Nervous System*; Funey's "Inquiry into Metanephrosis."

To avoid doubling up on articles, use peeling off whenever you can:

▷ The revised "The Habitat of the Badger"; the well-known *A Man of the People*.

The revised "Habitat of the Badger"; the well-known *Man of the People*.

The article that you peel off is the one from inside the title, not the one from the surrounding sentence:

▷ "A" late "Housewife's Lament"; *The* famed *Attack of the Hussars*.

A late "Housewife's Lament"; the famed *Attack of the Hussars*.

When you can't peel off an initial article, you should at least consider using a construction that dodges the need to double up on articles:

The original "A Physician Speaks."

or The original version of "A Physician Speaks."

Pasting on initial articles: A pasted-on article belongs to the surrounding sentence, not to the title. This group of examples concerns a volume called *Larousse Gastronomique*:

▷ Try *The Larousse Gastronomique*.

▷ Try [T]*he Larousse Gastronomique*.

▷ Try [*The*] *Larousse Gastronomique*.

▷ Try The *Larousse Gastronomique*.

Try the *Larousse Gastronomique*.

Paste articles onto titles only in your text, never in your reference list.

Interpolation into titles: Resist the urge to add bracketed information to titles. It's usually newspaper titles that give people this itch; because they're published for local audiences, their titles often lack identifications that outsiders need. But a word or two solves the problem more gracefully than interpolating:

▷ *The* [*Milford, Connecticut*] *Day*.

The Day, published in Milford, Connecticut.

And it's especially important to avoid interpolation on your reference list, where it would spoil the alphabetical order:

▷ *The* [*Springton, Lincolnshire*] *Sun*.

The Sun (Springton, Lincolnshire).

Citing Yourself

Citing other papers of yours: Always use an embedded citation rather than brackets alone when you're citing your own work.

▷ Further examination of the epistle [2,3,5,6,8] shows that it could not have been written during the earlier part of the Roman captivity.

This looks unexceptionable till your reader checks the reference list and finds that you have written all five of the papers you are citing. Depending on the authorship of the papers, you should write something along the lines of the following examples:

> My research on the epistle [2,3,5,6,8] shows . . .
>
> The research Banton and I have done on the epistle [2,3, 5,6,8] shows . . .
>
> The research my colleagues and I have done on the epistle [2,3,5,6,8] shows . . .

Citing the current paper: Mention of another portion of the paper you are currently writing should be complete in the text, with no bracketed number pointing to the reference list:

> ▷ I attempt to demonstrate [9] that Pernambuco is a special case.

The reader who looks up reference [9] and finds that it points to chapter 6 of the very paper he is reading will be disconcerted. Try something along the lines of the following examples:

> I attempt to demonstrate later that . . .
>
> In chapter 6, I attempt to demonstrate that . . .

Consistency is a virtue in cross-citation. It doesn't matter whether you write "chapter 6" or "chapter six" or "Chapter 6" or "Chapter Six," just as long as you stick to one method through the course of any one paper.

"Above" and "below" are among the most common ways of doing cross-citation. Some people object to them because a statement cited as "above" may lie physically lower on the previous page than the citation does on the current page; this objection strikes me as silly.

Remember that "above" as an adjective falls in the appositive (following) rather than the attributive (preceding) position— "the lemma above," not "the above lemma." I never heard anyone try to say "the below lemma," but that's wrong too. "Above-mentioned" is a vile locution; "the stanza mentioned above" takes up no more space than "the above-mentioned stanza" and spares your reader's eardrums.

"Supra" and "infra" are obsolete ways of cross-citing and should be changed to "above" and "below." Consign "aforesaid" and "aforementioned" to the dustbin, where they belong.

Another common way to cross-cite is with tenses, a past or perfect tense for what came before, a future tense for what will follow. Do not ball yourself up with complicated tense structures:

▷ Having had in Section 3 and having in the current section the advantage of dealing with questions that have lent themselves to an art-historical perspective, we turn toward the end of this section and then shall turn increasingly in future sections to problems that have required recourse to physical evidence.

If you find yourself enmeshed in one of these, stop, take a deep breath, and start over:

The questions in Section 3 and so far in this section have lent themselves to an art-historical perspective. But from now on, many of the problems we turn to will require recourse to physical evidence.

Now for a warning: Be on your guard against abundant cross-citation.

One kind of excessive cross-citation, the compulsive summary, can simply be eliminated. There are the scholars who close each section of their work with summaries of what has gone before and what will come after:

▷ This chapter has dealt with the over-all structure of the German Stock Exchange. In the next chapter, the workings of the Berlin Börse, the principal market, will be examined in detail.

There are the scholars who open each section with a set of summaries:

> ▷ Having laid out the general make-up of the German Stock Exchange in the previous chapter, we turn our attention in this chapter to a detailed description of the principal market of that Exchange, the Berlin Börse.

And then there are the scholars who do both. After a while, the reader begins to feel that he's engaged in some terrifically hazardous but slow-motion enterprise, like something in a bad dream. Not all summaries should be eliminated, just the ones that come like clockwork.

But sometimes you may find yourself using a great number of cross-citations that you cannot merely cut. These usually indicate a fundamental error in your organization. If you need to say over and over, "Section 7 will cover this," "The details are in section 7," "Section 7 explains this more fully," maybe you should change section 7 to section 2. Organization is the most elusive of all problems in writing. We recognize badly organized material when other people produce it, but spotting our own failures is more difficult. Heavy cross-citing is one of the few hints you'll ever have to guide you; heed its warning.

What to call yourself: Some characteristic faults of scholarly writing result from authors' attempts never to call themselves anything at all. They seem to confuse objectivity with disembodiment. This misconception leads to the dangling participle:

> ▷ Comparing Sir Philip Sidney with his younger brother Robert, who in 1618 was created earl of Leicester, Philip seems to have been the more gifted.

It leads to excesses of the passive voice:

> ▷ It is then observed that the absorbed exudate can be found to be mainly excreted by the kidneys, and by the use of

standard techniques much nitrogen can be established to be present in the urine during this period.

It leads to the presumptuous "we" in a paper by a single author:

▷ We have assumed a cardinality no more than n to the set.

It leads to the coy (and sometimes misleading) sobriquet:

▷ Thus Thackeray comes like a breath of fresh air into the musty, draperied apartments of established wealth. The author must confess to some sympathy for the victims of the invasion.

It leads to the overuse of "one," making one's writing, if one were but aware of it, sound as if one were a character in a skit by Noël Coward. It frequently leads all round Robin Hood's barn:

▷ It is thus the considered position of the present author in relation to his previous work [9] as well as to that of others [3,17] that certain too hasty and perhaps too general assertions may in the past have been made by the aforementioned.

Welcoming "I, me, my, mine" to the scholarly vocabulary can at a single stroke improve thousands of sentences. Compare the last example with the following version, revised almost beyond recognition:

I now think that in my essay on imitative signs [9] I overstated the case for onomatopoeia, as Bainton and Morrow do also [3,17].

The same technique works with the Thackeray example:

Thus Thackeray comes like a breath of fresh air into the musty, draperied apartments of established wealth. I must confess to some sympathy for the victims of the invasion.

But the first-person singular is no panacea. The examples about Sir Philip Sidney and the kidney disorder cannot be fixed up by splicing in a few pronouns. What they need is a firmer narrative stance:

> Sir Philip Sidney seems to have been more gifted than his younger brother Robert, who in 1618 was created earl of Leicester.

> Then the kidneys excrete the exudate they absorbed, and the urine contains much nitrogen.

The point about narration is best made by revising the *n*-cardinality example:

▷ We have assumed a cardinality no more than n to the set.

The reader who comes across this in the midst of a difficult mathematical exposition is justified in thinking "We who? You and who else? I never made any such assumption." So you try again:

▷ I have assumed a cardinality no more than n to the set.

This is a definite improvement over dragging your reader along with you by the heels, but it's not enough. What you need to do is lay out the story:

> The proof works only if the set has a cardinality no more than n.

If novelists wrote like scholars, *Great Expectations* would begin:

▷ The family name of the current author's father being Pirrip, and the christian name of the former Philip, our infant tongue could make of both names nothing longer or more explicit than Pip. So one called oneself Pip, and Pip was adopted to be called by.

When you're part of your story, bring yourself in directly, not in a submerged and twisted way.

A *Tale of Two Cities* in scholarly style would begin:

▷ The statement can be made with regard to the times that they were the best; that they were the worst seems to this author an assertion of equal weight.

When you have nothing to do with your story, leave yourself out.

We: Each of the several varieties of "we" requires separate consideration.

The "we" that means "we the authors of a joint paper" is never objectionable. Just don't shove yourselves in where the story of your paper can be told more directly without you.

The "we" that means "I" is always objectionable except in monarchs, popes, and the front columns of *The New Yorker*.

The "we" that means "you and I, reader" is the tricky one. As long as your reader's going along with you, it's fine. But you can't suck him in against his will. "We see," "we observe," and "we notice" are therefore dangerous. The reader who doesn't see, doesn't observe, doesn't notice resents the pretense that he does. This "we" is just another version of the rhetorical error often found in "obviously" and "of course." Anything you label obvious had better be very obvious indeed, or your reader may think you're high-hatting him.

The "we" that means "everyone" or "all the world" is unobjectionable when what you assert is really common knowledge. "We do not know" is therefore always safe, while "we know" again runs the risk of cutting the reader to whom your statement comes as news.

Myself: "Myself" is an intensive or a reflexive:

I myself have no doubts about the accuracy of Griggs's account [12].

I found myself in the classic position of the pure theoretician with a rough-hewn, inelegant, but eminently practical solution before him.

It is not a softened form of "I" or "me":

▷ Travis, Ichikawa, and myself [17,18] turned to Littré's dictionary.

Travis, Ichikawa, and I [17,18] turned to Littré's dictionary.

▷ Olson was able to identify the spore-print for myself.

Olson was able to identify the spore-print for me.

Until you get used to it, the first-person singular may strike your ear as harsh and assertive; don't try to duck around it with "myself."

Irrelevant Citation

Citation versus acknowledgment: There are two ways to learn about a source you've never actually had your hands on; you can read about it, or you can be told about it. The first way requires a citation; the second requires an acknowledgment.

Say that you've never worked your way through Brennan on torts, but you're struck by an apt observation another author attributes to him. You may make use of the observation without recourse to the original:

But joint perpetrators are severally liable without the right to contribution from each other [19].

Your reference is to Brennan, but through the secondary source:

19] E. K. Brennan.
The Law of Torts.
Cited in L. Wallichensky, *The Victorian Courtroom*, page 179. Indiana University Press, 1961.

If Wallichensky has misinterpreted or misrepresented Brennan, the fault is his, not yours. And you have withstood the harried scholar's chief temptation, citing unseen sources.

Now suppose, once again, that you learn about the Brennan secondhand, but this time over coffee, or in a seminar. You may still make use of him, but you have no secondary source to cite:

▷ But joint perpetrators are severally liable without the right to contribution from each other [19].

What would your reference read?

▷ E. K. Brennan.
The Law of Torts.
Cited in a private communication by Arthur Hadley.

What you must do is embed a mention of Brennan and acknowledge Hadley:

But according to Brennan on torts, joint perpetrators are severally liable without the right to contribution from each other. (Arthur Hadley was kind enough to point this out to me.)

or But joint perpetrators are severally liable without the right to contribution from each other.*

———————

* My colleague Arthur Hadley tells me that E. K. Brennan enunciates this principle in his classic work on torts.

Of course, you can save yourself all this grief by looking it up in Brennan yourself. (You might still want to thank Hadley for telling you about it.)

Analogy: A telling analogy is one of the best teaching devices known to man. Do by all means help your reader to see your point by drawing comparisons from general knowledge, from natural science, from world literature. These comparisons should require no citations, since the whole point is to make your material more accessible and vivid by relating it to something your reader already knows.

> ▷ The hydrogen, helium, and oxygen atoms respond to this pressure in turn, like the three little pigs responding to pressure from the big bad wolf [9].

That bracketed number disperses much of the charm of the analogy—to say nothing of how odd a treasury of fairy tales looks on the reference list for a physics paper. Any comparison so obscure that it justifies citation will probably collapse under its own weight:

> ▷ The hydrogen, helium, and oxygen atoms respond to this pressure in turn, much as Trinkhilda, Stefan, and wee Dormhart responded to pressure from Baldograd the giant sea-monster in Welke's translation of the Finnish epic [41].

Citing axioms: Do not cite authority for the fundamental assumptions of your discipline, or for common knowledge. The chemist who gives a citation for the existence of tin, the historian who gives a citation for the fact of Lincoln's presidency, the grammarian who gives a citation for the conjugation of "to be"—they give a shaky impression.

Citations in Draft

Although by the time you begin to write you should have a fair idea of the contents of your reference list, there may be changes along the way. Numbering and renumbering and re-renumbering is no fun, to say nothing of the fertile ground it provides for error. The best system for handling citations in draft is to assign each item on your reference list a non-numeric code, to leave the brackets in your text empty, and to enter the code in the margin.

(Putting the code in the margin rather than in the brackets keeps you from missing brackets when you go back to enter the numbers on your final draft.)

```
           on special techniques for teaching
   Rex     literature under open admissions [ , ].
   SS&A    There is much more information about
           the
```

For what to do on final draft and final typescript, see the section on manuscript preparation.

Quotation

A Plea Against Quotation

Most young scholars overquote. Their motives are unimpeachable. Scrupulously honest by nature and by training, they want no credit for words not strictly and solely their own. As a result, they violate a basic rule of composition: Quote only the quotable. Quote for color; quote for evidence. Otherwise, don't quote.

When you are writing well, your sentences should join each other like rows of knitting, each sentence pulling up what went before it, each sentence supporting what comes after. (That's how I think knitting works.) Quotation introduces an alien pattern—someone else's diction, someone else's voice, someone else's links before and afterward. Even necessary quotations are difficult to knit smoothly into your structure. Overquotation will result in something more like a bird's nest than like fine handiwork.

It's easy to see how overquotation occurs. Picture the upright student who is looking at C. A. Beard's *The American Party Battle*. He finds the following sentence:

A very large number of Democrats voted the Republican ticket outright.

This is just the point he himself was interested in, and Beard is sufficient authority for it, so he writes:

> According to Beard [3], a very large number of Democrats voted the Republican ticket outright.

Now his conscience begins to trouble him. He has used Beard's exact words without quotation marks. Is this perfidy? He begins to tamper with the sentence:

> ▷ According to Beard [3], an exceedingly large amount of Democratic voting power was applied to the whole of the G.O.P. slate.

The wording is now distinct from Beard's. It is also repulsive. He tries to improve it:

> ▷ According to Beard [3], many Democrats voted . . . many Democrats placed their votes . . . a large number of members of the Democratic . . . votes from persons of the Democratic . . .

He despairs. Beard put the idea about as well as it can be put, he decides, so he writes:

> ▷ According to Beard [3], a "large number of Democrats voted the Republican ticket outright."

The trouble with this quotation is that it's a red herring for the reader, who has a right to expect that quotation will be reserved for color or evidence. He examines the quotation quizzically. Certainly it can't be color that the author was aiming at. Beard's words seem perfectly straightforward, with no special tang or flavor. So he concludes that the writer must be quoting for evidence.

Bad examples are marked with an arrowhead (▷).

Evidence of what? Since the statement seems otherwise unexceptionable, the author must disagree with it. (All this goes through the reader's mind in a fraction of a second.) Perhaps Beard asserts this Democratic switchover on insufficient grounds, he conjectures. Perhaps the author is quarreling with "large" and thinks the number of Democrats voting Republican was modest. Perhaps "outright" is the key word, and the author thinks that there was actually much soul-searching among Democratic voters. The reader's curiosity is aroused—and dashed to the ground. There was no reason for the quotation marks. He flicks aside his irritation and reads on.

This episode is over almost as soon as it has begun. No reader really articulates these hypotheses as he goes along; no reader pauses long enough. But the expectations are real, the disappointment, however slight, is real, and the reader's confidence in the writer is now a little shaken.

Pity the reader. (That's as good a rule for writing as you will find—pity the poor reader.) And have mercy on your fellow authors. It's hard enough to write something worth reading. No one should be under the perpetual requirement to make his every word worth repeating.

Quotation to avoid plagiarism: Most of us who went to American grade schools can remember long hours of copying articles out of encyclopedias. "The abode of the penguin is a hard and difficult one." It was called doing research. Then in college we found that it was also called plagiarism. This disjuncture is so common and so upsetting that plagiarism has become a bugbear. Of course you mustn't steal other people's words and present them as your own. But neither must you quote what's not quotable. Quote what is vivid or memorable or questionable, strange or witty. Paraphrase the rest.

If your paraphrase agrees with the original in a key word or group of words, you are right to examine it closely. Heaven knows, there are few sentences written that can't stand improvement. Try taking a fresh piece of paper and writing the same idea without looking at the original. (There would be less overquotation if people took notes in their own words instead of defacing books with yellow laundry markers.) Still no luck? Try jotting a cryptic note, "↑ Dems v. all Repub," letting a day pass, and then rewriting the sentence from your note.

I see that like most instructors I have an exaggerated idea of how much time a student can give to my pet topic—you may not have a day. Take it if you can; take ten minutes if that's all you have.

If after all this there is still some agreement between what you have written and the original, and if the original is really in no way striking, let your version go without quotation marks. The language is our common property. That two people should express the same simple idea similarly is not such a surprise.

Tags: Writers inherit not just words but phrases and sentences from the past. No one, I hope, would feel he had to put quotation marks around a word he learned from someone else. But there is a class of phrases and sentences called tags that are felt as operating on one level like quotations and on another level like part of the common language.

Putting quotation marks around tag phrases is pedantry; the reader already knows the words are not the author's own.

▷ To apply "a little learning" dangerously, let us attempt to fit a curve to these data.

▷ Turning, then, to "*arma virumque*," there is the question of Owen's military service.

▷ Haspel's description is perhaps a bit of "gild[ing] the lily."

His use of quotes reveals the first author as a pedant, but a mere garden-variety pedant. The second author is more notable for his conceit. Does he really fear that we believe him capable of lapsing into Latin, let alone the Latin of Virgil?

But the third author is my favorite. He seems to be trying for Pedant of the Year award with his quotation marks and brackets, and he succeeds only in making himself look silly. What Shake-

speare actually wrote was "to gild refined gold, to paint the lily."
I hasten to add that Pedant #3 should have written:

> Haspel's description is perhaps a bit of gilding the lily.

Not:

> ▷ Haspel's description is perhaps a bit of painting the lily.

And certainly not:

> ▷ Haspel's description is perhaps a bit of "paint[ing] the lily."

Correcting tags is the most arrant pedantry of all.

Quotation marks around full-sentence tags are inoffensive but confining. When the tag is identical to the quotation, use quotes or not, as you like:

> A strict application of Barrett's guidelines would produce classrooms of tiny Fascists. "The letter killeth, but the spirit giveth life."

or
> A strict application of Barrett's guidelines would produce classrooms of tiny Fascists. The letter killeth, but the spirit giveth life.

When the tag departs from the quotation, leave the quotes off and bend to the common wisdom:

> ▷ So the proof works after all. "I am escaped with the skin of my teeth."

> So the proof works after all. I have escaped by the skin of my teeth.

For a quotation that you feel is almost a tag but not quite, use no quotation marks and a loose citation like "in the words of X" or "as X says":

> But, as Oscar Wilde put it, a man cannot be too careful in the choice of his enemies.

No bracketed number, of course.

There was a time when a warning would have been needed against larding scholarly writing with endless biblical and classical tags, but today the practice has pretty well died out. Most scholars now use tags lightly and cleverly when they use them at all—go and do thou likewise.

Quotation on the rack: If you quote, quote whole. If you paraphrase, paraphrase. Don't combine the two. Don't tear quotations apart and leave them to suffer all crippled and broken.

> ▷ Albert Schweitzer [27] stressed the "one truth" that, according to him, "something spiritual" lies beneath "all that happens in world history."

Either quote:

> Albert Schweitzer [27] wrote, "One truth stands firm. All that happens in world history rests on something spiritual."

Or paraphrase:

> It was Albert Schweitzer's view [27] that some spiritual essence underlies world history.

Imaginary quotation: You can say hello without saying the word "hello." Ditto for say yes, say no, say boo, say good-bye, say when. These expressions can introduce a pleasantly colloquial note into scholarly writing if you don't ruin their flavor by mistaking them for quotations.

> ▷ Edward's favorite sport was saying "No" to his ministers.
>
> Edward's favorite sport was saying no to his ministers.

The author does not intend to indicate that Edward repeatedly spoke the word "no"; "say no" here means balk or thwart or deny or disappoint. Use the quotation marks only when you mean that the exact word was said.

> Edward looked at his minister coldly. "No," he said. "No, I think not."

Quotation to fill up space: Any serious young scholar will be scandalized at the idea, but there are students who quote because they don't know what to say. A friend of mine calls it Tarzaning, swinging from quoted vine to quoted vine with little but thin air between.

To some extent, the practice may result from taking assignments with deadly literalness. The instructor who assigns a twenty-page paper usually does not mean longer than nineteen pages and shorter than twenty-one; the length is a hint about what sort of response he expects, not a requirement. Obviously I can't speak for all teachers everywhere, but many would rather have three pages of your own writing undiluted than twenty sodden with quotations.

For those who are no longer students, padding with quotations has no excuse. One of the pleasures of adulthood is saying nothing when you have nothing to say.

A Plea for Quotation

I know of only one place where scholars consistently underquote, and that is in subjecting texts to close analysis. There are situations in which you can't quote the material you're analyzing because it's simply too long. But readers rightly loathe the author who fails to reproduce a verse or two, a sentence, a stanza, or a short paragraph for which he's offering a reading:

> ▷ The balance of fricatives and dentals, the susurrative alliteration achieved in part by anaphora, and the robust march of the open assonants make this quatrain a small jewel of English sound color.

Without the quatrain, the sentence is a small jewel of vagueness. The higher the ratio of analysis to original, the more pressing the obligation to quote.

Mathematicians building on previous work seldom think of needing to quote, but failure to restate a crucial result, whether exactly or in a paraphrase, can cause the same sort of fury in the reader.

It is true that most scholarly writing reaches only a tiny audience. There are papers that no more than a handful of readers will examine closely. The temptation to write private communications for those few readers is understandable. "It's hardly necessary to quote from the Hermotimus," thinks the scholar. "Anyone who reads a paper of mine must know his Lucian backwards and forwards." So he leaves a line unquoted and misses a chance for welcoming the unforeseen reader—the bright ninth-grader in Moline, the retired librarian in Manitoba.

Failure to quote is not the shameful crime that failure to cite is. The reader can dig out for himself what you should have given him. But you've turned a cold shoulder to newcomers, you've contributed another stone to the edifice of scholarly snobbishness, and you may have cheated yourself of an additional reader or two.

Quote whole: When you are quoting a text for analysis, quote it in reasonable pieces. Don't cut it to ribbons.

> ▷ "Their son having fallen sick" begins the story parallel to 1 Kings 14. "The old man sent his wife," unnamed, as Jeroboam's wife was, "with ten loaves," the same number as in Kings, "biscuits," a more familiar term than the King James "cracknels," "and a cruse"—here the clinching argument, for the word was obsolete in the United States by 1866 [36] —"of honey."

This is like a Sears, Roebuck catalog without the pictures. Your poor reader cannot be expected to piece a quotation together from little bits and snippets. Give it to him whole, even if you have to repeat to make your point:

> "Their son having fallen sick, the old man sent his wife with ten loaves, biscuits, and a cruse of honey." Right from the beginning, the story is parallel to 1 Kings 14. The wife is unnamed, as Jeroboam's wife was. She takes ten loaves, the same number as in Kings; biscuits, a more familiar term than the King James "cracknels"; and a cruse of honey. "Cruse" is the clincher, for the word was obsolete in the United States by 1866 [36].

Epigraphs

The epigraph is among the most delightful of scholarly habits. Donald Knuth's work on fundamental algorithms would be just as important if he hadn't begun with a quotation from Betty Crocker, but not so enjoyable. Part of the fun of an epigraph is turning a source to an unexpected use. Use a quotation from Isaiah, not for an article on biblical criticism, but for one on the Industrial Revolution:

> Neither shall there be any work for Egypt which the head or tail, branch or rush, may do.

Use a quotation from Mauriac's Monsieur Puybaraud, not for an article on French literature, but for one on educational reform:

> Get as many diplomas as you can, my boy. You don't need them now, but one never knows.

There's nothing wrong with using more expected sources for your epigraphs—Engels for the first one, say, and Dewey for the second. But most scholarly writing needs all the leavening it can get, and unlikely epigraphs help.

Quotation and Citation

All quotations except tags need embedded citations—a word or two about the source as well as a bracketed reference number if you haven't mentioned the source recently. This needn't lead to a dull progression of "he said," "she said," "he wrote," "she wrote." Just be sure your reader knows where the quotation comes from without having to flip back to your reference list.

Putting a bracketed number at the end of a quotation sometimes looks odd, although it is correct; putting it by the embedded citation is often more graceful.

> Melbourne then got off another shot. "Things have come to a pretty pass when religion is allowed to invade the sphere of private life" [7].

or Melbourne [7] then got off another shot. "Things have come to a pretty pass . . ."

Epigraphs, whether they come from expected or unexpected sources, require only brief embedded citations—no bibliographic information and no bracketed numbers.

▷ There should be no false shame about accepting odds, but there frequently is.
> —F. V. Morley.
> *My One Contribution to Chess.*
> George W. Stewart, New York, 1946.

▷ There should be no false shame about accepting odds, but there frequently is.
> —F. V. Morley [26].

There should be no false shame about accepting odds, but there frequently is.
> —F. V. Morley.

Even if the article for which this is an epigraph is about Frank Morley and contains thirty other references to *My One Contribution*, the epigraph is cited only with his name. And if the article is about probability and statistics, all the more reason to cite the epigraph by the author's name alone; don't clutter up your reference list with extraneous material.

Tags require no citations at all.

Inlaid versus Displayed Quotations

An inlaid quotation is set into your text. "Cauliflower is nothing but cabbage with a college education." That's an inlaid quotation (from Mark Twain). A displayed quotation is set off from your text.

> If once a man indulges himself in murder, very soon he comes to think little of robbing; and from robbing he comes next to drinking and sabbath-breaking, and from that to incivility and procrastination.

That's a displayed quotation (from Thomas De Quincey). How do you decide which to use?

Inlays are unobtrusive; they save paper; they save time for the typist or the compositor; and they are a little harder to read than displayed quotations. Displays are showy; they use up paper; they take extra time for the typist or the compositor; and they are a little easier to read than inlaid quotations. So, as a rule of thumb, display long quotations (over fifty words, over two sentences, over two lines of verse) and inlay short ones. Display hard quotations (heavy in symbols, heavy in non-Roman letters, heavy in small details) and inlay easy ones. Many of the displayed examples in this book show what I mean by small details; it would be unreasonable to ask a reader to sort out differences that often amount to no more than a comma without the aid of displays.

▷ Shaw's first version of Drinkwater's opening line went: "Yr naht best plaized t'baw hint'rhupted in yr bi o gawdnin baw th'lawk o mai, gavnuh." The standard edition reads: "Youre not best pleased to be hinterrapted in yr bit o gawdnin baw the lawk o me, gavner." So he did make concessions.

Shaw's first version of Drinkwater's opening line went:

Yr naht best plaized t'baw hint'rhupted in yr bi o gawdnin baw th'lawk o mai, gavnuh.

The standard edition reads:

Youre not best pleased to be hinterrapted in yr bit o gawdnin baw the lawk of me, gavner.

So he did make concessions.

The only rigid rule about display format is that your display indentation must be different from your paragraph indentation— visibly different, preferably about four typed characters or two ems. Otherwise, let your eye and your common sense guide you. Display indentation may be larger or smaller than paragraph indentation. You may leave a little extra space above and below a display. You may space a display more closely than your text; you may also use a smaller type size for display than for text. You may indent at the right margin as well as the left, or you may use the right margin of your text. Pick a style and stick to it for the length of any one article.

Epigraphs are always displayed, and they alone may depart from the display format that you choose for the rest of a piece. You might use a display indentation of three spaces in your text and one of twenty spaces for your epigraphs; you might center your epigraphs or (in printing but not in typing) set them flush right, things you would never do for displays in your text. Or you might follow your standard display format with the one exception that the citation for an epigraph is usually set to the right and below:

A great empire and little minds go ill together.

—Edmund Burke.

The dash before the citation is optional but useful.

Tags are always inlaid, never displayed.

Either inlay a quotation or display it—don't do half one and half the other.

> ▷ His audience knew what to expect. "I suppose," he read,
>
>   that the high-water mark of my youth in Columbus, Ohio, was the night the bed fell on my father.
>
> Already there was laughter.

This is a split quotation (one with the attribution in the middle), and all split quotations must be inlaid:

> His audience knew what to expect. "I suppose," he read, "that the high-water mark of my youth in Columbus, Ohio, was the night the bed fell on my father." Already there was laughter.

That means you may not split a quotation so long or so complicated that it requires display. If the quotation is not split, it may be either inlaid or displayed (probably inlaid in this case, because it's easy):

> His audience knew what to expect. He read, "I suppose that the high-water mark of my youth in Columbus, Ohio, was the night the bed fell on my father." Already there was laughter.

or   His audience knew what to expect. He read,

>   I suppose that the high-water mark of my youth in Columbus, Ohio, was the night the bed fell on my father.
>
> Already there was laughter.

Punctuating Quotations

In the United States, the mark of primary quotation is a small, high double scratch (") and the mark of quotation within quotation is a small, high single scratch ('); elsewhere the conventions are reversed. Don't worry about punctuating quotations within quotations within quotations; worry about avoiding them. Quotes come in pairs, one at the start of the quotation and one at the end; in checking over your work, be sure that all quotes are indeed paired off. In some typefaces there's a difference between open-quotes and close-quotes, which makes checking the pairs easier; peer even more closely when open-quotes and close-quotes look the same.

Inlaid quotations (except for tags) always require quotation marks:

▷ Kierkegaard had no high opinion of academics: One way is to suffer; the other is to become a professor of the fact that another suffered.

Kierkegaard had no high opinion of academics: "One way is to suffer; the other is to become a professor of the fact that another suffered."

With displayed quotations, the display itself usually takes the place of quotes:

Kierkegaard had no high opinion of academics:

One way is to suffer; the other is to become a professor of the fact that another suffered.

The exceptions are rare, but suppose that in one piece you were displaying both equations and quotations. Using two different display formats is madness; your pages will look terrible, and your readers will never figure out what's going on. So you might want to use quotes around the displayed quotations.

If you have occasion to put quotes around an entire display, set the open-quote to clear, one character to the left of the display:

▷ Stamper's advice [76] bears repeating:
   "The statistician who looks for a bell-curve anywhere in nature above the atomic level has failed to grasp the essential nature of his tools."

   Stamper's advice [76] bears repeating:
   "The statistician who looks for a bell-curve anywhere in nature above the atomic level has failed to grasp the essential nature of his tools."

This is such a tiny detail that you may have trouble even seeing it —in the bad example, the open-quote is set above the "n" in "nature"; in the good example, it's set off by itself. Setting to clear is one of the marks of professional copy. It comes up again in numbering the items in the display:

▷ Latrobe [41] suggests the following division:
   1. Inherent powers are enjoyed by the possessors of natural right.
   2. Derivative powers are received from another. They may come from authority or interest.

   Latrobe [41] suggests the following division:
   1. Inherent powers are enjoyed by the possessors of natural right.
   2. Derivative powers are received from another. They may come from authority or interest.

Partial clearing is helpful in quoting dialog:

▷ Then comes the famous exchange:
   Medvienko: Why is it that I always see you wearing black?
   Masha: I am in mourning for my life. I am unhappy.

▷ Then comes the famous exchange:

Medvienko: Why is it that I always see you wearing
black?
Masha: I am in mourning for my life. I am unhappy.

Then comes the famous exchange:

Medvienko: Why is it that I always see you wearing
black?
Masha: I am in mourning for my life. I am unhappy.

Final punctuation: Life would be easy if all quotations were full sentences and stood on their own:

For the origin of the argument we must go back to Tertullian [27]. "It is certain because it is impossible." No later formulation was ever so forceful or attractive.

The master of the art was Finley Peter Dunne [8].
Th' dead ar-re always pop'lar. I knowed a society wanst to vote a monyment to a man an' refuse to help his fam'ly, all in wan night.
For forty years Dunne set the standard of dialect transcription.

But, as luck would have it, most quotations fall within your own sentences, and punctuating them becomes a trouble.

When you intend to put a quotation within a sentence of your own, start by chopping off from the end of the quotation any mark of punctuation except a question mark, an exclamation mark, or a period of abbreviation. There are only nine possibilities. The item you intend to quote can end with one of the marks of punctuation that you let alone:

What cat's averse to fish?

Glorious style of weakness!

All his emotions were bound up in Standers, Inc.

It can end with one of the five marks you chop off (a sentence period, a comma, a semicolon, a colon, or a dash):

▷ But leave us still our old nobility.

But leave us still our old nobility

▷ Make me thy lyre,

Make me thy lyre

▷ Remember that the most beautiful things in the world are the most useless;

Remember that the most beautiful things in the world are the most useless

▷ Trust thou thy Love:

Trust thou thy Love

▷ Shovel them under and let me work—

Shovel them under and let me work

Or it can have no final punctuation, in which case you let it alone:

This translation became the standard for literary German

This is as good a time as any to look at quotation marks within your quotation. If the quotation is going to be displayed with no surrounding quotation marks, let internal double quotes alone:

Call the world if you please "The Vale of Soul-making"

If the whole quotation is going to be enclosed in quotes, demote internal double quotes to single quotes:

Call the world if you please 'The Vale of Soul-making'

Notice that in both cases the sentence period before the close-quote has disappeared. Only five marks can fall in that position:

the sentence period, the comma, the question mark, the exclamation mark, and the period of abbreviation. Toss out the sentence period and the comma; keep any of the other three.

Now you're ready to drop the quotation into your own sentence, with quotation marks around it if it's inlaid, usually with no quotation marks if it's displayed. Unless what follows immediately after the close-quote is a comma or a sentence period, your work is done:

> Shelley's "Make me thy lyre" is an echo of a line from Walter Savage Landor [19].

> What did his readers think when they read, "But leave us still our old nobility"?

> The question "What cat's averse to fish?" summed up his attitude toward women.

> "All his emotions were bound up in Standers, Inc."—and none of them in his family.

> Tossing off an elevated sentiment like "Call the world if you please 'The Vale of Soul-making'" with a shrug was all a part of his pose.

Listing every possibility would be a bore; you get the point. If, however, a comma or a sentence period comes right after the close-quote, you must not let it stand:

▷ We readily hear the alliteration in "Trust thou thy Love", but we need to listen again for the assonance.

▷ Ruskin wrote, "Remember that the most beautiful things in the world are the most useless".

"What's wrong with those?" I can hear an angry reader asking. "They're logical, aren't they? And consistent?" Yes, they are, and the convention of pushing the comma and the period into the quotation is illogical and inconsistent. But before you decide to adopt another system, think about a lifetime of niggling controversy with typists and printers. There are better things to fight about. Go ahead; push the comma and the period under the quotation marks; it's only a convention.

> We readily hear the alliteration in "Trust thou thy Love," but we need to listen again for the assonance.

> Ruskin wrote, "Remember that the most beautiful things in the world are the most useless."

If the mark you've pushed under finds no other mark, you've finished. If another mark is there, you have one more step to go. A period that finds another mark disappears:

▷ He wrote, "What cat's averse to fish?."

> He wrote, "What cat's averse to fish?"

▷ The only epitaph he wanted was "All his emotions were bound up in Standers, Inc.."

> The only epitaph he wanted was "All his emotions were bound up in Standers, Inc."

A comma that finds a period of abbreviation stays:

> The only epitaph he wanted was "All his emotions were bound up in Standers, Inc.," and he got it.

A comma that finds a question mark or an exclamation mark may stay or go; letting it stay looks a little old-fashioned:

> He wrote, "Glorious style of weakness!," and he meant it literally.

or He wrote, "Glorious style of weakness!" and he meant it literally.

Final punctuation summary: At first, the whole routine for the final punctuation of quotations may seem like a nightmare to you, but after a while it will become almost second nature. Then all you'll need is a summary for the tricky cases that come up seldom:

1. Chop off from the end of the quotation any mark of punctuation except a question mark, an exclamation mark, or a period of abbreviation.

2. For a quotation within your quotation, demote double quotes to single quotes unless you plan to display the whole quotation without quotation marks.

3. For a quotation within that falls at the end of your quotation, omit a final sentence period or comma; keep any other mark of final punctuation.

4. Now drop the quotation into your own sentence, with quotation marks around it if it's inlaid, usually with no quotation marks if it's displayed.

5. If a comma or a sentence period comes right after the close-quote, push it under the quotation mark into the quotation.

6. A pushed-under period that meets another mark of punctuation inside the quotation disappears.

7. A pushed-under comma that meets a period of abbreviation inside the quotation stays; one that meets some other mark may stay or go, preferably go.

You can even, if you like charts, generate a chart of all the possibilities. Pretend that the last word of the quotation is "Hawaii" or, to get in the period of abbreviation, "C.I.I." (for Chartered Insurance Institute). Let # stand for a space. Then there are nine ways the quotation can end:

ii?	ii;
ii!	ii:
I.I.	ii—
ii.	ii#
ii,	

Quotation within and at the end of your quotation adds another six possible endings:

ii."   ii!"
ii,"   I.I."
ii?"   ii"

Now for the surrounding sentence. Pretend that the first word after the quotation is "ooze." Then there are eight possibilities:

#oo   : oo
? Oo   —oo
! Oo   . Oo
; oo   , oo

With the options for the pushed-under commas, that makes 124 possible combinations. The thing is laid out in all its glory below.* If you don't like charts, don't even look at it, because it's a dilly.

	#oo	? Oo	! Oo	; oo
ii?	ii?" oo	ii?"? Oo	ii?"! Oo	ii?"; oo
ii!	ii!" oo	ii!"? Oo	ii!"! Oo	ii!"; oo
I.I.	I.I." oo	I.I."? Oo	I.I."! Oo	I.I."; oo
ii.	ii" oo	ii"? Oo	ii"! Oo	ii"; oo
ii,	ii" oo	ii"? Oo	ii"! Oo	ii"; oo
ii;	ii" oo	ii"? Oo	ii"! Oo	ii"; oo
ii:	ii" oo	ii"? Oo	ii"! Oo	ii"; oo
ii—	ii" oo	ii"? Oo	ii"! Oo	ii"; oo
ii#	ii" oo	ii"? Oo	ii"! Oo	ii"; oo
ii."	ii' " oo	ii' "? Oo	ii' "! Oo	ii' "; oo
ii,"	ii' " oo	ii' "? Oo	ii' "! Oo	ii' "; oo
ii?"	ii?' " oo	ii?' "? Oo	ii?' "! Oo	ii?' "; oo
ii!"	ii!' " oo	ii!' "? Oo	ii!' "! Oo	ii!' "; oo
I.I."	I.I.' " oo	I.I.' "? Oo	I.I.' "! Oo	I.I.' "; oo
ii"	ii' " oo	ii' "? Oo	ii' "! Oo	ii' "; oo

* The remaining half of the chart appears on the following page.

	: oo	—oo	. Oo	, oo
ii?	ii?": oo	ii?"—oo	ii?" Oo	ii?" oo / ii?," oo
ii!	ii!": oo	ii!"—oo	ii!" Oo	ii!" oo / ii!," oo
I.I.	I.I.": oo	I.I."—oo	I.I." Oo	I.I.," oo
ii.	ii": oo	ii"—oo	ii." Oo	ii," oo
ii,	ii": oo	ii"—oo	ii." Oo	ii," oo
ii;	ii": oo	ii"—oo	ii." Oo	ii," oo
ii:	ii": oo	ii"—oo	ii." Oo	ii," oo
ii—	ii": oo	ii"—oo	ii." Oo	ii," oo
ii #	ii": oo	ii"—oo	ii." Oo	ii," oo
ii."	ii' ": oo	ii' "—oo	ii.' " Oo	ii,' " oo
ii,"	ii' ": oo	ii' "—oo	ii.' " Oo	ii,' " oo
ii?"	ii?' ": oo	ii?' "—oo	ii?' " Oo	ii?' " oo / ii?,' " oo
ii!"	ii!' ": oo	ii!' "—oo	ii!' " Oo	ii!' " oo / ii!,' " oo
I.I."	I.I.' ": oo	I.I.' "—oo	I.I.' " Oo	I.I.,' " oo
ii"	ii' ": oo	ii' "—oo	ii.' " Oo	ii,' " oo

Dicey situations: If you follow through the steps given above, you will never make a technical error in punctuating the ends of your quotations. But you can produce technically correct hash. Questions within questions, for instance, are difficult for a reader to make sense of, no matter how accurately you punctuate them. Especially in scholarly prose, where most questions are rhetorical, try another construction.

▷ Is it then necessary to return to Morrison [8] merely in order to ask, "Where are the Merovingian remains today?"?

It seems unnecessary to return to Morrison [8] merely in order to ask, "Where are the Merovingian remains today?"

or Is it then necessary to return to Morrison [8] merely in order to ask where the Merovingian remains are today?

Some of the combinations are highly unlikely. For exclamation within exclamation, I can conjure up:

Blast your "Ouch!"!

But what would question within exclamation be like?

Blast your "Who?"!

It's difficult to think of any piece of scholarly writing in which such sentences might occur.

In theory, the rules about final punctuation apply to quotations of all lengths. In reality, quotations of more than one sentence should be worked around to end with sentence periods, question marks, or exclamation marks. This example is technically correct but ill-advised:

> ▷ I have puzzled over Johnson's "Subordination tends greatly to human happiness. Were we all upon an equality, we should have no other enjoyment than mere animal pleasure" in the light of what we know about his social habits.

Displays of whatever length should be made to end with sentence periods, question marks, or exclamation marks. The example is again technically correct, but irksome to look at:

> ▷ London [22] addressed his subject in no uncertain terms:
>
>   A scab is a two-legged animal with a corkscrew soul, a waterlogged brain, a combination backbone of jelly and glue
>
> and went on to compare strike-breakers unfavorably to Benedict Arnold and Judas Iscariot.

One last detail requires consideration. Some material will not stand up to the ordinary conventions for punctuating quotations. In most computer languages, for instance, there's a character, call it a dot, that looks just like a period but performs a computational function. There's a world of difference between these two APL expressions:

```
GJ∇ρα∩∈←◻○∪∈6 .
```

```
GJ∇ρα∩∈←◻○∪∈6
```

Any attempt to treat them as ordinary quotations courts disaster:

▷ At this point, the user types out, "$GJ\nabla\rho\alpha\cap\epsilon\leftarrow\square$OU$\epsilon$6."

▷ At this point, the user types out, "$GJ\nabla\rho\alpha\cap\epsilon\leftarrow\square$OU$\epsilon$6.."

First, use displays for such material. Second, work the expression that ends with a dot around so that it falls in the middle of a sentence; you can always do this by calling attention to the dot, and give your reader a helping hand at the same time:

At this point, the user types out,

$GJ\nabla\rho\alpha\cap\epsilon\leftarrow\square$OU$\epsilon$6.

(with a dot at the end).

Third, work the expression with no dot at the end around so that it falls at the end of a sentence; in this case, and only in this case, you may use the end of the display as if it were a sentence period:

At this point, the reader types out

$GJ\nabla\rho\alpha\cap\epsilon\leftarrow\square$OU$\epsilon$6

The computer should respond with a description of the set.

The problem might also come up in talking about punctuation; use the same solution. You can help your typist by writing "no period" in the margin; or your printer by writing "stet," which means let it stand.

Quote-cap: A quotation construed as a sentence, no matter how short, begins with a capital letter:

According to Jones [9], Freud said something along the line of "Nuts!" and went on his way.

A quotation construed as a fragment, no matter how long, begins with a lower-case letter (unless the fragment begins the sentence it lies within):

> During the interview, the subject said "waving the wiwwy pwetty once" for "wearing the really pretty ones."

> "Wearing the really pretty ones" came out "waving the wiwwy pwetty once."

A quotation mortised into a subordinate clause with an introductory word like "when" or "whether" is not to be construed as a full sentence. Among the introductory words that can cancel out a full sentence, "that" is the most common.

▷ Vanbrugh [26] said that "The want of a thing is perplexing enough, but the possession of it is intolerable."

Vanbrugh [26] said that "the want of a thing is perplexing . . ."

or Vanbrugh [26] said, "The want of a thing is perplexing . . ."

▷ Though "Slumber is more sweet than toil," he was famous for the long hours he worked.

Though "slumber is more sweet than toil," he was famous . . .

or Though he wrote, "Slumber is more sweet than toil," he was famous . . .

The first word of the first part of a split full-sentence quotation is capitalized; the first word of the second part is not (unless it's a proper noun or a proper adjective).

▷ "God is decreeing to begin some new and great period in His Church," he wrote, "Even to the reforming of the Reformation itself."

"God is decreeing to begin some new and great period in His Church," he wrote, "even to the reforming of the Reformation itself."

The comma-quote convention: Just to make life more difficult, there is a convention that requires a comma to separate any transitive verb analogous to "say" from a whole-sentence quotation that is its direct object.

Lamb [64] said, "Boys are capital fellows in their own way, among their mates; but they are unwholesome companions for grown people."

"Say" and "write" are at the head of the list to which the convention applies. Other candidates are: reply, respond, argue, declare, announce, remark, whisper, read. It's impossible to give a complete list, and perfect consistency, agreeable though it might be, is probably impossible as well. Don't lose any sleep over it. The scholarly writer will not, I hope, include in his list such words as "groan," "snort," "sigh," and "gasp." These words take only cognate objects ("sighed a sigh") except in vulgar fiction.

In standard order, the comma comes right after the verb:

Jonson [6] wrote, "Where it ends a former syllable it sounds longish."

A word or a phrase may intervene:

Graves wrote in his *Spiritual Quixote* [9], "Go to the tavern, and call for your bottle and your pipe and your Welsh rabbit."

In inverted order, the comma slides under the quotation marks (as you already know a comma should):

"Under our garb He took our nature," wrote Grosseteste [15].

In a split quotation there are two commas, one separating the verb from the part before, one separating it from the part after:

"Well ink," says Palmer, "is the plant V. Beccabunga."

The comma-quote convention applies only to full-sentence quotations:

▷ He writes, "a Mindy weeke" after every accounting, so we assume that Sunday was still thought of as the last day in the week.

He writes "a Mindy weeke" after . . .

The convention applies only to verbs, not to infinitives, participles, and gerunds:

▷ To say, "I think not" is all very well for the non-specialist.

To say "I think not" is . . .

▷ Writing, "Nothing may come of this" more than once in his diary [6], Cavendish nevertheless plunged ahead.

Writing "Nothing may come of this" more . . .

▷ Saying, "Dress and tonsure profit little" did not prevent his wearing a habit.

Saying "Dress and tonsure profit little" did . . .

And it requires a comma only between verb and quotation, not between the quotation and the rest of the sentence:

▷ Chaucer wrote, "Fare now well mine own sweet herte," during this period in his life.

Chaucer wrote, "Fare now well mine own sweet herte" during this period in his life.

The comma-quote convention is suspended for sentence quotations of one or two words, but only for those in normal order:

> She said "Bosh" to his arguments.

> "Bosh," she said to his arguments.

It is also suspended when you switch into the imperative, a rare occurrence in scholarly prose:

> Say "Nothing begets nothing" ten times aloud before looking at Elliott's metaphysics.

Colon-quote: Use a colon to introduce a quotation only at the end of a sentence. The following example may be technically correct, but it's hideous to look on:

▷ Motley [43] wrote: "As long as he lived, he was the guiding-star of a whole brave nation, and when he died the little children cried in the streets," immortalizing himself as well as William.

> Motley [43] immortalized himself as well as William when he wrote: "As long as he lived, he was the guiding-star of a whole brave nation, and when he died the little children cried in the streets."

Quoting Format

What do you do if your quotation crosses a paragraph boundary? Ignore it, unless the paragraphing has a strong impact on the quotation. If it has, display the paragraphs.

> Crayne's tirade continued unabated:

>> You are the most miserable excuse for a son any father ever felt shame over. You are scarcely human, scarcely an animal.

>> You are a stone.

What do you do if your quotation crosses a verse boundary? Use slashes to show the lines in short, inlaid quotations:

> It is difficult to believe that a major poet could write, "Pleasures newly found are sweet / When they lie about our feet."

Display the verses of longer quotations:

> The sickly greens at dinner were blamed on the local shop, and the "Song Against Grocers" [19] resulted:
>
> God made the wicked Grocer
> For a mystery and a sign,
> That men might shun the awful shop
> And go to inns to dine.

With complicated poems, you may be able only to approximate, but do the best you can to follow the format of the original. A copy of the original will be more help to a typist or a printer than your version; make a clean photocopy and insert it in your text.

As for other kinds of format, letterheads, titles, captions, headings, and such, display is seldom satisfactory:

▷ It was some time before Voltaire wrote again:

Aix-la-Chapelle

6 February 1770

My dear le Riche:

> The number of the wise will always be small. It is true that it has been largely increased, but it is nothing in comparison with the number of fools, and unfortunately they say that God always favors the heaviest battalions.

With a little caginess, you can avoid the problem:

It was the 6th of February 1770 before Voltaire wrote again to le Riche, from Aix-la-Chapelle:

The number of the wise . . .

Changes in Quotations

Changes you should not show: Occasionally a scrupulous fit will come over a young scholar and produce monstrosities of false conscience:

> ▷ Pater's description of art as ". . . proposing frankly to give nothing but the highest quality to your moments . . ." is now a commonplace. "[S]he has been dead many times, and learned the secrets of the grave . . ." no longer reads like a line of living prose, let alone poetry, and "[s]he is older than the rocks . . ." sounds older than the rocks itself.

Not one of these ellipses is needed. The ellipsis is for omission from the middle of a quotation, not from either end. Nor are the brackets around the upper-case and the lower-case "s" necessary. Bringing a quotation into conformity with the quote-cap convention does not constitute altering it, and bracketing such changes looks not punctilious but weird.

> Pater's description of art as "proposing frankly to give nothing but the highest quality to your moments" is now a commonplace. "She has been dead many times, and learned the secrets of the grave" no longer reads like a line of living prose, let alone poetry, and "she is older than the rocks" sounds older than the rocks itself.

In quoting titles, you will often need to alter capitalization and punctuation to fit your style; these changes too are conventional and need not be set off with brackets. Suppose that you're citing a journal that styles itself all in capital letters:

▷ *THE AMERICAN HERPETOLOGIST.*

▷ *T[he] A[merican] H[erpetologist].*

The American Herpetologist.

Pushing commas and periods onto the ends of quotations and demoting double quotes to single ones for quotation within quotation are two more conventional changes. Proceed blithely.

Omission: Show omission from the middle of a quotation with an ellipsis, jocularly known as a dot-dot-dot. These dots are periods. Do not space them out; do not position them above the line; do not substitute asterisks.

The ellipsis is an ugly mark of punctuation, and the conventions of ellipsis owe more to a recognition of this ugliness than to logic. Here is a passage (from John Wesley's journal) on which to practice ellipsis:

> Thence I rode to Cardiff, and found the society in as ruinous a condition as the castle. The same poison of Mysticism has well-nigh extinguished the last spark of life here also. I preached in the Town-hall, on "Now God commandeth all men every where to repent." There was a little shaking among the dry bones; possibly some of them may yet "come together and live."

Ellipsis from the middle of a sentence:

> The same poison . . . has well-nigh extinguished the last spark of life here also.
>
> `poison#...#has`

(Below each example, the typewriter spacing is shown with cross-hatches.) For ellipsis from the beginning of a sentence that falls

in the middle of your quotation, you may leave the first word of
the rest of the sentence lower-case or cap it:

> I preached in the Town-hall, on "Now God commandeth
> all men every where to repent." . . . possibly some of them
> may yet "come together and live."
>
> `repent."##...#possibly`

or I preached in the Town-hall, on "Now God commandeth
all men every where to repent." . . . Possibly some of them
may yet "come together and live."

> `repent."##...#Possibly`

Ellipsis from the end of a sentence that falls in the middle of
your quotation:

> I preached in the Town-hall . . . There was a little shaking
> among the dry bones; possibly some of them may yet
> "come together and live."
>
> `hall#...##There`

Logically, you might think that the omission of a whole sentence would look like this:

> ▷ Thence I rode to Cardiff, and found the society in as
> ruinous a condition as the castle. . . . I preached in the
> Town-hall, on "Now God commandeth all men every
> where to repent."
>
> ▷ `castle.##...##I`

Not so. The same three dots indicate an omission of any size:

> Thence I rode to Cardiff, and found the society in as
> ruinous a condition as the castle . . . I preached in the
> Town-hall, on "Now God commandeth all men every
> where to repent."
>
> `castle#...##I`

Using logic again, you might think that omission from the end of one sentence and the beginning of the next would look like this:

▷ I preached in the Town-hall . . . . . . possibly some of them may yet "come together and live."

▷ hall#...##...#possibly

Wrong again. Never double up on ellipses, no matter how much logic seems to demand it.

I preached in the Town-hall . . . possibly some of them may yet "come together and live."

hall#...##possibly

or I preached in the Town-hall . . . Possibly some of them may yet "come together and live."

hall#...##Possibly

Never use an ellipsis at the beginning of your quotation:

▷ Lewis [27] finds at the heart of comedy ". . . the observations of a thing behaving like a person."

Lewis [27] finds at the heart of comedy "the observations of a thing behaving like a person."

Use an ellipsis at the end of your quotation only to show breaking off mid-thought, where the ellipsis means "and so on":

The line is frequently rendered "In the sweat of thy brow shalt thou eat bread," but what we actually have in the King James is "In the sweat of thy face . . ."

Just in case you happen to see it some time and wonder about it, the ellipsis is sometimes used as a mark of final punctuation to indicate trailing off:

▷ If they only knew what madness lies behind this apparently normal mask . . .

But it's a shabby device and has no place in scholarly prose. Therefore the arrowhead.

An ellipsis may indicate that you've left out a word, a phrase, a sentence, or a paragraph, and there's no way for your reader to tell how much is gone. It's bad form to use an ellipsis for a large omission; stop the quotation and then start up again:

> ▷ Harman [14] writes in her memoirs, "The first charge against me was that of stinginess . . . I had discovered that distasteful food presented less hardship to the purse than delicious, well-cooked meals."
>
> Harman [14] writes in her memoirs, "The first charge against me was that of stinginess." She lends some weight to the charge when she boasts in a later chapter, "I had discovered that distasteful food presented less hardship to the purse than delicious, well-cooked meals."

The messy, imprecise conventions for ellipsis reinforce my contention that you should quote as little as you can to start with, and as whole as you can when you do quote. On the other hand, the judiciously placed ellipsis can make the difference between an apt, entertaining quotation and one that meanders off on its own track, ignoring the purpose you had in mind. Use ellipses to help knit quotations firmly into the fabric of your own prose, and only for that reason.

Alteration: Show alteration within a quotation by bracketing the material that is yours. Your contributions may be addenda, by way of explanation:

> Darwin then goes on, "I also crossed a bard with a spot [C. livia], which is a white bird with a red tail and red spot on the forehead, and which notoriously breeds very true."

They may also be substitutions. You may want to substitute a noun for a pronoun. In this example, the original reads "he":

According to Macaulay [22], "In order that [Frederick the Great] might rob a neighbor whom he had promised to defend, black men fought on the coast of Coromandel and red men scalped each other by the Great Lakes of North America."

You may sometimes want to alter the syntax of a quotation to fit in with the point you're trying to make. Here Edwards obviously referred to himself in the first person and in the present tense:

▷ Oliver Edwards told Dr. Johnson that he had "tried too in [his] time to be a philosopher: but [he didn't] know how, cheerfulness was always breaking in."

(The use of the brackets is technically correct, and the explanation for the arrowhead comes in a moment.) Another reason for substitution might be to replace an unfamiliar word or usage. Here the original reads "scumble":

▷ "This done," Dugdale says, "he did [soften] the offense with pretty words and wailings."

Finally, you may wish to get the author you're quoting out of hot water. Here the original used the coy sobriquet "Caledonians":

▷ We read in Chambers [6], "It appears that during these events the [Scots] had again become formidable."

Or again, Disraeli said "myself" here where the grammar of reflexives won't permit it:

▷ Disraeli then stepped back, according to observers [16], let his hands fall to his sides, and spoke very simply. "Lord Salisbury and [I] have brought you back peace—but a peace I hope with honor."

These uses for bracketed alterations appear in descending order of advisability. Adding an explanatory note is always acceptable, though a long one is better off in a sentence by itself:

> ▷ *The Missouri Monthly* [24] reports, "Grapes [from which wine is produced in Gasconade and other central and north-central counties] are grown in the Ozark region, and Missouri is second only to California in viticulture."

Question even simple substitutions. The Macaulay example seems blameless to me, but the Oliver Edwards quotation has been pointlessly mangled. The author reveals no overriding design of his own and should instead have written:

> Oliver Edwards told Dr. Johnson, "I have tried too in my time to be a philosopher: but I don't know how, cheerfulness was always breaking in."

More substantial changes are all the more questionable. The alteration of the Dugdale would be better handled as an addition than as a substitution:

> "This done," Dugdale says, "he did scumble [soften] the offense with pretty words and wailings."

The Chambers is no longer quotable once it's been sanitized, and should be paraphrased instead:

> We read in Chambers [6] that during these events the Scots regained their strength.

And the alteration of Disraeli's words is outrageous. "Myself" for "I" or "me" is an error, but an error of a particular kind. It indicates unsureness, timidity. Disraeli was a stylist; as anyone writing about him should know, he was perfectly capable of sacrificing grammar to rhetoric. What was it that made observers say he spoke simply? His manner, his posture, his tone of voice—

and that foxy "myself." The author who takes it upon himself to correct his betters is on mighty shaky ground.

At the risk of being repetitious: Quote seldom; quote whole.

Modernization: Quotations from old sources will be easier to read if you modernize difficult punctuation and spelling. The longer the quotation, the more help your reader can use; archaic spellings that seem colorful and charming in a brief quotation become fatiguing in a long one. The mere modernization of spelling and punctuation need not be shown with brackets; an explanation of your policy early in your text (perhaps in a footnote) covers all cases. Work with a light hand.

This is the moderate position on modernization. Two sterner views exist.

One argues against any modernization whatsoever, invoking the principle of unswerving fidelity to sources and the harsh demands of the scholarly calling. Writers of this persuasion are fond of reproducing photocopied documents for us to read, and the nastier the handwriting the better they like it.

The other view on the subject demands total modernization— no old-fashioned usages, even the ones that are amusing and easy to read; no outdated syntax; no obsolete vocabulary. Proponents of this cause argue that the original author saw nothing colorful in the mechanics of his writing, so neither should we. They regard antiquarian interests as prurient.

Steering between these two extremes requires taste and wit. Your readers will bless you for it. Take as an example a passage from Thomas Dallam's book about his visit to Turkey in 1599. Here is how the alter-nothing school would give it:

▷ Yow ar come hether wythe a presente from our gratious Quene, not to an ordinarie prince or kinge, but to a mightie monarke of the worle, but better had it bene for yow yf it had bene sente to any Christian prince, for then should yow have bene sure to have receaved for yor paines a greate rewarde; but yow muste consider what he is unto whom yow have broughte this ritche presente, a monarke but an infidell, and the grande Enemye to all Christians.

Even for his day, Dallam was a poor hand at spelling. Here is
how the alter-all school would give the same passage:

> ▷ You [have] come [here] with a present from our gracious
> Queen, not to an ordinary prince or king, but to a mighty
> monarch of the world. [It would have been better] for you
> if it had been sent to [a] Christian prince, for then . . . you
> [would] have been sure to [receive] for your pains a great
> reward. [Instead] you must consider what [kind of person]
> he is [to] whom you have brought this rich present—a
> monarch but an infidel, and the [foremost] enemy [of] all
> Christians.

Midway between the two is this version:

> You are come hither with a present from our gracious
> Queen, not to an ordinary prince or king, but to a mighty
> monarch of the world. But better had it been for you if it
> had been sent to any Christian prince, for then should you
> have been sure to have received for your pains a great
> reward. [Instead] you must consider what he is unto whom
> you have brought this rich present—a monarch but an
> infidel, and the grand Enemy to all Christians.

The object is to retain the flavor that makes the passage worth
quoting instead of paraphrasing, and to retain only the flavor, not
every gristly bite.

Americanization: Unfortunately for quoters, there are three small,
mechanical issues on which the United States parts company with
the rest of the English-speaking world. We have our way of
spelling a number of disputed words, our way of abbreviating
personal titles, our way of punctuating quotations; they have
theirs. Which way should you follow when you quote them?
Either, just as long as you're consistent.

Suppose you wish to quote the following passage, which illustrates all three differences:

> The kerbstone broker delivered up his judgement. 'Our organisation's not up to it, Mr Mawkers', he said sadly. 'It'd be an honour, but the answer's no.'

Here are the points to notice: kerbstone, judgement, single quote as the mark of primary quotation, organisation, Mr, comma outside the close-quote, honour. If you decide not to Americanize, you must Americanize nothing. The displayed version of the quotation will look exactly as it does above:

> Cranston depicts the scene with his customary gentle humor:

>> The kerbstone broker delivered up his judgement. 'Our organisation's not up to it, Mr Mawkers', he said sadly. 'It'd be an honour, but the answer's no.'

So will the inlaid version; it's a piece of good luck that we exactly reverse the conventions for single and double quotes:

> Cranston depicts the scene with his customary gentle humor: "The kerbstone broker delivered up his judgement. 'Our organisation's not up to it, Mr Mawkers', he said sadly. 'It'd be an honour, but the answer's no.' "

If, on the other hand, you decide to Americanize, you must Americanize everything except the titles of books and articles and any proper names in your quotation. The Centre for Industrialisation is so spelled even when you Americanize. The displayed version of the quotation will look like this:

> Cranston depicts the scene with his customary gentle humor:

>> The curbstone broker delivered up his judgment. "Our organization's not up to it, Mr. Mawkers," he said sadly. "It'd be an honor, but the answer's no."

Notice: curbstone, judgment, double quote as the mark of primary quotation, organization, Mr., comma inside the close-quote, honor. The inlaid version will look like this:

> Cranston depicts the scene with his customary gentle humor: "The curbstone broker delivered up his judgment. 'Our organization's not up to it, Mr. Mawkers,' he said sadly. 'It'd be an honor, but the answer's no.' "

Choose the method you find easier (neither is a breeze) and stick to it through the course of any one paper.

Correction: The simplest rule about correcting mistakes in quotation is to correct nothing. But as long as there are apples there will be worms, and sometimes you'd really like to quote something with a flaw in it. Consider your options: Is there some way to quote only the unmarred portion? If the mistake is important, shouldn't you be paraphrasing instead of quoting? If it's not that important, couldn't you just let it go uncorrected? Only after rejecting these other possibilities should you substitute your correction in brackets for the original error.

Here, for instance, the author is quoting a line for its singularity; the original exists in one edition only, so variant readings are impossible; the mistake was "thsi," almost certainly a typographical error; and the woman who wrote the line is dead, which puts her beyond the reach of requests for verification:

> How many people today know Realow's mournful, resonant line "Revolving, revaluing, we resolve [this] revelation"?

Even at that, you should probably add a sentence about what you changed and why.

Sic: "Sic" is Latin for "thus." Enclosed in brackets, it is inserted into a quotation after a questionable expression to assure the doubtful reader of its accuracy:

Sperling's daughter wrote an affectionate note to him after his appointment: "You old crumudgeon [sic], give 'em 'ell," she said, and went on to point out such practical details as the new wardrobe that the tropical climate would necessitate.

"Crumudgeon," a small family joke, supports the author's assertion of affection; without the "sic" his reader might assume the word was a typo. This is an unsneering use of "sic."

In general, however, the expression is both condescending and hostile. To correct an error in a quotation is merely condescending; to leave it in and sic it is an attack. Be warned, and do not take up arms unknowingly. Avoid using "sic" just to show how precise and knowledgeable you are, and above all make sure that the error you point out is really wrong.

> He who sics the blameless phrase
> Hoping he will gather praise
> Makes himself a double fool,
> Wrong and pompous. Mind the rule:
> Sic less, and you won't be sorrier;
> Sic more, and *sic transit gloria.*

If on consideration you choose to slip the gimlet "sic" between the ribs of your enemy's words, go to it. Serious quarrel in high style is one of the joys of the scholarly life.

Italics mine: One way to fit a quotation to your purposes is to emphasize the part you're most interested in by putting it in italics or underlining it. You must then show that the emphasis is yours by inserting "italics mine" in brackets at the end of the quotation. Use the expression for both italics and underlining; everyone recognizes the two as interchangeable. That's how to do it; but don't.

Go easy on italics everywhere. They have a thoughtless air about them, an "Oh, I can't be bothered to rework this, I'll just italicize it and let you figure it out." They are ugly to look at and difficult to read. They lend themselves easily to abuse, to attempts at wrenching stress from syntax that won't permit it. These are reasons for questioning any old italics, and adding italics to quotations has other dangers as well. Almost always, you should be paraphrasing or quoting only the part that interests you. If a pious respect for other writers' words doesn't persuade you, consider the possibilities for unconscious humor:

> ▷ As late as Hazlitt's time it was still possible for him to write, "You will hear more good things on the outside of *a stage-coach from London to Oxford* than if you were to pass a twelvemonth with the undergraduates, or heads of colleges, of that famous university [italics mine]." So little had the science of equine management advanced that the journey was likely to be made in a single run; the practice was still common of driving horses out to their limit, and eventually to the grave.

The author who unwittingly reveals that Hazlitt's words are no more to him than data for a history of animal husbandry must forgive us if we smile at him. We are all fanatics about our subjects, but we should try to keep fanaticism in check:

> As late as 1810 it was still possible to take a stagecoach from London to Oxford [15]. So little had the science . . .

Changes in epigraphs: Choose as epigraphs quotations that require no omission or alteration. An epigraph is a cheerful little kite flying over the solid earth of your prose. Don't weigh it down with ellipses and brackets.

No brackets: Even on student papers, parentheses may not be used for indicating interpolations into quoted matter. If your typewriter has no brackets, draw them in by hand:

```
Mill believed that "advice, instruction,
persuasion, and avoidance by other people
```

```
 ... are the only measures by which society
can justifiably express its dislike or dis-
approbation of [an individual's] con-
duct."
```

Permission to Quote

If you hope to publish material that contains a quotation of more than five words of poetry or fifty words of prose from a published source under copyright or a quotation of any length from an unpublished source, you had better start getting permission as soon as possible.

For copyrighted material, send the publisher a precise description of the source, including the edition, the page numbers, and the exact words you hope to use. Tell what use you intend to make of the quotation—the easiest way to do this is to send along a copy of the relevant section of your draft. And describe the circumstances under which you hope to publish, what journals or publishers you're submitting to, and what payment (if any) you can expect.

Permission to quote from unpublished material is a matter for negotiation, diplomacy, and sometimes law. If you run into difficulty, seek advice from your publisher or from some older, cooler head with experience in your field.

Be aware that most publishers and journals consider getting permission to quote the author's responsibility. A manuscript with many quotations and no permissions may be rejected just because it's too much of a headache to contemplate all the negotiations that would be necessary to publish it.

What happens if you're denied permission to quote, or granted it only on payment of a prohibitive fee? If the quotation was not crucial to your exposition, forget it. Otherwise, give an unusually precise embedded citation and add to it the information about why you cannot quote. You can be safe in assuming that your reader will immediately seek out the passage you had hoped to quote. In fact, now your worry is that the passage will be given undue weight, which is why you shouldn't use this device for unimportant quotations.

One of the conditions of permission is usually that you send a copy of your work to the publisher. Under any circumstances, it's always a pleasant gesture to send a copy to the author from whom you've quoted.

Other Uses for Quotation Marks

Despite their name, quotation marks have other uses besides marking off quotations, which it seems wise to describe briefly for the sake of completeness.

Quotes and italics are interchangeable for setting off words considered as words:

The "rack" of "rack and ruin" is like "wreck."

Italics are preferable to quotation marks for lists of such words. Sometimes you can avoid them both because of the way you construct your sentence. The object is to save your reader from any slight confusion; when no confusion is possible, no quotes or italics are needed.

▷ The infant's first ten words, in order of acquisition, were: "mama," "juice," "airplane," "Jane," "noisy," "kitty," "cracker," "bad," "fan," and "stink."

The infant's first ten words, in order of acquisition, were: mama, juice, airplane, Jane, noisy, kitty, cracker, bad, fan, and stink.

Quotes may set off the first occurrence of an unfamiliar word or expression when a definition follows at some distance:

Tukey's technique is to "slash" the outlying numbers—to subtract from the positive outliers or add to the negative ones the mean value of the set.

Do not set off the word with quotes after the first occurrence. No quotes are needed when the definition comes immediately after the unfamiliar word:

> Blaney suffered from hidrosis, excessive sweating, which the doctors of the time thought of as a fatal sign.

Quotation marks and expressions like "so-called" and "alleged" are interchangeable (not overlapping) for setting off words used with ironic force:

> Then these "morons" suddenly became able to read and write, to calculate, and to take up school subjects. One of them later became a teacher herself.

Finally, you may see in other people's writing quotation marks used to set off colloquialisms—in other people's writing but not yours. If you use a word, use it wholeheartedly. Don't condescend to it. If it's not a good word, find another.

> ▷ Charles showed a marked tendency to "fly off the handle" in these crises.

Why pass on to your reader an expression you feel you have to handle like a dead fish?

> Charles showed a marked tendency to get excited in these crises.

> or Charles showed a marked tendency to fly off the handle in these crises.

In all of these uses, quotation marks follow the standard patterns for fitting in with the punctuation of the surrounding sentence. Periods and commas slide under the close-quotes, other marks stay outside.

Quotations in Draft

Repeated copying of quotations invites errors. If you can, hold off
on transcribing a quotation until you're doing your final draft, and
then copy it straight from the original. All you need in previous
drafts is a reminder about what you intend to quote. A note
to yourself in the margin will keep you from missing a quotation
that needs to be filled in; I use a pair of quotation marks for this
purpose, but any old thing will do.

```
       sent a note to Browning about her
""     reactions. "-sweet tooth-" He read the
       note aloud at parties to show how little
```

If the material you're quoting is very difficult, you may want to
make a photocopy and use that in your final draft instead of
attempting to transcribe it.

The Footnote

Although the new way of doing citation and reference jettisons the bibliographic footnote, the content footnote is another story. When you hear the comment "The best part was the footnotes," you can be sure that doesn't mean the ibids and op. cits.

The content footnote can be abused, of course. There are scholars who footnote compulsively, six to the page, writing what amounts to two books at once. There are scholars whose frigid texts need some of the warmth and jollity they reserve for their footnotes and other scholars who write stale, dull footnotes like the stories brought inevitably to the minds of after-dinner speakers. There are scholars who write weasel footnotes, footnotes that alter the assertions in their texts. There are scholars who write feckless, irrelevant footnotes that leave their readers dumbstruck with confusion.

The footnote should never be your first choice for expressing an idea. Integration is a powerful virtue in prose—"seamless masterpiece" didn't get to be a cliché for nothing. Never footnote without first asking yourself whether a little more skill and a little more foresight might not make it possible to work the idea into your text.

On the other hand, vitality is a greater virtue than unity any day. The footnote is an awkward tool, inelegant, all thumbs, but it has the breath of life to it. In many contexts the appearance of a footnote parallels the moment when we draw our chairs closer to a speaker and bend forward: Now we're getting to the good stuff, now we're getting to the heart of it. Clumsy and halting though

footnotes undoubtedly are, they've given us too much enlightenment and pleasure for us to turn our backs on them now. By
using footnotes judiciously you can fill your reader in on general
information he lacks, satisfy his curiosity about fine points, whisper
delicious tidbits in his ear, and share with him an occasional
small frolic.

No scholar should be ignorant of the two classical works on the
subject of footnotes:

> Robert Benchley.
> Shakespeare explained.
> In *The Benchley Roundup*, pages 33–35. Harper & Brothers,
> 1954.
>
> Frank Sullivan.
> A garland of ibids for Van Wyck Brooks.
> In Robert P. Falk, editor, *The Antic Muse*, pages 55–58.
> Grove Press, 1955.
> Originally published in *The New Yorker*, 19 April 1941.

Both appear frequently in anthologies; they should have a tonic
effect on your footnote style and help you correct any bad habits
you've fallen into.

Fundamentals

Footnotes are parentheses. Your text must be grammatically and
logically detachable from your footnotes; the footnotes needn't
be detachable from the text. Here is a footnote that makes no
sense without the text:

> and it was Kemble's wish to establish a system so that his
> letters to Mrs. Siddon* might be preserved against the time

---

* Who was no mean correspondent herself, her letters for the period
1805–07 alone having been collected in three volumes [27].

While this scarcely merits accolades for beauty, it is acceptable footnote style. But here is an unacceptable footnote, one that the text attempts to depend on:

> ▷ that Edward Manette and the Duke of Burgundy had done for the sake of the King.* She was of a mind to allow her
>
> ---
>
> * Charles's consort at the time was a bourgeoise, one Amité Duvalle. Her father, a clothier in Amiens, cut her off for the immorality he would certainly have welcomed had the family been of either better or worse birth.

The "she" in the text cannot take its referent from the footnote; the text must read independently. When the error is grammatical, it's fairly easy to catch. But the text must also be logically independent of footnotes. Here is an example of information too important to be relegated to a footnote:

> ▷ for the 36 subjects* who participated throughout this new
>
> ---
>
> * Volunteers predominated in this group. Only two of the conscripts stayed the course.

To slide essential qualifications into a footnote is at best bad form; at worst, dishonesty. Your reader should be able to take your text without the footnotes and understand its weaknesses as well as its strengths. The prospect of making bold statements in text and then correcting them in cautious footnotes tempts some young scholars; in the words of St. Paul, be not deceived.

How long is a footnote? Longer than a word or two, which you could simply slip into your text in parentheses; shorter than half a page. If a footnote threatens to run longer than half a page, do something to it. Perhaps you should incorporate it into your text; perhaps you should turn it into an appendix and mention the appendix in your text; perhaps you've just run away with yourself and what you need to do is cut.

Footnotes should not include tabular material or material with

---

Bad examples are marked with an arrowhead (▷).

subscripts or superscripts because they will eventually be set tight
—single spacing on a typewriter, small type with little leading
(space between the lines) in print. On a typewriter, an exception
can be made for one-line footnotes. For material to be set in type,
not even the one-line exception works; the small type sizes often
lack superscripts and subscripts—as well they should, for the
sake of the reader's eyesight. Mathematicians get around this re-
striction by incorporating their footnotes into their texts and calling them remarks:

> although the midmean in this instance is defective.
>
> *Remark:* A correction can be made with $\frac{1}{2} x^2 y^2 z$ in most
> cases.
>
> The wing variables remain unstable. Until more of the kind

Remarks are not so flexible as footnotes—you can't put a remark
in the middle of a sentence, where an asterisk or a dagger would
do no harm. But they are a handy option to consider if your subject requires fancy notation.

Modest displays can occur in footnotes by means of double-
indenting:

> in June on the occasion of the King's official birthday.* His
> health was beginning to fail and he was no longer so eager
>
> ---
>
> * No one else liked George either. Byron has a farcical description of
>   him in heaven memorizing the hundredth psalm, and E. C. Bentley
>   wrote the unkind couplet:
>
> > George the Third
> > Ought never to have occurred.

But don't try anything complicated in laying out your footnotes;
they will only look chintzy and embarrass you.

Footnotes or endnotes? In the old-fashioned style, when nine
out of ten notes were bibliographic, the shift to endnotes made
good sense. The reader who had constantly to readjust his eyes for
no better reward than a loc. cit. or an ibid. passim was just as

happy to have all the notes bunched at the end. With the elimination of the bibliographic note, footnotes come into their own again. Even the tired-eyed, astigmatic reader is happy to glance down from time to time if he knows that your footnotes are informative and amusing and if you don't ask him to do it too often.

"Not too often" is begging the question, of course. How often is too often? Footnotes that could have been gracefully incorporated into your text try your reader's patience; so do footnotes of slim relevance unless they're really funny. A useful corrective to excessive footnoting is financial: A typed page with a footnote on it costs about half again as much as one without. The ratio in printing is not quite so punitive, but footnotes must be set separately and then combined with the text, offering numerous opportunities for confusion and error. There are no absolute standards, but think twice before you decide to footnote.

Documentation occurs in footnotes as it does in text, by means of bracketed reference numbers. These numbers do not carry over from text to footnote, from footnote to text, or from one footnote to the next.

in the fossil dinoflagellates of the Mesozoic and the Cenozoic [12].* Paleontologists currently think that the kind of

---

* Ehrenberg also laid the groundwork for later investigations of the acritarchs [12].

The repetition may feel odd to you, but it's necessary.

Signal footnotes with the following symbols in order, starting over on each new page: * † ‡ § ** †† ‡‡ §§. (If you get into the doubled signals, you're probably footnoting too heavily.) Unlike bracketed numbers, the footnote symbols follow punctuation:

▷ until no new geological information*, no matter how much

until no new geological information,* no matter how much

Avoid signaling a footnote with a symbol you're using for some other purpose. If you're using the asterisk to talk about Kleene * (a mathematical function; the name is pronounced, whimsically, cleanie-star), banish the asterisk from your list of footnote signals—even if Kleene * appears on only one page of your text. If your sections are marked §, drop that symbol from your list of footnote signals.

Explanatory Footnotes

Definitions: Before you footnote a definition, there are two tests to apply. Can you substitute a more familiar term?

▷ his paronomastic* facility resulted in his being asked to give

---

* Word-shunting, making jocular or suggestive use of similarity between different words or of a word's different senses.

his facility at puns resulted in his being asked to give the

The line between linguistic exuberance and showing off is narrow, but it should be observed. If you cannot replace the term, can you incorporate the definition into your text?

▷ converting the semivowels* to true consonants in all but the

---

* The letters w and y.

converting the semivowels, the letters w and y, to true consonants in all but the heightened speech of the class that is

Use footnotes only to define irreplaceable terms and only when the definitions cannot be fitted into your text:

down the Ophel* in the direction of the Pool of the Cap

---

* A swelling on the southern slope of the Mount of the Temple—a long, narrow, rounded spur between the mouth of the central valley of Jerusalem and the Kidron.

Definitions must occur at the first use of the term, not later:

▷ reverted to the terza rima* in his version of the classical but

---

    * Lines of five iambic feet with an extra syllable rhymed aba, bcb, cdc, and so on. The last tercet is usually converted by an extra line into a quartet, yzyz, to avoid leaving a line unrhymed.

The clue here is "reverted" in the text; if you catch yourself defining a term midstream, you must search back for the first use and insert the definition there.

Equivalent measures: In dealing with unfamiliar measures and coinage, you should always help your reader get his bearings. Don't, however, automatically reach for a footnote. Sometimes you can simply substitute a more familiar term:

▷ Indented a mut quad* on either side and leaded out to a

---

    * A variable unit of measure the width of the capital M in the alphabet under consideration.

indented an em on either side and leaded out to a full or

Sometimes you can work an explanation into your text:

▷ swigging pint* after pint of home brew. They turned the

---

    * The Imperial pint is 20 ounces.

swigging pint after pint of home brew—and the Imperial pint is 20 ounces. They turned the evening into an awful

Reserve footnotes for complicated explanations. Coinage, for instance, seldom lends itself to facile equivalents:

paid for with three solidi* and delivered to her home after

_____

* Estimates of the value of the solidus vary from $3 [14] to $25 [36]. One solidus was enough to buy food for the family of a freedman for a day [28] but not enough to pay for Orideon's reading the omens [19].

Identifications: Footnotes can identify minor figures in your cast of characters, especially those who make only one appearance:

engaged to Gustav Kirchhoff* only the year before. A shameless flirt, she had some impact on the life of the

_____

* Gustav Robert Kirchhoff (1824–87), German physicist who, with Robert Bunsen, developed spectrum analysis. He never recovered from Helga's jilting him and made her another proposal of marriage after the death of her second husband, when they were both in their seventies.

figures such as Torelli* who were better known at court for

_____

* Pompeo Torelli (1539–1608), Italian dramatist. His *Merope* (1589), the first treatment of this subject, was later taken up by Voltaire and Matthew Arnold.

Translations: In order to satisfy all your readers, you should in general provide both the original and a translation for any passage you quote that was written in a language other than English. Omit the original only when it is of no literary or linguistic interest; omit the translation only for student papers or manuscripts circulating in draft among your colleagues. Never omit the translation in anything that's being published. (An exception might be made for a foreign tag or a pun or joke.)

Footnotes are the best way to meet this obligation. It's up to you whether to put the original in the text and the translation in a footnote or vice versa.

Ma 'l suon che di dolcezza i sensi lega,
col gran desir d'udendo esser beata,
L'anima, al dipartir presta, raffrena.*

***

* In Hilbertson's translation:
   But to my joy-besotted soul the sound
   Carries a hope for heaven now
   And holds my soul earth-bound.

the words of the Secret, "so that it may become acceptable
by her merits, in whose honor it is offered."* The tradition
of mediation is very powerfully felt in this part of the old

***

* "Ut in cujus honore solemniter exhibetur, ejus meritis efficiatur
acceptum."

If the translation is your own, you needn't give a citation for it
unless you've published it elsewhere.

Glosses: Brief glosses on prose quotations fit well into the text if
you enclose them in brackets; use footnotes only for lengthy
glosses.

wrote, "It seems, Mother [Mrs. Bixler, his stepmother], that
the time has come for me to set out again on my own and

said, "The redeemed language* of the speeches he gave to

***

* Allenby seems to use this expression in a casual way, with no reference to the technical terminology of Augustinian criticism.

Even very short glosses on poetry should appear as footnotes:

It shall not touch, with breath of bale,
The pleasance* of our fairy-tale.

***

* Alice Liddell's middle name was Pleasance.

You make me marvel wherefore ere this time
Had you not fully laid my state* before me
That I might so have rated my expense
As I had leave of means.

---

* Variant *place*.

The same is true of glosses on tables and graphs. Here the population for the whole table except one entry is twenty:

13.44	13.22	8.19	12.65	13.19
10.81	9.37	10.13	9.91	10.12
4.66*	10.87	9.49	10.14	11.59

---

* $N = 15$.

Special notation: Footnotes should not contain subscripted or superscripted material. Within that constraint, a good rule of thumb for explaining unfamiliar notation is to use no more than one footnote per expression. There is obviously a good deal of drama and common sense in introducing new notation at work, rather than in the abstract:

$$v_\epsilon(f)\dagger = \{h \mid |f(x) - h(x)| < \epsilon \text{ for all } 0 \leq x \leq 1\} \quad \epsilon \text{ fixed}$$

---

† The operator v (near) represents the case where only an approximation of $f(x)$ is wanted.

But your reader cannot absorb too many new pieces of information at once:

$$\triangleright \quad \sigma(f)\dagger = \{h \mid f(x) = 0 \text{ iff}\ddagger h(x) = 0 \text{ for all } x \epsilon \mathcal{C}\S\}$$

---

† The operator σ (sameroots) represents the case where we need to know only whether $f(x)$ is zero.
‡ If and only if.
§ ¢ denotes the set of complex numbers.

Here the author should have begun with the definitions and then combined them in a working expression. The same reasoning applies to all special notation, not just to mathematical expressions.

Enlargement: The use of footnotes for detail usually results from the attempt to write for two audiences at one time. The general reader, our scholar reasons, is interested in results; the specialist is interested in method. So, put the results in the text and the method in footnotes, have your cake and eat it too.

There are people who can pull this trick off perfectly, and others who muck it up. What are the guidelines for success?

First of all, these footnotes must only enlarge, never mitigate. To make flat statements in your text and then qualify and soften them in footnotes is to treat the general reader with a contempt he readily identifies and returns.

Second, this use for footnotes precludes all the other kinds set out in this section. If you think about it, all of the other explanatory footnotes are intended to lend a hand to the reader who lacks specialized knowledge. Intermingling these with footnotes intended to segregate specialized knowledge is confusing and disruptive. If you want to use footnotes for information of interest only to your colleagues, you must incorporate all your helps to the general reader into your text. Begin your first footnote with an explanation of the scheme you intend to follow: "The footnotes in this article are meant for specialists." That way both kinds of readers know what to expect and can proceed intelligently.

The Footnote Aside

The best-beloved footnote is the aside—the tidbit, the comment, the sidelight, the joke. Most of the delight of these footnotes comes from their context and their content, but it is possible to give a few general tips.

Avoid the cultivation of a schizophrenic style. The author of the text and the author of the footnotes should be recognizably the same person. Picture the desiccated scholar who raises his eyes from the crumbling yellow pages of his notes, peers dimly over his glasses, smiles a vague, wan smile—and suddenly turns a cartwheel. His audience is disconcerted and distressed. Young scholars sometimes adopt an artificially prim style in their texts and then, in their footnotes, let their natural high spirits get the best of them. Neither the lackluster text nor the frenzied footnote is a goal to strive after, and the combination of the two is dreadful.

Length should continue to serve as a rough guideline for whether a remark belongs in the text or a footnote. An aside of a word or a phrase or a short sentence belongs in the text, often in parentheses. Save your footnotes for longer excursions, remembering that conciseness is everywhere a virtue, but especially in jest.

Don't pull your punches. Avoid all introductions if you can; avoid like the plague introductions that use the impersonal pronoun and the passive voice:

▷ which the downward-sloping demand* seems to require in

----

* One is irresistibly reminded of Anthony Hope's "Economy is going without something you do want in case you should, some day, want something you probably won't want."

which the downward-sloping demand* seems to require in

----

* "Economy is going without something you do want in case you should, some day, want something you probably won't want"—Anthony Hope.

The aside, like the epigraph, should not be weighted down with heavy, irrelevant citations. If you're quoting someone in an aside, give a brief, unscholarly citation and let it go at that.

The acknowledgment: A special use for the footnote aside is to thank a colleague who's done you a good turn. Help on an entire manuscript is usually acknowledged in a special section at the beginning or the end of the text, but help on a single point can be mentioned in a footnote.

It is virtually impossible to express gratitude without using the first-person singular. You will only sound stilted and unappreciative if you try:

▷ possibly by olfactory clues.* When male pairs are joined in

---

* This suggestion was first brought to the author's attention by Gretchen Pritchard, whose assistance is acknowledged with appreciation.

possibly by olfactory clues.* When male pairs are joined in

---

* My thanks to Gretchen Pritchard for this suggestion.

The quibble: An important use for footnote asides is segregating quibbles. It's unattractive to clutter up your text with split hairs; finick in your footnotes:

Debutante, with Rex Harrison.* Her subsequent career is

---

* Harrison was born in 1908 and christened Reginald Carey, not "Reginald Cary" [13], not "Reginald Carew" [26], and certainly not "Rex Carew" [18].

The only trouble I foresee about this advice is that the mean-spirited, jesuitical fussbudgets I have known always see themselves as perfectly reasonable, just a little more fastidious than the common run of persons, that's all. Relegating quibbles to your footnotes requires that you recognize them.

Footnotes in Draft

The best system for handling footnotes in draft is to run them in with your text, double-spaced, marking the division with bars:

helped Heath with his work.* Bennett was at

* Major General Heath's chief preoccupation
at this time was a proclamation on snip-
ing during the invasion. The manuscript
survives in a dozen drafts, which must
have taken weeks of Bennett's time. The
invasion never took place and the famous
proclamation never saw the light of day.

the end of his patience with his family,
and his financial situation was endangered

The section on manuscript preparation talks about how to handle
footnotes in final draft and final typescript.

Scholarly
Peculiarities

The list that follows is neither exclusive nor comprehensive. Other kinds of writing share many of the failings described here, though they turn up more often in scholarly prose; and scholars have, heaven knows, other faults than these. But even so sketchy and incomplete a listing owes a debt to the masters. It would be churlish to neglect to thank them, and irresponsible to fail to recommend them to you.

Since the Oxford University Press first published H. W. Fowler's *A Dictionary of Modern English Usage* in 1926, the book has been the stern teacher and kindly guide to all who wish to write well. What can I say about Fowler? What can the minnow say in praise of the whale? Go out and buy a copy today, read through one letter a week, and in half a year you will have made a friend for life.

Among the many other good books on usage, my two favorites are Wilson Follett's *Modern American Usage* (Hill & Wang, 1966) and Eric Partridge's *Usage and Abusage* (Penguin, 1963). Although some of the modern grammars are enlightening and exciting, I find the traditional grammars more useful for practical writing. Their stress on proscriptions and prohibitions, which the modernists abhor, makes for lopsided analysis, but lopsided in just the way I need. Barnes & Noble does a public service by keeping George O. Curme's classic *English Grammar* in print in their college outline series.

And then there's the little book, *The Elements of Style* by William Strunk, Jr., and E. B. White (Macmillan, 1959). If you are

condemned to a desert island and allowed only one book to help
with composing notes to send out to sea in bottles, choose Fowler.
If you're allowed another, take Strunk and White.

The Abstract Abstract

The purpose of an abstract is to summarize, not to tease. Many
authors find it painful to trot their results out naked before the
world; they want to seduce, to captivate, to tantalize. What results
is the abstract of the seven veils:

> ▷ An advance in the definition of certain operators is made
> possible by the application of several recent results in com-
> plexity. Full details are supplied, and illustrative examples
> are included. Data on related findings are presented in the
> final section along with implications for further research.

In other words, what's in this paper is a secret. A good abstract
should be concrete:

> The operators Shift, Reply, and VVX [5,14,9] are not so
> weak as they first seemed. An application of Browning's
> Theorem [2] and his more recent work on conjunctivity
> [1,3,4] suggests that these operators impose hidden con-
> straints on their members, which may constitute a uniform
> but as yet undefined set.

Notice that an abstract can use pointers to your reference list; an
abstract published separately from the paper it abstracts can have
its own short reference list.

Mathematicians have special difficulties with abstracts; they
tend to feel that anything short of a full, formal statement of their
ideas is meaningless. But in conversation with other mathematicians they can get their drift across. In fact, a good device for

---

Bad examples are marked with an arrowhead (▷).

writing abstracts is to pretend that you're in a phone booth, making a long-distance call to a colleague. You want to give him the gist of your latest paper, and you have change for only three minutes.

Acknowledgments

Not even the most heartfelt sentiment can survive stale language. Many an advisor before yours has been thanked for understanding and guidance; many a colleague for useful contributions; many a typist for accuracy and neatness; many a spouse for patience. Not one has escaped gratitude for services above and beyond the call of duty.

As always, specificity is the best cure for cliché. Yes, your advisor was, like all others, kind, helpful, firm, and encouraging; but who else suggested a way out of the bind you got yourself into in chapter 6? Yes, your spouse was, like everyone else's, stoic, Job-like, and emotionally and financially supportive; but who else programmed your recursive functions?

> ▷ I am also grateful to my colleagues Paula Hibbin and Ralph Feinster for their helpful comments.
>
> I am also grateful to Paula Hibbin for telling me about the work of the Syracuse group and to Ralph Feinster for two thorough readings of the manuscript, which resulted in numberless small improvements and clarifications.

Bad Words

The young scholar who begins to take his writing seriously and look for help will notice that an incredible amount of the advice he gets is about specific words. In careful writing, "aggravate" does not mean vex; "anticipate" does not mean expect; "meticulous" does not mean exact; "decimate" does not mean destroy. "Hopefully" cannot serve as an absolute. The idiom is "different from," not "different than." "Charisma" is a vogue-word; "triphibious" is a malformation; "firstly" is a barbarism.

All this is good advice, but young scholars, overwhelmed by its volume and particularity, may not know how to take it. Some freeze with terror and find they cannot write at all; some give up the hope of writing carefully and adopt a pose of sloppy cynicism. Both responses are overwrought and gloomy.

Calm down. If you work hard at making your writing simple, forceful, and entertaining, you will automatically avoid most missteps, and the ones you do make will be forgiven you. The reader who is carried forward by a piece of writing may flinch at occasional errors, but they will not detain him. You may never make a mark as a stylist, but you will have done your job.

And cheer up. Lists of disputed words result from changes in the language and from different rates of change—the spoken language moves more quickly than the written. Some changes catch hold. An 1887 manual of usage forbids "ice cream" for "iced cream"; that one was settled so long ago that it seems odd that anyone would fight about it. Some changes do not survive. The same manual forbids "die with" for "die of"; again, the matter has been settled. Some changes remain at issue for a long time. I have before me articles on "apt, likely, liable" in usage guides published in 1887, 1926, 1957, 1964, and 1975. Our children's children may still worry over the distinction.

But because the bulk of the language is highly conservative and because most changes do eventually either win out or die, there are never at any one time more than a thousand words in dispute. Of that thousand you may have use for only, say, three hundred. If you have reason to be concerned about scholarly prose, you are not the man in the street. You must already have mastered thousands and millions of facts, details, and fine discriminations. What are a few hundred more, if you need them to share with your reader everything you know?

Bending Over Backwards

Most of us had, in the sixth or seventh grade, a schoolteacher who tried to give us "grammar." Either he didn't know what he was talking about or we were fooling around and looking out the window, but there are several errors common in otherwise educated writing that seem to result from his teaching. Distinctions have been garbled, and a mystical significance attaches to some words.

"As" for "like": Yes, you must not use "like" for "as":

▷ Blottoes smoke good like a cigarette had ought to.

That is the uneducated error you were warned against. But the educated error, "as" for "like," is just as bad:

▷ In their haste and confusion, the city officials were acting as children.

The simple rule in such comparisons is that if the word links to a noun or a pronoun, it's "like"; if it links to a whole clause, it's "as":

In their haste and confusion, the city officials were acting _____ children.

children = noun

In their haste and confusion, the city officials were acting like children.

In their haste and confusion, the city officials were acting _____ children do.

children do = clause

In their haste and confusion, the city officials were acting as children do.

But notice that "as . . . do" is nothing more than a dodge for the dreaded "like."

"If it were" for "if it was": There are two kinds of conditional clauses, simple conditions and conditions contrary to fact. Constructions of the "were/had been" variety are used only for conditions contrary to fact. Test the clause in question by adding an imaginary parenthetical statement of fact. If the parenthesis begins with "but," the condition is contrary to fact; if the parenthesis begins with "maybe," the clause is a simple condition.

> If there _____ no alternative to interviews, we would have gone ahead with this lengthy and inaccurate technique.

> If there _____ no alternative to interviews (but there was)—condition contrary to fact.

> If there were no alternative to interviews, we would have gone ahead with this lengthy and inaccurate technique.

> If there _____ no chance for appeasement, Talleyrand had a plan for victory.

> If there _____ no chance for appeasement (maybe there was, maybe there wasn't)—simple condition.

> If there was no chance for appeasement, Talleyrand had a plan for victory.

"May" for "can": Yes, it's "may" rather than "can" for granting permission:

▷ Can I eat a piece of cake?

I can hear my grandfather's voice: "Oh yes, you can. You have a mouth, tongue, teeth, a good digestive system. Certainly you can. You *may* not."

But the words are linked in another way that has nothing to do with let and license. "Can" is at one end of the continuum of possibility, with no nuance:

> The normal child of six can handle a spoken vocabulary of about fifteen hundred words.

"May" is somewhere in the middle; it has a "maybe" or a "perhaps" built into it:

> He may read as many as two hundred words.

At the far end, "might" is dubious; it suggests that the chances are fifty-fifty, or less:

> He might even write his own name.

It's important, then, when you're talking about possibility rather than permission, to reexamine the knee-jerk preference for "may." Using it in place of "can" casts doubt on perfectly straightforward statements:

▷ The reader may find a fuller explanation of irreducibility in chapter 4.

If you've been so traumatized that any "can," even a blameless one, gives you the jimjams, remember that "will" is at the same end of the continuum.

> The reader can find a fuller explanation of irreducibility in chapter 4.

or The reader will find a fuller explanation of irreducibility in chapter 4.

"Well" for "good": Yes, the use of "good" as an adverb is a vulgar error:

▷ That kid sure done good.

But the use of "well" as an adjective for anything but health is the educated version of the error:

> ▷ It would be well for us to examine these assumptions more closely.

The copulas—the verb "to be" and its analogs—link their subjects with adjectives, not adverbs. Test the verb in question. If it's analogous to "be" or "seem," it's a copula, and you need an adjective; if it's not, you need an adverb.

As a result, she sounded very _____ that night.

sounded, like seemed—a copula

As a result, she sounded very good that night.

As a result, she sang very _____ that night.

sang, like did—not a copula

As a result, she sang very well that night.

"Whom" for "who": This is my favorite, because I went to a school where we were required to render the cheer "Two, four, six, eight, whom do we appreciate?" Yes, "who" for "whom" is a bad mistake, but the reverse is just as bad:

> ▷ There was a good deal of speculation as to whom the representatives appointed from the wards with elections in dispute might be.
>
> ▷ Mallowby spoke for the justice of the cause of the Pretender, whom, as he averred, every man in the kingdom knew was honest, modest, and wise.

If you cannot tell "who" from "whom" in a simple sentence, you need to go to a basic grammar and sort them out. There are only fourteen possible instances, and only three or four of them are common. But everyone has trouble with the pair in convoluted, misshapen sentences, and correcting "whom" to "who" is not the answer. The answer is rewriting.

Capitalization

Is it because so many of our scholarly folkways are German in origin that scholars tend to overcapitalize? The names of academic disciplines do not need capitals unless they are being used as shorthand for administrative departments. So we have:

> Geology and Geophysics is at war with Biology over the lecture hall at the end of the corridor.

But:

> No discovery in geology and geophysics has had greater impact on the lives of ordinary people.

The use of capitals to personify and solemnize rapidly becomes tedious:

> ▷ Thus Art, her raiment torn and bedraggled, once more took up the Sword against the traitor Craft.

Most nouns and adjectives derived from proper names lose their capitals; to retain them is pedantic:

> ▷ Paisley did everything he could to show his contempt for the conference; he sighed, he yawned, he ate his way noisily through an entire tray of Napoleons, and eventually he pretended to fall asleep.

A sound, conservative dictionary is your best guide to the use of capital letters.

Articles ("a," "an," and "the") are capitalized at the beginnings of sentences, sentence quotations, and titles. They are not capitalized when they attach to proper nouns:

▷ This work was supported by a grant from The National Science Foundation.

This work was supported by a grant from the National Science Foundation.

The Cliché Redivivus

There is a certain kind of dry, scholarly humor that delights in tinkering with saws and sayings:

George was unable to see the European forest for the English oak.

In the conference on metrification, Lavoisier was every inch a diplomat—or, as it became, every centimeter.

I have nothing against this practice; it tickles me. But if you too enjoy it, remember that a little goes a long way and beware of twisting your exposition out of shape just for the chance of getting off a good one.

Coherence

Especially in the mathematical sciences, there are some scholars who seem to distrust ordinary discourse coherence. Every sentence, every fresh clause, must begin with a connective: thus, thence, whence, whither, therefore, hence, and, then, so, again. In advanced cases you get combinations: "And so, then, these results are therefore . . ." If you have fallen into this habit, try excising all connectives and then restore only those you need for emphasis. Take it as a general rule that no sentence is allowed to fly off from its predecessor willy-nilly. If it has, no amount of glue in the form of adverbs and conjunctions will hold it down.

The Colonated Title

Pick a scholarly work, any scholarly work; what's its title? Something-something, *colon*, something-something-something. Am I right? The use of title and subtitle is justified by the desire to be both catchy and precise:

Nose to the Grindstone: A Life of Arnold Bennett.

Setting a context is another justification:

The Manley Clinic sleep treatment: A study of drug abuse among physicians.

But the habit can become so ingrained that scholars reach for colons automatically where none are needed:

▷ The economy of the French capital: Paris, 1750–1800.
The economy of Paris, 1750–1800.

Conclusions

Begin at the beginning and go on till you come to the end; then stop. That's excellent advice, and every scholar should heed it. There is no rule of composition that says you must end with a summary of everything that's come before—honestly there isn't. The mark of a good summary is revelation: "Remember this, reader? And that? Well, here's how they fit together." If you have revealed all before you start to summarize, then stop.

Emphasis

Because so much scholarly writing is calm, deliberate, and measured, some scholars overdo it when they want to be forceful. The ideal is for all emphasis to be structural, none mechanical—for the shape and motion of your sentences to carry your stress all by themselves. When you feel yourself itching for italics or an underline, look first to see whether the passage shouldn't be rewritten:

> ▷ During this phase, some of the internal *and external* stimuli to which the females were exposed affected their behavior.
>
> During this phase, both internal and external stimuli affected the females' behavior.

> or During this phase, some of the internal stimuli to which the females were exposed affected their behavior, but external stimuli also began to affect them.

> or External as well as internal stimuli affected the females' behavior during this phase.

When you must italicize, choose a key word or two; italicizing a whole passage actually de-emphasizes it by making it more difficult to read:

> ▷ The student should realize that *the fundamental bias of this work is theoretical* and that *applications are merely sketched, not worked out in detail.*
>
> The student should realize that the fundamental bias of this work is *theoretical* and that applications are merely sketched, not worked out in detail.

(Better yet, do away with the italics altogether.)

Underlining and italics are interchangeable conventions for emphasis. Total caps, on the other hand, should never be used for stress.

▷ This approach is the WORST possible and induces fluctuations beyond the capacity of most measuring instruments.

(Use an underline or italics, or do away with the mechanical emphasis altogether and let the sentence stand on its own.) Capitalizing "the" or "a" for stress is a barbarism:

▷ Henry was, after all, The King, and his mere motion was sufficient for the deed.

(Use an underline or italics if you insist, but be aware that the effect is paltry.)

Except in the rendering of dialog, exclamations are rare in writing, and scholarly writing is the least exclamatory of all. Adding an exclamation point to a plain declarative sentence makes it not emphatic but pathetic:

▷ There has been, up to now, no complete account of the acquisition and disposition of some 216 millions of acres of public lands in Texas!

(Start the sentence with "surprisingly" and end it with a period; better yet, ask yourself whether it really is such a surprise.) If you are ever in doubt about whether a sentence merits an exclamation mark, try shouting it out the window. There will be virtually no correct uses in scholarly writing.

Equanimity

The scholar who wants to write well should cultivate bad temper in his reading. Read you must, whether the writing is good or bad. But do not smile sweetly as you read through the pages of graceless, stilted, maundering bombast your discipline requires of you. (If there is any field in which all scholars write like angels, I apologize.) Fume; fuss; be angry. Your anger will keep you up to the mark when you turn to writing yourself, and it may have a good effect on your students and your colleagues.

Hyperqualification

Most scholarly prose is hedged round with caution and qualification, as well it should be; the world of scholarship is no place for hysterical exaggeration. But doubling and tripling up on qualifications gives your writing the texture of an unmolded custard, soft and runny at the edges. To be both accurate and forceful requires ingenuity:

▷ Many of the members of the sample population showed some tendency in the direction of being not very stable.

The sample tended toward instability.

▷ One of the chief preoccupations of most if not all of the representatives was the likelihood of some kind of reform in a rather short time.

Reform was in the wind.

▷ It is almost certain that the greater number of the semiconductors will eventually prove to be of almost no commercial value, but for many the strong possibility remains that they will seem rather interesting to the theoretician and continue for some time to attract a great deal of attention in many laboratories.

Most semiconductors may be useless, but they are fascinating.

Two qualifiers require special attention, "relatively" and "comparatively." In sentences where the terms of the comparison are stated, they are redundant:

▷ The interest of the older children was relatively greater and more sustained.

The interest of the older children was greater and more sustained.

▷ Nitzler was comparatively inexperienced for a district official.

Nitzler was inexperienced for a district official.

In sentences with no terms of comparison, they are meaningless:

▷ Knowlton had hit on a relatively inexpensive solution to the problem.

Relative to what?

Knowlton had hit on an inexpensive solution to the problem.

or Knowlton had hit on a solution to the problem that cost less than any previous solution, but it was still too expensive to put into production.

or Knowlton had hit on a fairly inexpensive solution.

Correct, sensible uses for these words are few and far between.

Initialisms and Acronyms

With initial mania everywhere, it would be surprising if no scholars were infected. Treat the disease with a dose of plain, old-fashioned words:

▷ Negotiations then began between the Cooperative Wholesalers Society (CWS) and the Milk Producers Revenue

Board (MPRB). The CWS wanted price supports; the MPRB wanted free competition.

Negotiations then began between the Cooperative Wholesalers Society and the Milk Producers Revenue Board. The wholesalers wanted price supports; the board wanted free competition.

Introductions

If you find yourself writing an introduction that seems to be nothing more than a table of contents, why not substitute a table of contents?

> ▷ The first section reviews the current literature on aphasia. The second section discusses melodic therapy techniques. Then in the third section there are three case histories. Finally, the fourth section brings up open questions for future research.

> 1. Review of the Literature on Aphasia   1
> 2. Melodic Therapy Techniques   8
> 3. Three Case Histories   17
> 4. Future Research   22

The table of contents says everything the introduction did and more—it has page numbers too.

Inventing Terms and Notation

The topic at hand is assigning names to new discoveries, not foolishness like "sendee" for recipient.

Be sure that what you want to name is really new. A discovery at the far edge of your area of specialization may be a commonplace in someone else's. Rediscovery leads to a proliferation of terms and obscures the unity of knowledge across fields.

Be sure that your discovery is worth naming. Although it's difficult to foresee the results of your work, the stony truth is that nine out of ten new concepts never get much further than their author, a colleague or two, and a few graduate students. There's no point in beating your brains out over a great name for something with no applicability to anyone's work but your own. "This technique," "this result," "my finding," "my approach," "the new variable" may be sufficient.

Consider the local definition. Suppose, for instance, that your Type 4 behavior is, in common language, fear. Rather than call it "Type 4" or, worse still, "phobic disquietation," you can in an introduction define "fear" as nothing more or less than Type 4 for the length of this paper. Your reader will be able to keep it straight from Types 1, 2, 3, and 5, and you will have struck a blow for modesty and common sense in nomenclature. In a long paper, you would be wise to remind your reader now and then that by "fear" you mean only Type 4, lest he get confused and think you're talking about the general phenomenon.

Consider the context. You are not Adam and Eve in the Garden of Eden. If there already exist three phenomena called lutes, flutes, and oboes, calling the fourth member of the family a wheelbarrow is cloddish. Give some thought to the verbs that cluster around any noun you're considering. We're stuck with such monstrosities as "to walk a tree" and "to stack a goal," but we certainly don't need more.

Don't jump in. Hold off on naming a new idea until it has assumed its full shape in your mind. A poor name, hastily chosen, can mislead your readers and can even subtly restrict your own ability to realize the extent of your invention.

Keep it simple. A moment's thought should convince you that "dumping" is a better way to describe a dumping sort of concept than "geotropic activation," better, catchier, and more likely to make a name for you. Simplicity is especially important in inventing new notation. I once saw a paper with w, $\overline{w}$, $\overline{\overline{w}}$, $\ddot{w}$, $\hat{w}$, ω, $\overline{\omega}$, $\overline{\overline{\omega}}$, $\ddot{\omega}$, $\hat{\omega}$, ω, $\overline{\omega}$, $\overline{\overline{\omega}}$, $\ddot{\omega}$, $\hat{\omega}$, w'—shall I go on? If you care nothing for your reader's weary eyes, think of dealing with hot-tempered typists and crabby printers for the rest of your life.

Always give your reader some indication of how you intend a new notation to be said aloud. There's nothing more tiresome than reading through an entire paper subvocalizing "little left squiggle, straight bar, little right squiggle."

Don't blow your own horn. If you're Sweeney, leave it to someone else to call your technique Sweenification.

Get help. Any editor who works with printers will be happy to tell you that ζ' costs a third less than $\hat{\zeta}$. Any philologist worth his salt will be overjoyed to help you with prefixes and suffixes and roots from Greek and Latin. He suffers, after all, much more than you do from words like "calmative," "nounal," and "cavitron."

Inversion

There is a common delusion among scholars and other people who write formal prose that relatives and comparatives require inversion afterwards. They do not.

> This proposal won more favor than did its predecessors.

or This proposal won more favor than its predecessors did.

> The polyvalent functions have as many uses as have the bivalent ones.

or The polyvalent functions have as many uses as the bivalent ones have.

The inverted versions are not bad enough to require arrowheads, but a comparison with ordinary, everyday diction makes it clear that the versions in natural order are better:

▷ She's twice as smart as am I.

She's twice as smart as I am.

In many cases, the periphrastic verb, the one that repeats the verbal idea, can simply be omitted:

> This proposal won more favor than its predecessors.

> The polyvalent functions have as many uses as the bivalent ones.

A Little Latin

AD; BC: Anno Domini, in the year of the Lord; before Christ.
Few works are of such vast historical scope that these abbreviations are necessary. But if your period is 35 BC to AD 76 then you should notice that "BC" goes after the year and "AD" goes before it. If you prefer, you may write the abbreviations "B.C." and "A.D."

No one objects to "the third century BC," but there are some pernickety people who will not allow "the third century AD" because "annus" means year. Well, so it does, but it also means age or time or season. Since we have no other handy way of expressing the idea, using "AD" with centuries seems a harmless sort of shorthand. "CE" has been proposed (for "Christian Era" or "Common Era"), but because it has never become popular it slows the reader down instead of speeding him ahead, as shorthand should.

A.m.; m.; p.m.: Ante meridiem, before noon; meridies, noon; post meridiem, after noon.

By this system, noon is 12 m. and midnight is 12 p.m. But there are also people who write noon "12 n." and midnight "12 m." And on the twenty-four-hour clock noon is 12 and midnight is 24. To avoid confusion, write out the words "noon" and "midnight."

C., c̄: Cum, with.

Use these only in notes to yourself, not in writing for other people to read.

▷ Silicon is found mainly c̄ oxygen as SiO_2.

Silicon is found mainly with oxygen as SiO_2.

C., ca.: Circa, about.

The use of these expressions with approximate dates and figures is justified only in parenthetical dating and in lists and tables. Avoid them in ordinary sentences:

▷ An amnesty was declared at the time of his death c. 1542.

An amnesty was declared at the time of his death, in about 1542.

▷ The distance was ca. 300 miles.

The distance was roughly 300 miles.

In parenthetical dating, you may also use question marks:

Edward George Bateman (ca. 1790–1864).

or   Edward George Bateman (1790?–1864).

On lists and tables, you may also use the ~ sign:

	3,114	4,228	5,109	1,134	c. 4,500
or	3,114	4,228	5,109	1,134	~4,500

If all the figures on a table are approximate, you'll say so in the heading and have no need for marking off individual numbers.

Round off figures that you must give as approximations:

▷ Ca. 1.482 atmospheres.

Ca. 1.5 atmospheres.

E.g.: Exempli gratia, for the sake of example.

Natural, unabbreviated English words make for more graceful expression:

▷ The American Romantics, e.g. Burchfield and Stettheimer, thought of themselves as rebels.

The American Romantics, such as Burchfield and Stettheimer, thought of themselves as rebels.

Etc.: Et cetera, and so on.

The least of the objections to "etc." is that it is a foreign expression for which you can easily substitute unabbreviated English.

Its sloppy vagueness is unsuited to the rigor and precision of scholarly thought, and it is addictive at the ends of lists, even when it makes no sense:

> ▷ Many of these back-formations (for example, "ethic," "burgle," etc.) serve useful functions.
>
> Many of these back-formations (for example, "ethic" and "burgle") serve useful functions.

"For example" gives notice that only some members of a set are to be mentioned; "etc." then drags in all the other members. The two expressions are at loggerheads.

I.e.: Id est, that is.

There are few settings in which simple apposition will not do the job, and do it less stiffly:

> ▷ In his masterpiece, i.e., *Huckleberry Finn*, he overcame these tendencies.
>
> In his masterpiece, *Huckleberry Finn*, he overcame these tendencies.

When apposition is not enough, "that is" is better than "i.e."

N.B.: Nota bene, note well.

In general, your writing itself should help your reader to note well what you're saying, without any need for flags and arrows. In those few cases where you need a flag, there are other expressions with more impact than "N.B."

> ▷ The reaction then occurs very quickly. N.B.: The resulting gas is fatal in concentrations as low as one part in ten billion.
>
> The reaction then occurs very quickly. Warning: The resulting gas is fatal in concentrations as low as one part in ten billion.

Viz.: Videlicet, namely. (From videre licet, it is permitted to see.)
This expression is archaic and should be used only for humor.
But be cautious about using such effects. Some young scholars
adopt a half-mocking tone when they set out to write—archaisms,
convolutions, the excessive use of "one," all of it conscious, all
of it arch. Sometimes this style can be funny, but more often it's
sad. The message comes through: "I'm not sure just where I stand
on this, so I'm going to pretend it's all beneath me."

The search for an authentic voice in which to write is very
difficult if you go at it directly. Concentrate instead on getting your subject across to your reader. That job is hard enough
to eradicate self-consciousness and the need for defensive
irony.

Motivation

"Motivation" is the term mathematicians use for the context of a
piece of work, where it comes from and what it leads to. Motivation is the mortar around bricks in the scholarly edifice, and every
article needs some.

Often the use that you make of your secondary sources will
indicate where your work fits. When explicit motivation is necessary, be on guard against grandiose, far-reaching statements. Early
in my career, I had the task of correcting an extraordinary essay
from a student that began, "All the world is turning to thoughts
of mortuary science." All the world need not be turning to
thoughts of your subject, but neither should you present it in a
vacuum.

▷ One of the most pressing problems facing us today is the
identification of the locus of histamine reactions.

▷ The locus of the histamine reactions is unknown.

If we knew the locus of the histamine reactions, we would
be a step closer to preventing allergies.

▷ Who has not, on reading Milton, been struck by the impact of recessive accent on his meter?

▷ Milton's meter displays certain characteristics of recessive accent.

Recessive accent accounts for much of the "figured bass" effect that observers have noted in Milton's meter.

The examples are exaggerated for the sake of brevity; motivation usually resides, not in any individual sentence, but in the attitude that informs a whole piece of work.

Nor

Since scholarly writers have a corner on the "nor" market, they bear the responsibility for keeping the word in working order. There are only two constructions in modern English in which "nor" can occur. The first is in partnership with "neither."

Neither Knowles nor Sunderman makes this distinction [12,35].

The second is as a clause-level coordinating conjunction, meaning approximately "and . . . not" or "and . . . no."

Frick was disenchanted with the railroads, coal, and oil, nor had he any interest in the money market for itself.

The clause that follows this "nor" is inverted, "had he any interest" rather than "he had any interest." If you stick to these two uses for "nor," you'll be in good shape.

Below the clause level, "nor" cannot appear without "neither."

▷ The mixture does not settle nor go into solution.

▷ Not in the Senate nor in the House was there a murmur of protest.

Test the items the "nor" is attempting to connect to see whether they're clauses.

          settle

▷ nor

          go into solution

          in the Senate

▷ nor

          in the House

If they're not, rewrite:

The mixture does not settle or go into solution.

or   The mixture neither settles nor goes into solution.

Neither in the Senate nor in the House was there a murmur of protest.

or   Not in the Senate or in the House was there a murmur of protest.

Like all coordinating conjunctions, "neither . . . nor" must link grammatically parallel items.

▷ The staging was a success neither in 1728 nor 1750.

          in 1728

▷ nor

          1750

The staging was a success neither in 1728 nor in 1750.

or   The staging was a success in neither 1728 nor 1750.

Paragraphing

Two points here:

The first is to notice that even after a very short introduction, parallel items require parallel paragraphs. You may introduce A,

B, and C as parallel and treat all three together with an introduction. You may put the introduction in one paragraph and A, B, and C together in another. But if you give B and C their own paragraphs, A must have one too.

The second is a plea for paragraphing by eye. Scholars think big thoughts, and big thoughts make big paragraphs, but there's no excuse for the endless paragraph that goes on page after everlasting page. Give your reader a breather. Make it a rule never to let more than thirty lines go by without looking back to see whether you can't break them up. That means you must paragraph more frequently than usual for material to be printed in narrow columns—all to the good. Experiment with an occasional short paragraph for a change, even with a one-sentence paragraph.

Passivity

I wish that scholars were the only ones who practiced the vice of passivity, but they are among the worst and should be chided for it. The passive voice ("Y is done by X," as opposed to the active, "X does Y") is a perfectly lovely voice, useful for placing emphasis correctly, for facilitating parallel construction, for ducking ambiguous or uninteresting agency, and for sheer variety. But it is not the normal working voice of English discourse. Passive after passive, one on top of the other, can dull the most sparkling ideas and turn golden work to dross.

The experimental sciences outdo everyone else on this score. You can read through paper after paper in which nobody ever does anything, nobody ever produces anything, nobody ever acts. Things are done, results are produced, actions are accomplished, as if by unseen hands. You get the feeling that our laboratories are staffed by disembodied spirits.

If you suffer from this addiction, look first for passives with "by." There you've already admitted the agency and can undertake the transformation from "was done by X" to "X did" with little trauma. Steel yourself to the use of the indefinite pronouns. "Someone said" may at first sound strange compared to your old familiar "it has been said," but you can learn to like it. Eventually, if you have courage and determination, you can cure yourself of even the most insidious passives, the kind you use when you don't know, or don't want to say, who did what.

Here is a terrible example—terrible, but as anyone who reads scholarly prose will attest, not untypical:

> ▷ In what might be called the official Victorian world-view, a fairly clear-cut distinction was made between love and friendship. Friendship was conceived of as a relationship between members of the same sex based on shared interests and values; love was founded on the attraction of opposites, who were intended by their union to be bound in a complementarity of virtues and skills by which the basis for the foundation of a family could be laid.

Simple transformations from the passive to the active are impossible here. What the author must do is rethink, asking himself over and over "Who does what?" so that his answers will take that form.

The first passive, "might be called," is an attempt to wiggle out of responsibility. The author wants to use an expression but he doesn't want to own up to it. The second passive, "was made," further distances that same expression. The author must face squarely the question whether he likes the phrase "official Victorian world-view." If he likes it, he should use it straight out; if he doesn't, he should use something else.

> The official Victorian world-view made a fairly clear-cut distinction between love and friendship.

> or The Victorians made a fairly clear-cut distinction between love and friendship.

The third passive, "was conceived of," seems to result from the author's fear that we have forgotten what he's talking about. Having started in the minds of the Victorians, we should be able to continue there for a sentence or two without nagging reminders.

Friendship was a relationship between members of the same sex based on shared interests and values.

Now you should notice that there are two more passives here, "based" and "shared." Most past participles in English are passive. The wise writer will avoid other passives in sentences with past participles, to keep the passives from piling up. The wily writer will avoid past participles themselves when some other construction is more direct.

In friendship, members of the same sex shared interests and values.

Passive #6, "was founded," is a knee-jerk passive; the author has no reason for it, he's just gotten so much in the passive habit that anything else sounds bare to him.

Love was the attraction of opposites.

In the final portion of the sentence, we see the author being choked to death by his own passivity. "Were intended," "to be bound," "could be laid"—these are bad, but what's worse is that the twisted, backward construction has led the author to write nonsense. "Intended by their union to be bound in a complementarity" doesn't mean much, and "the basis for the foundation" is—what? The subsoil? There is no quick fix here. The only solution is to start again. What do you mean? What are you trying to say?

Love was the attraction of opposites, whose complementary virtues and skills laid the foundation for a family.

I have a theory that passivity is tied up with personification. In strong personification, as you may recall, a non-human thing takes on human characteristics—the smiling sun, the sobbing wind, that sort of thing. Now look at a typical passive construction:

▷ The primary computation service has been provided by a large, central batch facility.

Why does the author write that instead of "a large, central batch facility has provided"? Aside from the automatic passivity that infests all scholars, he may feel that the active is too direct, too active. In the back of his mind there's the hazy idea that the facility didn't really provide the service, it just, well, it just somehow was provided. If my guess is correct, he feels the active as a mild personification. Then it must be said that mild personification is a good device, a worthy device, and one to use freely. Write without fear:

A large, central batch facility has provided the primary computation service.

No reader will imagine that the batch facility ran around with a towel over its arm, providing service, any more than he will think that the sun really smiles or the wind really sobs.

Personal Fads

Most personal fads are not only harmless but tonic. Scholars spend their days and nights in intimate struggle with the language, and no one should go through that without developing a set of preferences and prejudices, even quirks. Readers prefer writing with some flavor, some tang—anything rather than bland, impersonal pabulum. Personal peculiarities are harmful only when they get in your way, either by restricting your access to the whole range of the possibilities of the language or by obtruding themselves between your reader and your subject.

For restricting access, consider the case of "get." Many scholars seem to have something against the word. They go to great lengths to avoid it. Acquire, gain, obtain, derive, procure, earn, reap, gather, glean, collect, incur, be in receipt of, fall heir to—anything but "get." The word must be ten thousand times more frequent in normal speech than it is in scholarly writing, and it's a great loss because many of its substitutes are stiff.

▷ The family was unable to procure assistance and turned to crime.

The family was unable to get help and turned to crime.

"Get" is too protean a word to get along without.

For obtruding on your reader, repetition is what's usually at fault. Everyone has pet phrases and constructions that grow wearisome with reuse. I once read through a thirty-page paper in which the expression "the case that" occurred more than a hundred times (I counted). It is the case that so-and-so, it is not the case that so-and-so—there's nothing wrong with the expression, but after that many uses it began to sound like nonsense syllables. Catching such repetitions requires a high degree of self-awareness. In this as in many other instances, your best hope is to have a friend or a colleague read your work with a critical eye. You can earn the favor by reading his.

Respective

"Respective" and "respectively" are such complicated words that defining them is like a short excursion into the New Math. Their function is to link the members of two sets with identical cardinality in a one-to-one correspondence in the order of their enumeration. Got that? In other words, if you say that A, B, and C relate to X, Y, and Z respectively, you're saying that the two groups pair up A–X, B–Y, and C–Z. The times when that needs to be said are, to put it mildly, rare. Often it's understood without saying:

▷ The experimental animals were then returned to their respective cages.

Here is an author who does not trust his readers' common sense. If each animal were put in another animal's cage, that would require comment; but if, as we expect, each animal goes back to his own cage, we don't need "respective" to keep us on the track.

The experimental animals were then returned to their cages.

Even in the rare instance when you do need "respective" or "respectively," rewriting will usually do the job more neatly.

▷ Backhart, Miles, and Babbidge stood for Devon, East Anglia, and Wales respectively.

Backhart stood for Devon, Miles for East Anglia, and Babbidge for Wales.

Both versions say the same thing, but the second says it with more grace.

The Waffle

This is another case of hyperqualification, but at the level of sentences and paragraphs instead of words and phrases.

▷ We would like to have more information about the small-scale flow, but our model can account for all the information in laboratory experiments. Observations in nature are, however, all too few. The fact remains that under experimental conditions much of value can be learned. But the field work will undoubtedly mean that we must correct many of our assumptions. In the meantime, nevertheless, the work in vitro will continue.

Any waffle this tightly woven is immediately apparent, and no one would veer back and forth this way in so short a space. But if the ideas are large ones, with a good deal of exposition, you do frequently see what amounts to "A but B but A but B."

Outlining is the best cure for waffles. I don't mean the kind of outlining done beforehand, because not one person in a hundred can work that way. But the outline you do afterward is a different story. Write a sentence of outline for each paragraph of text—a sentence rather than just a label, because what you're looking for are shifts signaled by words like "but" and "on the other hand," which won't show up with labels.

By the way, this kind of outlining is helpful for paragraphing too. A paragraph that can't be outlined in a single sentence should often be two paragraphs.

Which-Hunting

I understand that if you tape-record a person who's carrying on a normal conversation, he follows the normal English pattern for relative pronouns, "that" for restrictive clauses, "which" for nonrestrictive. He does, that is, unless you tell him that he's addressing an audience, or dictating a formal letter or a paper. At that point, he starts substituting "which" for "that." This is another of those bending-over-backwards errors, the ones that result from affecting an unnatural, prissy diction in writing.

The first cure, then, is to listen to what you write. For many people that will be sufficient.

▷ The novel which is emerging in the Third World does not fit our standard categories.

If you're lucky, that will sound awful to you, and you'll change it easily and automatically to:

The novel that is emerging in the Third World does not fit our standard categories.

Don't give up if you can't hear it right away. Your ear has undoubtedly been battered by all the bad prose you've had to read, but the damage is not permanent.

If you have a good grasp of comma punctuation, all you need to know is that which-clauses are set off by commas.

These regulations, which Elizabeth had no intention of following, went into effect the following summer.

No commas, no "which":

▷ He preferred the settlement which his sister had proposed.

He preferred the settlement that his sister had proposed.

But if you're weak on both "which/that" and commas, you'll have to think about the grammar of restrictive and non-restrictive clauses. Restrictive clauses ("that" with no commas) are essential, defining, irremovable. Non-restrictive clauses ("which" with commas) are parenthetical, descriptive, detachable. The trouble comes in deciding what you mean to say. In most cases, you can't decide the sentence by itself; you need to look around at the context.

The leaf _____ the grub has used for shelter now becomes its food.

"That" with no commas or "which" with commas? There's no way to tell by looking at the sentence in isolation. Check the context to see how the clause relates to the noun it's modifying. If "the leaf" is a fresh expression, not mentioned before, or not sufficient in itself for your reader to know what leaf you're talking about, the clause is restrictive.

The leaf that the grub has used for shelter now becomes its food.

If you've already talked about the leaf, your reader knows full well what leaf you mean, and you're just reminding him, the clause is non-restrictive.

The leaf, which the grub has used for shelter, now becomes its food.

Another way of checking the same distinction is to try out imaginary uprooting.

The training _____ the Agency gives is free except for books and supplies.

"That" with no commas or "which" with commas? Again, only the context can answer the question. But try ripping out the clause and putting it after the sentence.

The training is free except for books and supplies. The Agency gives the training.

If that makes sense in context, the clause is non-restrictive:

The training, which the Agency gives, is free except for books and supplies.

But if the uprooted version is nonsense—if the reader must ask, "What training? What are you talking about?"—then the clause is restrictive. A restrictive clause uprooted would have to go before the sentence.

The Agency gives training. The training is free except for books and supplies.

If this is the only version that makes sense in context, what you want is "that" with no commas:

The training that the Agency gives is free except for books and supplies.

As a desperate last measure, if you're completely at a loss, use "that" with no commas. It's the more common construction by maybe ten to one, so the odds will be with you.

THE
REFERENCE

To write a reference, you must have the work you're referring to in front of you. Do not rely on your memory. Do not rely on your memory. Just in case the idea ever occurred to you, do not rely on your memory.

The tidy, thorough scholar will take down a full reference on an index card whenever he reads anything worth mentioning, keep a card file of these references, and construct his reference lists quickly and effortlessly from his file. If you are untidy and disorganized, like most of us, you may find yourself throwing together your reference list at the last minute. The temptation to write a reference without having the work before you will be powerful. Resist it. A vague recollection is worthless; a vivid recollection is probably the product of your imagination—ingenious, no doubt, but of little use to your reader. Don't rely on your memory.

It is best to write out a reference when you first encounter a work you may later refer to. Now you can remember how you found it. Later it will be part of your mental furniture. You will no longer remember that you once puzzled over its obscure publisher, its misleading Library of Congress entry, its pseudonymous authorship. Now is the time to write a reference, to save your reader from repeating your puzzlement.

If you failed to write out a reference you now need, get hold of the source again. You will be surprised to see that the incisive expression you remember is a misquotation; the diagram you recollect shows something else; the memorable anecdote illustrates another point; the book you can see as if it were before you doesn't exist. If you don't write references out at first encounter, you will waste many hours tracking them down in the library. Better you than your reader.

What should a reference say? As always, you can figure out the answer by putting yourself in your reader's place. Your text has captivated him. He wants to know more. It's your responsibility to help him. Of course you should make your references crisp and uniform whenever possible, because crisp, uniform reference lists are easier to read than muddy, jumbled ones. But you must never sacrifice information to form. If an informative reference must be messy and peculiar, it must—better that than a sleek and shiny one that lacks crucial data.

The objection is often made "But no one would be looking at my paper who doesn't know Brazzleton's work. No reader would be able to make out what I'm talking about without that background." Much scholarly writing is done at universities, in departments of like-minded people, all of whom correspond with like-minded people at other universities. The young scholar feels that he is writing for his thesis committee and his friends and that fellow at Toronto who's working along the same lines—a little world. He forgets that the written word is the instrument of a great world, a democracy of the mind. You may never reach the reader from that great world, the unexpected reader, the anonymous reader. But you must remember the possibility that he exists and by no action of yours exclude him. It is in writing references that the fellowship of scholars takes its most concrete, practical form. The careless or deliberate withholding of information about how to find sources is a betrayal of that fellowship. Writing a good reference is an occasion for thoughtful generosity.

I want to tell a story that illustrates two of these points.

The great mathematician G. H. Hardy was sitting one day in his study in Cambridge when he noticed in the afternoon's mail an odd letter. The letter covered many pages, and each page was different from the one before. Only two of the pieces of paper were new when the writer used them, one a piece of ordinary stationery, the other a piece of butcher's paper. All the rest of the pieces of paper were obviously recovered from wastebaskets, uncrumpled and smoothed out, the original contents effaced so that the writer could use the backs. The handwriting was the badly formed, childish scrawl of the nearly illiterate, written very small to conserve paper, and written in smudged pencil to boot.

"Dear Sir," the letter said, "I am but a poor Indian sweeper boy, and you will think me foolish for even dreaming that I might be able to look at your splendid papers. Having done so, I have only demonstrated my unworthiness to attempt to understand your brilliant mind, because it seems to me that these papers are full of mistakes, and how could this be so? Let me show you what I have thought so that you can tell me the errors I am making and set me on the right path again."

Hardy read this with a tolerant smile. Prominent mathematicians get a steady trickle of mail from madmen and mathematical incompetents who believe that they have proved the four-color theorem or trisected the angle with a straightedge. Often the letters are amusing.

This one was not. As he read on, Hardy realized that he was seeing for the first time a fundamental error in his work. In a few badly written pages, the sweeper boy was demolishing several years of research. Hardy was astonished, embarrassed, and then (he really was a great man) delighted. Never before had he seen such insight, such unorthodox approaches, such delicious mathematical wit. He sent to India, but the boy would not come alone, so he went and fetched him. The Indian sweeper boy, whose name was Ramanujan, became Hardy's colleague and his best friend.

This story illustrates the possibility that your scholarly work may reach far beyond the little world you know. It also illustrates the wisdom of writing down a reference on first encounter—because of course I am unable to recall where I read it. The harder a time

I have confirming it, the more certain it seems that I have made it up, or misremembered it, or colored it more highly than the original will permit. C. P. Snow describes the incident in his introduction to Hardy's autobiography, but his version is a little different from the one I know, and less detailed. So I repeat the story with much trepidation, less to support the first point than the second.

If you must not rely on your own memory, even less should you rely on someone else's. If your only access to a reference is through a secondary source, then you must refer to the secondary source as well as the primary one. The principle of secondary reference is not just scholarly etiquette; it's scholarly ethics.

To invent an extreme case, let's say that I'm trying to recall where Paul speaks of himself as a citizen of no mean city in order to refer to it in a paper I'm writing on Roman law. I flip through the Epistles with no luck. I don't have a concordance at home, and the library's shut. Stumped. Suddenly I remember that I once read something about that line in an essay on Luther's Pauline commentaries. I search out the essay, leaf through it, and there it is: Such-and-such, so-and-so, citizen of no mean city, Acts 12:39. May I then write my reference to Acts 12:39?

No.

Secondhand information must be presented as secondhand. To treat it as if it came from the horse's mouth is dishonest. Unless I confirm the reference, I must give it as

Acts 12:39.
Cited in S. Pilov, Luther's commentaries on Law and Gospel in Paul. A *Light to Light the Gentiles*, page 341. J. A. Allen, London, England, 1969.

Since the Bible is sitting right there in front of me, I can use the only permissible device for avoiding a secondary reference by writing my reference straight from the primary source.

As you will see if you look at Acts 12:39, treating a secondary reference as if it were primary is not only dishonest but dangerous. There is no verse 39; chapter 12 ends with verse 25. What happened to Pilov? Maybe he dozed off as he was checking that item on his reference list; maybe (perish the thought) he was relying on his memory. Whatever the reason, unless I give the reference as secondary, the responsibility for the error in my paper is mine. I make enough mistakes on my own without taking the blame for other people's too. So if you cannot confirm a reference in its primary source, give it in secondary form for your own sake as much as for your reader's.

To bring this little fable to a happy conclusion, let's say that after only five more minutes of searching I find the primary source, write my reference to Acts 21:39, and sigh with relief.

Panorama

The next sections cover in great detail the construction of a reference and the compilation of a reference list. But first, here is a sample list (on the right) with labels (on the left).

The purpose of the right-hand side is to give you something to look forward to as you work on your references. Some of the decisions you must make about setting up an individual reference depend on visualizing your final list and where you want the reference to fall in that list. So this is what the end of the process typically looks like, a numbered alphabetical listing with some cross-references from one item to another.

The purpose of the left-hand side is to serve as a quick review of the most common components of a reference list. The labels are in alphabetical order, and the examples are of the simplest cases, not of the tricky and unusual ones. When you have a hard case or need an explanation, go to the index. But when all you need is to jog your memory, here are some short reminders.

Since the pattern of your research may lead you to make frequent use of a kind of reference the rest of the world would call uncommon, some space is left at the end of the list for additional entries.

Author's name as he gives it   1] M. Atamer.
                Book title   *Prehispanic Art in Mexico,*
                                  page 279.
                                  Pennsylvania State University
                                  Press, 1958.

                                  Karl Bantry.
                                  The Modern Temperament.
                                  Schocken, 1971.
                                  2] Pages 49–61.
Compound reference   3] Page 134.
                                  4] Pages 197–203.

Corporate author   5] The Brighton Conservatory.
                                  Catalog of primitive
                                  instrument collection.
                                  Oxton House Press, Brighton,
                                  England, 1969.

Cross-reference   Kathleen Chaudry, see Slater
                                  [25].

                              6] N. L. Dahlgard.
                                  Formability in Sheet Metal.
                                  University of Newfoundland
Date of publication   Press, 1964.

                              7] P. G. Enriquez, editor.
                                  Infant Development.
Edition after the first   Macmillan, third edition 1974.

Editor-compiler   8] Raymond Fukada, editor.
                                  Teaching Machines.
                                  University of Virginia Press,
                                  1969.

                              9] Oliver Goldsmith (1730–74).
                                  The Complete Plays.
Editor-preparer   Edited by C. E. Mott. Cambridge
                                  University Press, 1960.

                             10] J. A. Hein.
                                  My turn: The dwindling supply
                                  of sunshine.
Extended date   *Newsweek* XXXII(17):39, 21 July
                                  1973.

First edition (no mention)

11] L. Insdorf.
The French Fable, pages 206–
220.
Dutton, 1961.

Foreign title

12] H. O. Jarvin.
Los Entremesos. (*The Snacks.*)
Calledoros, Maracaibo,
Venezuela, 1975.

Joint authors

Journal article

13] M. Klingfield, B. C. Mangino,
and J. A. Betts.
Foci of cortical degeneration.
Cerebrum XIV(2):134–191,
1964.

Major publisher (no address)

14] M-A. Lepesant.
Kafka's Dreams.
Cornell University Press, 1959.

Multivolume work

15] Herman Matthews, editor.
The Death of the Frontier.
Four volumes. Random House,
1963–72.

Non-book title

16] F. J. Narendra.
Counterforce attacks: A
strategy for limiting nuclear
warfare.
Foreign Affairs Quarterly IX
(1):34–39, 1970.

Obscure publisher

17] Eleanor Ortel.
Pitching Pennies.
The Wheelwright Press, 1348
Milburne Street, Springton,
Ohio 40873. 1957.

One volume of multivolume
work (cross-reference)

18] A. J. Pantini.
The Road West, pages 59–82.
Volume II in Matthews [15],
1968.

One volume of multivolume
work (no cross-reference)

19] R. D. Quinn.
Drama in Britain.
Volume IV in R. M. Costa,
editor, *Modern Drama.* Viking,
1967.

PhD thesis

20] Jill Rawlick.
Shakespeare on Film.
PhD thesis, City University of
New York, 1969.

Pinpointing after title

21] V. Rowlins.
Quarks and Hadrons, pages
47–59.
Harcourt Brace Jovanovich,
1976.

Pinpointing without pages
(for works in many editions)

22] Siegfried Sassoon.
Memoirs of a Fox-Hunting Man,
chapter 9.
St. Martin's Press edition,
1971.

Portion of a compilation
(cross-reference)

23] A. Scalia.
Motor skills at fourteen
months.
In Enriquez [7], pages 300–
342.

Portion of a compilation
(no cross-reference)

24] Peter Seever.
The salvation of Lake Huron.
In Carla S. Braceland, editor,
*The Biology of the Great
Lakes,* pages 79–142. Double-
day, 1970.

Pseudonym

25] Anne Slater (pseudonym of
Kathleen Chaudry).
Sail a Tall Ship.
Grove Press, 1967.

Review

Secondary reference

Translation

Translator

26] R. L. Snowden, Jr.
Review of Mark Heidman, *The Melville Knot.*
The New Republic XLI(31):34, 1971. Cited in Lepesant [14], page 433.

27] Claude Trussé.
A Stroll in the Lobby. (Un Tour au Foyer.)
Translated by S. Griman. University of Toronto Press, 1961.

I find it entertaining to try to construct the article for which this would be the reference list.

Reference Format

Style

The three basic blocks: Easy references fall into three blocks:

    I. Author.
    II. Title.
    III. Bibliographic information.

For instance, the two most common references are to books and journal articles:

    author → Clement Simms.
    title → *Small-Scale Aquaculture.*
    bibliographic → Princeton University Press, 1968.
    information

    author → Sharon Fiedler.
    title → Elements of pattern in Matisse.
    bibliographic → *Art Notes* XII(2):47–81, 1971.
    information

All of the references in the panorama are easy references; they fit the three-block format naturally.

The two optional blocks: To help your reader, you will sometimes add one or both of the two optional blocks:

IV. More bibliographic information.
V. Annotation.

The bibliographic information in block III describes the work you have before you; the bibliographic information in block IV describes some other version of the work that you happen to know about and that your reader may find more accessible than the one you're using. For instance:

> author → C. L. Granger.
> title → Courtship among the Duhbir.
> bibliographic → In Frances Rounds, editor, *Marriage and*
> information *Family Structure*, pages 38–96. Harper
> & Row, 1971.
> more → Originally in *Anthropos* XI(1):211–296,
> bibliographic 1968.
> information

In other words, you're working with the version that appears in the compilation edited by Rounds, but your reader might more easily put his hands on the original publication in the journal.

For the sake of convenience, I will call a block of annotation that's not bibliographic block V even when there's no block IV. Annotation might be special information on the author, a comment on the work, or a cross-reference to a related work—anything that your reader might find useful.

References with all five blocks are rare. For the sake of illustration, here are two examples:

> author → M. H. Schultz and R. S. Varga.
> title → L-splines.
> bibliographic → *Numerische Mathematik* 10(2):345–369,
> information 1967.
> more → Also published as Stanford Technical
> bibliographic Memorandum on Splines #334207–
> information Bromo–002, September 1967.
> annotation → Chapter 2 of Schultz [3] gives a smoother
> presentation of these results.

author → V. Nabokov.
title → The nearctic members of the genus Lycaeides Hübner.
bibliographic information → *Bulletin of the Museum of Comparative Zoology*, Harvard University, 101(4): 1–149, 1949.
more bibliographic information → Collected in A. C. Simon, *Color and Camouflage*. Ohio State University Press, 1954.
annotation → The author is the Nabokov better known outside lepidopterist circles for *Lolita* and *Ada*.

Bite-sized chunks: Each block starts with a capital letter and ends with a period. One or more phrases within a block may also end with periods; break the information up to make it as readable as you can. For instance, block III of a book reference usually has the publisher and the date of publication separated by a comma:

Hopkinson and Blake, 1969.

But that format doesn't work when you're listing the address of an obscure publisher:

▷ The Press in the Barn, RFD Route 7, Miller's Falls, Oregon 94883, 1962.

Use a period to separate the zip code from the date in this case:

The Press in the Barn, RFD Route 7, Miller's Falls, Oregon 94883. 1962.

Bad examples are marked with an arrowhead (▷).

Or again, block III of a reference to a portion of a compilation usually has a comma between the word "editor" and the title of the compilation:

> In F. N. Osman, editor, *The Quest for Rectitude*, pages 230–251. Scribner's, 1942.

But when the compilation has a very long title, then editor, title, and pages are too much to swallow all at once:

▷ In Simon Ashe, editor, A *Vision of the Future: Psychology, Sociology, and the Overthrow of Theology in Hawthorne,* pages 160–184. Louisiana State University Press, 1971.

A period after "editor" is a help in this case:

> In Simon Ashe, editor. A *Vision of the Future: Psychology, Sociology, and the Overthrow of Theology in Hawthorne,* pages 160–184. Louisiana State University Press, 1971.

On a typewriter, two spaces follow a period used to break up the information in a block. Below the examples the spacing is shown with crosshatches.

▷ In R. T. Banta, editor, <u>The Romance of the Nile,</u> pages 38–69. Princeton University Press, 1972.

▷ 38–69.#Princeton

> In R. T. Banta, editor, <u>The Romance of the Nile,</u> pages 38–69. Princeton University Press, 1972.

38–69.##Princeton

Open versus compressed format: In the open format, each block starts a fresh line:

> Evan Graham.
> 18th century keyboard fingering.
> *Musica* XII(3):41–102, 1965.

When a block runs over one line long, the second and following lines are indented:

> E. D. Hiatt, editor.
> *The Speculative Tradition in the Middle Ages.* Volume II:
>   *Technological Innovation in Medieval Agriculture and Weaponry.*
> Pergamon, 1956.

The indentation should be neither puny nor gross:

> ▷ *The Speculative Tradition in the Middle Ages.* Volume II:
>   *Technological Innovation in Medieval Agriculture and Weaponry.*
> ▷ *The Speculative Tradition in the Middle Ages.* Volume II:
>   *Technological Innovation in Medieval Agriculture and Weaponry.*

In the compressed format, the blocks are run together with no indentation. On a typewriter, each of the periods that separates the blocks is followed by two spaces.

> Michael Dewer. A raving maniac. *The New York Review of Books* XIX(4):5–9, 18 May 1971.
> ```
> Dewer.##A . . . maniac.##The
> ```

Because it's easier to read, most of the examples in this book are in the open format. The compressed format is usually just as suitable unless your references are exceptionally complicated and messy.

Numbered examples: At the time when you construct your references (on first encounter with the works, naturally) they won't be numbered. Most of the examples that follow are numbered, as if they were taken from a finished reference list, to get you accustomed to the system and to demonstrate the uses of cross-reference.

One bracket: Because the bracketed number is always at the left margin of your reference list, you may if you like use only the right bracket:

> 51] L. E. Vanderhaben.
>   Scott Fitzgerald and the will to tragedy.
>   *Perspectives* VIII(3):47–58, 1963.

That's the style I've followed in this book because I like its sleekness. But if you prefer, you may use both brackets:

> [51] L. E. Vanderhaben.
>   Scott Fitzgerald and the will to tragedy.
>   *Perspectives* VIII(3):47–58, 1963.

In your text, the numbers always need both brackets even if they chance to fall at the left margin now and then.

I. Authors

Normal order: List authors' names in normal order, not in reverse order.

> ▷ Perkins, Edward.
>   Edward Perkins.

Reverse order doesn't do much harm to simple names and may even be some help in alphabetizing, but it makes hash of joint authors:

▷ Sewell, E. R., Pastern, B. L., and Cooper, D. G.

   E. R. Sewell, B. L. Pastern, and D. G. Cooper.

To say nothing of the occasional noble you must refer to:

▷ Dorset (Sackville, Thomas), 1st Earl of.

   Thomas Sackville, 1st Earl of Dorset.

Initials: This is a small point even for a book that deals with little other than small points, but people's initials are spaced out:

▷ M.J. Bruner.

▷ M.J. Bruner.

   M. J. Bruner.

   M.#J.#Bruner.

The crosshatches show the correct spacing.

What name?: It is an elementary courtesy to an author to give his name as it appears on his work. For a book, the title page is the thing to follow, not the spine or the dust jacket or the library catalog entry. For a journal article, the name at the head or the foot of the article is the thing to follow, not the table of contents or the running head at the top of the page or the annual index.

   In theory, this rule applies to your own work as well as other people's. Suppose, for instance, that an author who usually calls himself "Ralph V. Schreiber" gets an article published and finds to his surprise that his name has been rendered "R. Schreiber." How should he list himself in a reference to his own article? By strict and narrow propriety, the answer is "R. Schreiber." But since it was an impropriety that worked the alteration to start with, it's forgivable for him to restore his name to the version he prefers, and he needn't even use brackets for his restorations.

Adding information: You have no obligation to search out the parts of an author's name hidden by initials. Even when you know this information, you have no obligation to give it unless you think it will be helpful to your reader. When you do add information, use brackets around your contributions. Suppose you're referring to an article on which the author's name appears as "W. B. Clark." Your entry may follow the original:

W. B. Clark.

Or you may plump it out:

W[illa] B[aines] Clark.

Joint authors: The names of joint authors appear in block I as they do on the original, but with the following exceptions. Regardless of the style of the original, write out "and" before the final name:

▷ Michael I. Shamos, Daniel P. Hoey.
▷ Michael I. Shamos & Daniel P. Hoey.
Michael I. Shamos and Daniel P. Hoey.

Regardless of the style of the original, if there are three or more authors use a comma after every one but the last:

▷ W. Lehnert, J. Meehan and R. Schank.
W. Lehnert, J. Meehan, and R. Schank.

Joint authors with the same last name should have listed themselves on the original:

Bergan Evans and Cornelia Evans.

If they didn't, fix the entry up:

Ruth [Wallerstein] and Margaret Wallerstein.

Pseudonymity: The reference to a work published under a pseudonym uses the pseudonym as block I. (This is just an extension of the rule about giving an author's name as he prefers it.) Enclose whatever additional information you have to contribute in parentheses—parentheses rather than brackets because you may want to include a cross-reference, and brackets within brackets look awful.

▷ Samuel Clemens.

▷ Samuel Clemens (Mark Twain, pseudonym).

Mark Twain.

or Mark Twain (pseudonym of Samuel Clemens).

When you have entries for one author under more than one name, use cross-references to help your reader see the connection:

5] John Canaday. See also Head [19].
Kitchen implements of the Neargos.
In J. L. Mattison, editor, *Tools and Totems of the Congo People*, pages 18–22. Crowell, 1973.
. . .

19] Matthew Head (pseudonym of John Canaday [5]).
Congo Venus.
Dutton, 1949.

Sometimes you may not know who stands behind a pseudonym:

Pauline Réage (pseudonym).

Anonymity: Block I for a work of unknown or unacknowledged authorship reads:

Anonymous.

Use the last block to give further information:

> 3] Anonymous.
> The running dogs of intellectual imperialism.
> *The Old Mole,* 9 February 1969.
> Attributed to Michael Ansarra.

You needn't try to keep a secret once the cat's out of the bag:

> ▷ Anonymous.
> Against prelacy.
> London, 1641.
> Known to be the work of John Milton.

> John Milton.
> Against prelacy.
> London, 1641.
> The pamphlet was unsigned.

Do not confuse corporate authorship with anonymity:

> ▷ Anonymous.
> Final report of the President's Committee on Expansion.
> St. Louis University, 1935.

> St. Louis University, President's Committee on Expansion.
> Final report, 1935.

Honorifics: Titles of education, occupation, and honor do not ordinarily appear in block I. (For that matter, they should never have appeared in the original works. An author who feels compelled to list himself as "PhD" or "Professor of Entomology" or "Member of the American Academy of Arts and Sciences" has the scent of snake oil about him, no matter how respectable the designation he lays claim to. Of course, the fault may be not his but his publisher's. Few publishers realize the strength of the academic bias against honorifics, and many an innocent author has been made to look braggardly against his will.)

You may sometimes want to mention an author's special qualifications in the last block:

9] N. J. Froissart.
Notes on cheilostomatoplasty aftermath.
Proceedings of the 17th Annual AASP Convention,
American Association of Surgical Practitioners, 1974.
The author is the head of surgery at Mount Zion Hospital in Kansas City, where Stamitz and Benton [18,19, 22] developed the procedure.

The main entry for a noble or a royal should follow the style you adopt in your text. If you call the poet "Rochester" or "Lord Rochester," alphabetize the item under R:

38] S. A. Richards.
Review of Graham Greene, *Lord Rochester's Monkey.*
Tarnation II(7):57–61, 1975.

→ 39] John Wilmot, second earl of Rochester.
Revile this hand.
In C. L. Bel Geddes, editor, *The Complete Poems,* page 202. Aquila Publishing, Isle of Skye, Scotland, 1971.

40] Friedlind Rumsfeld.
A History of Wadham College, pages 278–291.
Oxford University Press, 1922.

On a long list, a cross-reference under W would not be amiss. Notice that a cross-reference standing alone needs no number:

58] Pamela Wilkins.
Banishment and disgrace: Lord Rochester at court.
The Restoration Quarterly VII(3):102–164, 1969.

→   John Wilmot, see Rochester [39].

59] E. N. Worthy.
New light on the kidnaping affair.
The Journal of the Rochester Society XXI(3):41–60, 1971.

If you call him "Wilmot," the main entry goes under W and the cross-reference under R.

Corporate authors: Some flexibility is desirable in describing corporate authors. Suppose for instance that you're referring to a pamphlet put out by the Leeds branch of the Royal Society for the Prevention of Cruelty to Animals. If your article is about Leeds, you might want to do the entry for the pamphlet as:

Royal Society for the Prevention of Cruelty to Animals, Leeds Branch.

If your article is about RSPCA, you might want to do the entry as:

Leeds Branch, Royal Society for the Prevention of Cruelty to Animals.

It's not a matter of major importance as long as you get the information across.

Editors and translators: There are two kinds of editors, the one who compiles the work of several authors and the one who prepares the work of a single author. The first may sometimes be called a compiler or an anthologist; the second is almost always called an editor.

The compiler-editor is listed in block I if you are referring to the whole compilation, in block III if you are referring to part of it:

    15] Aimee Rolinson, editor.
    The Language of Labor: An Anthology.
    Smith David & Company, Atlanta, Georgia, 1967.

    6] R. Winston Hyat.
    The lingo of high steel, with a few notes on the Plains Dakota.
    In Aimee Rolinson, editor, *The Language of Labor: An Anthology*, pages 46–87. Smith David & Company, Atlanta, Georgia, 1967.

If you refer to both the whole compilation and a part of it in the same list, use a cross-reference in block III of the reference to the part.

    11] E. D. Klemke, editor.
    Essays on Wittgenstein.
    University of Illinois Press, 1972.

    . . .

    24] S. A. Rownia.
    Patterns of influence in the later years.
    In Klemke [11], pages 42–57.

The preparer-editor almost always appears in block III:

    114] Robert Wood.
    Ruins of Palmyra.
    Edited by M. H. Chevale. Boston University Press, 1958.
    Originally published in London, 1753.

The only exception to this rule is that occasionally you may want to compare two or more editions of one author's work. Then your reference list may be easier to read if you put the preparer-editors in block I. Suppose you are comparing two editions of Washington Irving. Your reference list might read:

3] Saxe Commins, editor.
Selected Works of Washington Irving.
Random House, 1945.

4] Amos Dodd, editor.
Washington Irving: The Complete Works.
New York, 1863–66.

But there is nothing wrong with using the alternative form:

10] Washington Irving.
The Complete Works.
Edited by Amos Dodd. New York, 1863–66.

11] Washington Irving.
Selected Works.
Edited by Saxe Commins. Random House, 1945.

Just be sure to treat both editors the same way.

Translators, like preparer-editors, usually appear in block III:

4] Theodore Blatch.
Thomas Erastus and Ecclesiastical Discipline.
Translated from the French by Sylvia Schauerbach.
University of South Dakota Press, 1967.

But again, if you are comparing two or more translations you may want to list the translators in block I. Suppose you are comparing the first translation of Euclid into English with the first translation into French. Your reference list might read:

2] H. Billingsley, translator.
The Elements of Geometry of the Most Ancient Philosopher Euclide of Megara.
London, 1570.
Facsimile edition published by the Society for Historical Mathematics, Norton Road, Masham, Yorkshire.
. . .

13] D. Henrion, translator.
Les Quinze Livres des Eléments d'Euclide.
Paris, second edition 1623.
Originally published in 1615. There are about twenty
copies extant, one of them in the Archives Nationales
in Paris.

But the alternative form, with Euclid in block I and the translators
in block III, is equally good.

If it's not apparent, let your reader know what language the
translation is from:

21] K. J. Lindskog.
Dreams of Flight.
Translated from the Swedish by A. Richards. Sussex
University Press, 1975.

Writing some notes and front matter is a regular part of the job
of editing or translating and requires no special mention in your
reference.

▷ R. L. Chee, editor and author of an introduction, an ap-
pendix, and explanatory notes.
Biological Controls.
University of Texas Press, 1975.

R. L. Chee, editor.
Biological Controls.
University of Texas Press, 1975.

But sometimes your reference is to the annotative material. This
is how it might look for an editor-preparer:

9] Rolf Eberle.
Foreword to Turbayne [43], pages x–xxviii.
. . .

43] Colin Murray Turbayne.
The Complete Poems.
Edited by Rolf Eberle. University Press of New Eng-
land, 1969.

For an editor-compiler:

14] D. M. Julianelle, editor.
Introduction to *Ethnic Geography*, pages i–xxxii.
Harper & Row, 1958.

And for a translator:

18] Rosario Sawyer.
Moorish Influences in the Cathedral Architecture of Mexico.
Translated from the Spanish by F. A. Wright. Scribner's, 1968.
. . .

44] F. A. Wright.
Appendix to Sawyer [18], pages 689–714.

Even if you make no other mention of the main work, it's worthwhile to write a reference to it for the sake of cross-reference. Without the opportunity for cross-reference, the entry gets pretty complicated.

▷ F. A. Wright.
Appendix to Rosario Sawyer, *Moorish Influences in the Cathedral Architecture of Mexico*, pages 689–714. Translated from the Spanish by Wright. Scribner's, 1968.

II. Titles

Block II of an easy reference is the title of the work; in references to journal articles, portions of compilations, and volumes of multi-volume works there are titles in block III as well.

What is a book?: Since the punctuation of a title depends on whether the work is a book or a non-book, it is necessary to ask what a book is.

A book is a fat thing bound by itself, or the equivalent in some other medium of a fat thing bound by itself. A non-book is a thin thing or a thing that's part of something else, or the equivalent in some other medium of a thin thing or a thing that's part of something else.

A book is a book. One volume of a multivolume work is a book, and so is the whole multivolume work.

Anything that contains articles by different people is a book, even if it's thin. A journal is a book. A magazine is a book, and so is a newspaper. A conference proceedings is a book.

An article in a journal or a magazine is a non-book, even if it takes up one whole issue. What if it's later published as a book? Then the book is a book, but the article remains a non-book.

Is a PhD thesis a book? Yes, but a Master's thesis is not, and neither is any other homework assignment before the PhD. What if a Master's thesis is later published as a book? Again, the book is a book, but the thesis remains a non-book.

A short novel is a book; a long novella is not. A short story is not a book. A poem is not a book unless it's book-length and bound by itself. Chapters of books are not books.

A pamphlet, leaflet, brochure, or booklet is not a book. A report is usually a non-book, although if it's very long and bound by itself you may want to call it a book.

Letters, memos, and notes are not books. Recipes, formulas, equations, and theorems are not books. Laws are not books, although they do tend to go on.

An opera is a book; an aria is a non-book. A musical is a book; a song is a non-book. A record album is a book; a band, a side, or a cut is not. No sketch, print, or painting is a book. A sculpture is not a book.

In both religious and classical studies there are any number of works that were never titled. We call them by conventional names, and these names, being proper nouns, are capitalized. But they're not titles, and they're not underlined or italicized. The Bible and the books of the Bible, the Socratic dialogues, the Koran, the Rig Veda, and many other works are named but not titled. The Fleta and the Britton, from the reign of Edward I of England, follow this pattern; so does the Penal Code.

When you have a choice, your bias should be toward classing works as non-books; the less punctuation in your reference list, the easier it is to read. Make a decision and stick to it—don't punctuate a borderline case as a book in your text and a non-book in your reference list.

Book titles: In both your text and your reference list, book titles get uppers-and-lowers punctuation (capitalize the first word, the first word after a colon, and all other words except articles and unstressed conjunctions and prepositions). Book titles also get underlined or italicized. Underline straight through:

▷ <u>Oxford Reformers</u>.

<u>Oxford Reformers</u>.

Do not underline the period at the end of the block:

▷ <u>Citizen Involvement</u>.

<u>Citizen Involvement</u>.

If your reference list is fairly simple and you're using the open format, you may omit the underline or italics from book titles; the uppers-and-lowers punctuation alone will be enough to do the job.

> 22] Jane Henry.
> A Systematic Study of the Marine Algae of the American East Coast.
> Dodd, Mead, 1971.

Never omit the underline or italics in the compressed format, or in your text.

In uppers-and-lowers punctuation you encounter the problem of how to capitalize hyphenated words. Your bias should be against upper case, in favor of lower case.

▷ *An Affair of Far-Reaching Consequences.*

An Affair of Far-reaching Consequences.

Non-book titles: In your text, non-book titles are punctuated with uppers-and-lowers and surrounded by quotation marks. In your reference list, neither the uppers-and-lowers nor the quotation marks are necessary. Use sentence punctuation (capitalize the first word, the first word after a colon, and no other words except proper nouns and proper adjectives). Omit the quotation marks.

Sources for a survey of English porcelain.

Even data bases that lie can be compromised.

The Chinese brush: A critical study of the period 1848–1910.

Titles within titles: Critical works give rise to titles within titles. Here are the possible combinations and how to handle them. If you have no italics, use this chart:

Inner Title	Outer Title	Inner Style	Outer Style
non-book	non-book	"Uppers and Lowers"	Unquoted sentence punctuation.
book	non-book	Uppers and Lowers	Unquoted sentence punctuation.
non-book	book	"Uppers and Lowers"	Uppers and Lowers.
book	book	"Uppers and Lowers"	Uppers and Lowers.

If you have italics, use this chart:

Inner Title	Outer Title	Inner Style	Outer Style
non-book	non-book	"Uppers and Lowers"	Unquoted sentence punctuation.
book	non-book	*Uppers and Lowers*	Unquoted sentence punctuation.
non-book	book	"Uppers and Lowers"	*Uppers and Lowers.*
book	book	Uppers and Lowers	*Uppers and Lowers.*

Non-book within non-book looks the same whether you have italics or not:

An addendum to Marinovski's "Motions in Log Space."

Book within non-book varies:

Citizen Kane, The Great Gatsby, and some
conventions of American narrative.

Citizen Kane, The Great Gatsby, and some conventions of American narrative.

Without italics, both non-book and book within book look the same:

Collected Essays on Yeats's "A Prayer for
My Son."
Lawrence, Sartre, and "Women in Love."

With italics, non-book within book looks like this:

Collected Essays on Yeats's "A Prayer for My Son."

And book within book looks like this:

Lawrence, Sartre, and Women in Love.

Odd originals: A number of important works of the twentieth century deliberately violate typographical conventions. If you follow the style of the original, your reference looks odd; if you don't, it looks prissy.

i: six nonlectures.
I: *Six Nonlectures.*

The joke would cease to be a joke if it ceased causing us discomfort.

When odd typography is a convention rather than a flouting of convention, ignore it. Some journals, for instance, style themselves and all the articles in them in full caps. Convert such titles to the usual pattern.

> ▷ S. P. Bower.
> AFFERENT IMPULSES TO THE CEREBELLAR
>   HEMISPHERES.
> *THE JOURNAL OF NEUROPHYSIOLOGY* 130(1):
>   55–75, 1957.

> S. P. Bower.
> Afferent impulses to the cerebellar hemispheres.
> *The Journal of Neurophysiology* 130(1):55–75, 1957.

Short titles: Shortened versions of titles should never appear on your reference list. The chapter on special schemes gives some uses for short names in your text, in your footnotes, and in a special section between your text and your reference list. But on the reference list itself, a title should appear in its entirety.

> ▷ Edmund Burke.
> *The Sublime and Beautiful.*

> Edmund Burke.
> *Philosophical Inquiry into the Origin of Our Ideas on the
>   Sublime and Beautiful.*

The only reason ever to eliminate part of a title is to avoid uninformative repetition.

> ▷ W. B. Yeats.
> *The Collected Poems of W. B. Yeats.*

> W. B. Yeats.
> *The Collected Poems.*

Title-colon-subtitle: Regardless of the style of the original, add a colon if it's needed to separate title from subtitle.

▷ *Public Electricity Supply and Demand.*

  Public Electricity: Supply and Demand.

▷ Ancient Egyptian language and writing techniques for translation.

  Ancient Egyptian language and writing: Techniques for translation.

Regardless of the style of the original, subtract an awkward comma or colon separating title from subtitle (or sub-subtitle, as in the third example):

▷ Security considerations: IV.

  Security considerations IV.

▷ Lectures in obstetrics, 7.

  Lectures in obstetrics 7.

▷ *Welles and Salisbury: 1818–1826: The Quiet Years.*

  Welles and Salisbury 1818–1826: The Quiet Years.

If the original uses a dash to separate title from subtitle, you may change it to a colon.

The trumpeting subtitle: It is the custom in some scholarly circles to draw a discreet veil over any subtitle that seems crude or hucksterish—the custom, but a bad one. Give your reader the title whole, not a bowdlerized version.

▷ The whore of Babylon.

  The whore of Babylon: Being an inquiry into the iniquities of the pope of Rome, the beast with seven heads, most assiduously compiled and brought together with great care and its author hopes some purpose.

▷ *Wires and Wiring.*

Wires and Wiring: An Indispensable Guide for Every Engineer and Student.

Even less is there any excuse for suppressing an informative subtitle:

▷ *The Nuer.*

The Nuer: A Description of the Modes of Livelihood and the Political Institutions of a Nilotic People.

With subtitles as with main titles, the only reason to eliminate part of the original is to avoid useless repetition.

▷ Louise d'Epinay.
From la Chevrette to la Briche: The Collected Correspondence of Louise d'Epinay.

Louise d'Epinay.
From la Chevrette to la Briche: The Collected Correspondence.

Changes in titles: In order to bring titles into conformity with your reference style, you may change upper-case letters to lowercase and vice versa; you may add and subtract underlines or italics; you may add and subtract colons. You may shorten a title to avoid repeating information given in another block of the reference.

Otherwise, change nothing. Do not correct punctuation. Do not correct or Americanize or modernize spelling. Do not feel that you need to make the titles on a reference list uniform. The young scholar is sometimes upset at the sight of an inconsistent reference list:

6] Martin Bennett.
The arithmetical limits of logspace.

7] Rosemary Browne.
The arithmetic limits of log-space.

Consistency is a virtue in many places, but not here. Bennett is entitled to his preferences, Browne to hers.

The slighter the variation, the harder your task in copying it exactly: judgment/judgement, catalog/catalogue, traveled/travelled. Be scrupulous. Check and double-check and check the final version again one last time.

Foreign titles: Foreign book titles are underlined or italicized because they're book titles, not because they're foreign. Foreign non-book titles are not underlined or italicized.

Unless a foreign title is so highly cognate with English that its meaning is immediately apparent, it's a courtesy to provide a translation for your monolingual reader:

> Sylvie Blanchette.
> L'agrandissement. (The blow-up.)
> In J.-P. Lache, editor, *Six Contes Modernes*, pages 293–370. Flammarion, 1971.

If you are referring to a translation, giving the original title is helpful when your reader is likely to have heard of it.

> Karl Marx.
> *Pre-capitalist Economic Formations. (Formen die der Kapitalistischen Produktion Vorhergehen.)*

Since this work is generally called the Formeñ, your reader will want to connect the nickname with your reference.

Every language has its own rules about capitalizing words in book titles. Following the rule of the mother tongue requires uniformity; it would be rude to capitalize Spanish titles by Spanish rules and Portuguese titles by English rules. A further difficulty is that many title pages are printed in full caps, so that you can't tell what the native punctuation would be in uppers and lowers. If you prefer nonetheless to follow foreign conventions for foreign titles, you must be both erudite and dogged. But if you're afraid that your performance may not live up to your ambition, impose English rules on all titles regardless of origin.

Untitled works: If a work has no title, describe it in block II.

> ▷ Thomas R. MacMahon.
> *Frontiers in Psychometrics* LIV(2):24, 1975.
>
> Thomas R. MacMahon.
> Letter to the editor.
> *Frontiers in Psychometrics* LIV(2):24, 1975.

Only as a last resort, when you can't figure out any sensible description for a work, should you write:

> E. T. Heald.
> Untitled.
> In Evelyn Zeller, editor, A *Celebration*, pages 16–18. University of Oklahoma Press, 1968.

III. Bibliographic Information

A brief note here, just so you won't be confused about what comes between blocks II and IV: Block III is the workhorse of the reference. Having said who wrote the work you're referring to and what it's called, you must now give your reader the information he needs to get the source for himself. That information varies tremendously from one kind of source to another, and there's no such thing as a Platonic ideal of block III, just a practical answer to the practical question "How do I find this?" The chapter on easy references describes the many answers you can give to that question.

IV. More Bibliographic Information

If you work in a field where most of the sources are current, published, and easily available, you may never need to use block IV to add bibliographic information to a reference. But if your field and your tastes incline you to sources that are difficult to come by, you may frequently be in a position to help your reader out.

Are you referring to a rare work? Your inexperienced reader will want to know how to get hold of another copy. Are you referring to an expensive hardcover? Your impoverished reader will bless you for mentioning the cheap paperback as well. Are you referring to a pirated Taiwan edition? Your reader of tender conscience will appreciate knowing about a version on the up-and-up. Are you referring to an early edition? Your young reader will want to know about current versions. Are you referring to an archival source? Your homebound reader will be grateful to you for telling him about any published materials on the subject.

One of the kindest uses you can make of block IV is to suggest a translation for monolingual readers:

15] Rudolf K. Goldschmit-Jentner.
   Die Begegnung mit dem Genius.
   Fischer Bücherei, Frankfurt and Hamburg, Germany, 1954.
   Translated as *Brilliant Encounters* by Edward Miel.
   Bantam, 1972.

You have no obligation to exhaust yourself chasing down information for block IV. When you know something that your reader may find useful, tell him:

38] Michele Wexler.
   The vanity racket.
   Partisan Review XLII(5):39–54, 1969.
   Also in *Women at War*, Dell, 1973, in a longer version.

If what you know is too vague to be of any use, don't abuse your reader's interest by being airy:

▷ S. A. Shepard.
The lives of the Massachuset Indians.
Readings in Anthropology 12(3):113–168, 1964.
Later collected.

V. Annotation

The occasions for using the last block are rare, but sometimes, for instance, you would like to warn your reader about a flawed source:

13] H. Mendes-Citié.
Orthogenesis in the Trans-Jordan Flora.
University of Illinois Press, 1921.
The author's evolutionary beliefs have been totally discredited, but his drawings remain valuable illustrations of the region's plants and flowers.

Sometimes you would like to connect two sources with a cross-reference:

22] Juan Fernandez.
A constructive proof of Fowker's theorem.
The Amateur Mathematician VII(8):47–48, 1962.
This is the most elegant proof, but not the first one [16].

Sometimes you may know some special information about a source too fascinating to keep to yourself. Play this tune with a light hand:

14] Benjamin Hardan Howett.
Memoirs.
Cassell's, London, 1862.
The E. M. of the dedication is probably Edward Morris.

And sometimes you may want to commend a source to your reader for some special reason. Since every reference constitutes a recommendation, use block V this way only when you have something unusual to pass on. If you were to attempt to summarize the virtues of every source, your reference list would begin to look like *TV Guide*.

Pinpointing

To pinpoint a reference is to describe exactly what pages, verses, figures, lines, and so on you're discussing—usually what pages.

Simple versus compound: In a simple reference, the page numbers to which you're pointing go where they fit most neatly, either in block II or in block III:

> 38] N. K. Prosnitz.
> *Sequences of Evolutionary Branching*, pages 247–283.
> W. H. Freeman, 1966.
>
> 5] Dorothy Beale.
> A small adventure.
> In *The Collected Stories*, pages 41–65. Viking, 1971.

In a compound reference, the page numbers go after the main entry:

> P. T. Alonzo.
> *Minority Voting Rights.*
> Basic Books, 1971.
> [4] Pages 39–51
> [5] Pages 106–130.
> [6] Page 271.

Be reasonable: No task in writing a reference requires more taste and judgment than pinpointing. At one extreme there's the author who has used only four pages from a thousand-page book but won't tell his reader what the four pages are. At the other extreme there's the author who pinpoints every second or third page of his source, cluttering up his reference list to no advantage. Steer clear of both extremes.

The page numbers that you give should reflect accurately the use you've made of your source. If you summarize the central argument of a whole book or article or pamphlet or build on its central thesis, the most accurate reference you can write is to the whole work, with no pinpointing:

41] M. G. Souther.
   Eugene O'Neill and the Lace-curtain Irish.
   Miami University Press, 1974.

If you use a hunk of material, identify the beginning point and the end point. Do not construct a compound reference of rags and tatters.

▷ G. S. Jestin.
   Work-to-Rule as a Tactic in the Early Labour Movement.
   Longman's, 1955.
   [18] Page 41.   [21] Pages 50–52.
   [19] Page 43.   [22] Pages 54–55.
   [20] Pages 45–48. [23] Page 56.

Draw this together into one coherent mass:

18] G. S. Jestin.
   *Work-to-Rule as a Tactic in the Early Labour Move-
   ment,* pages 41–56.
   Longman's, 1955.

To some extent, the way that you pinpoint depends on how much work your source has done for you. Suppose, for instance, that you've talked about two poems. One appears in a collection that has a table of contents; the other appears in a collection that has none. The reference to the first poem may have a page number or not, as you prefer.

> C. J. Danehauer.
> Frost-heaves.
> In *November and Other Poems*, page 56. Yellow Gate Press, Pickering, Rhode Island, 1968.

or C. J. Danehauer.
> Frost-heaves.
> In *November and Other Poems*. Yellow Gate Press, Pickering, Rhode Island, 1968.

The reference to the second poem needs a page number.

> Aaron Higgins.
> Safety shoes.
> In W. M. Cooperman, editor, *The Industrial Revolution in Poetry*, page 139. Penguin, 1959.

Pinpointing without pages: In referring to a work that has appeared in many editions, pinpointing by chapter or section is preferable to pinpointing by page.

▷ Jane Austen.
> *Mansfield Park*, pages 40–46.
> D. C. Heath edition, 1958.

> Jane Austen.
> *Mansfield Park*, chapter 3.
> D. C. Heath edition, 1958.

The two versions are not identical; chapter 3 extends from page 39 to 51. But the chapter reference is more useful, since in your reader's edition pages 40–46 may fall in chapter 2 or chapter 4.

Pinpointing quotations: There are two schools of thought about pinpointing quotations. The first holds that every quotation must have an exact page reference. This has much to recommend it, if for no other reason than that it curbs excessive quotation. The second school (which I incline to) relaxes this rule for the sake of brevity. The difference shows up when you're using a portion of material from a source *and* quoting from the middle of it. School #1 says that you must write a compound reference:

E. L. Grannis.
Simulated navigational geometries.
The Journal of Applied Mathematics XI(4):201–330, 1976.
   [15] Pages 235–248.
   [16] Page 239.

School #2 permits a simple reference in this case:

15] E. L. Grannis.
   Simulated navigational geometries, pages 235–248.
   The Journal of Applied Mathematics XI(4):201–330,
   1976.

You must decide for yourself what method you prefer in what circumstances.

Shorthand: There's no way to make a reference list an easy read, but you can keep it from being any more forbidding than it has to be. An important consideration is that hyperpunctuated material is much harder to read than ordinary text, and the reference list is the very exemplar of hyperpunctuation.

For that reason I strongly recommend that you do not abbreviate "p." for "page," "ch." for "chapter," and so on. Even over the course of a very long list, these abbreviations will save you only a line or two because of the way that references are set up. Typically the unabbreviated version works out to be no longer than the abbreviated one:

▷ Carol Kulakowski.
Marxist Views on the Arab Oil Economy, pp. 304–329.
University of Missouri Press, 1973.

Carol Kulakowski.
Marxist Views on the Arab Oil Economy, pages 304–329.
University of Missouri Press, 1973.

This is true in the compressed format too:

▷ L. C. Loke. *Hervey at Court*, pp. 237–280. Leslie Frewin
Publishers, 1969.

L. C. Loke. *Hervey at Court*, pages 237–280. Leslie Frewin
Publishers, 1969.

Abbreviation is usually a false economy. It saves little or nothing in space and costs your reader extra effort in looking at it.

Should you write "pages 113–28" or "pages 113–128"? The one-character saving is not worth even the very slight increase in difficulty in reading the shorter version.

"Pages 35 f." means pages 35–36; write it out. "Pages 119 ff." gives your reader no idea when to stop; write out the end point as well as the beginning point, "pages 119–133."

"Passim" means here and there, as in "pages 209–240 passim." Since no one thinks that you're referring to every word or every sentence in that portion of your source, the expression is usually silly.

Needless Information

If you were a publisher or a bookseller, you might wish to indicate how long an item is, by what process and in what profusion it is illustrated, how many informative tables, glossaries, and indexes it contains—all in order to justify the price you intend to ask. But if you're writing a reference, you can forget about all this information unless it is so unusual as to require mention in block V.

▷ Basil Willey.
Nineteenth-Century Studies: Coleridge to Matthew Arnold.
Introduction by Philippa Ashby. 293 pages, 16 pages of illustrations, 4 in color. With a chronology of English letters, 1800–1888. Columbia University Press, 1971.

Basil Willey.
Nineteenth-Century Studies: Coleridge to Matthew Arnold.
Columbia University Press, 1971.

Easy References

Easy references fit the three-block reference format smoothly and naturally:

      I. Author.
     II. Title.
   III. Bibliographic information.

Books

In the best of all possible worlds, you would refer only to first editions of English-language books put out by major American and English publishers, and your references would all look like these:

5] R. Dudley Edwards.
   A New History of Ireland.
   University of Maryland Press, 1973.

32] W. D. Routt.
   Eratosthenes of Alexandria: The Sun, the Moon, and the Numbers.
   Random House, 1962.

18] Deirdre Liam.
*Excesses of Etiquette: The European Courts of the 17th
Century.*
Chatto & Windus, 1959.

Every book reference is an elaboration on this simple format.

Publishers: It seems a sensible rule to follow the publishers' own style in describing them. Unfortunately, many publishers are as fickle as thirteen-year-olds about how to style themselves. The book in front of me was published by Hill and Wang; or by Hill & Wang; or by Hill and Wang, Inc. All three forms appear on the one book. So common is this multiplicity of designations that a better rule is: Follow the title page, but not slavishly. Since you are describing rather than filing suit, you may leave off legal bumph like Inc., Ltd., and Cie. And no harm will result from calling the publishers Crowell instead of Thomas Y. Crowell Company, so long as you avoid shorthand your reader will not recognize. Just be sure to give any one name in the same form through any one list—not "Scribner's" in item [12] and "Charles Scribner's Sons" in item [37]. Choose one or the other and be faithful to it.

Old-fashioned references gave a city for every publishing house, which was always either too much information or not enough. "New York: G. P. Putnam's Sons" is silly in one direction; "New York: The Bandersnatch Press" is silly in the other. Give as complete an address as you can for an obscure publisher:

2] A. K. Amady.
Songs and Tunes of the Wetherfield Hills.
Kammen & Condry, Mason City, Iowa, 1957.

54] B. K. Liapunov, editor.
Exploring local parks.
The Angleworm Press, 42 Vernon Street, New Haven,
Connecticut 06511. 1974.

Give no address for a major publisher:

> 9] Lawrence Johns.
> *Assemblage and Collage.*
> Simon and Schuster, 1968.

Between dark obscurity and bright fame there is a great middle ground where you must let your knowledge of the patterns of publication in your field guide you. When you think that an address will help your reader, give it to him.

For foreign publishers, city and country should be in the English version:

▷ Bellini, Firenze, Italia, 1962.

Bellini, Florence, Italy, 1962.

▷ Stammenverlag, Hollerstrasse 143, Köln, Deutschland, 1934.

Stammenverlag, Hollerstrasse 143, Cologne, Germany, 1934.

The reader who looks up a publisher in an English-language source book under "Deutschland" is not going to get very far. And the reader who writes away to "Firenze, Italia" may never get his letter sorted into the bag marked "Florence, Italy."

No publisher: When a place of publication is listed with no publisher, tell your reader what you know:

> 31] R. Colt Hoare.
> *A Tour through the Island of Elba.*
> London, 1814.

When there is no information about publication, say so:

> 42] S. D. Gaites.
> *The Foundations of German Nationalism.*
> No publisher, 1917.

Bad examples are marked with an arrowhead (▷).

Often you will want to annotate such a reference:

34] M. R. Helder.
The History of the Helder Family.
No publisher, approximately 1875.
Mattie Helder's will lists a printing press among her possessions, on which she probably produced this volume. The only extant copy is in the Wisconsin State Archive.

Until quite recently, of course, publication was a haphazard phenomenon, and even today there are many books published off the beaten track. The fine points of bibliographic provenance are interesting, but your main object in writing a reference is to help your reader get his hands on your sources. Keep that in mind when you deal with works that, although published, are for all practical purposes archival.

Books that list no publisher because they are still in manuscript present one last possibility; see the section on works not yet published.

Series and imprints: Publishing books in series and under special imprints appears to be thoughtful and purposive, so there are many series and imprints, some genuine, some spurious or at least short-lived. You may therefore decide for yourself, based on your preference and knowledge of the source, whether to include such information in block III. Avoid repeating the publisher's name in the series or imprint name.

▷ Priscilla Braids, editor.
Views of the Baroque.
An Iowa History of Arts and Letters Book. Iowa State University Press, 1968.

Priscilla Braids, editor.
Views of the Baroque.
A History of Arts and Letters Book. Iowa State University Press, 1968.

or   Priscilla Braids, editor.
    Views of the Baroque.
    Iowa State University Press, 1968.

Dates, editions, and reprints. If a date appears on the title page of a book, give that as the date in your reference and thank your lucky stars. If there is no date on the title page, you may have a difficult task before you. What you are aiming for is the date of publication; if the work you are referring to has been published more than once, you would like to give dates for both the current and the original publication.

Let's consider first a modern work that is not a reprint. On the page behind the title page, copyright and printing history are usually given. Look first for a copyright date; if there's only one, use it in your reference. If there are several copyright dates, use the latest one unless it's a renewal.

© 1937, 1955, 1967, 1973.

Copyright 1927, copyright renewed 1954.

The date to use in the first case is 1973, in the second 1927. Lacking a copyright date, use the first printing date of the latest edition.

First published 1906. Second edition 1907, reprinted 1908, 1910, 1911, 1914, 1916, 1918, 1919, 1922, 1923, 1925, 1927. Third edition 1931, reprinted 1934, 1936, 1938, 1940, 1947, 1949, 1951, 1954, 1958.

(This publisher seems short on warehousing.) Here the date to use is 1931. Always mention along with the date any edition other than the first:

8] H. W. Fowler and F. G. Fowler.
    The King's English.
    Oxford University Press, third edition 1931.

A reprint of a modern work—and that includes most paperbacks —will usually present more difficulties. Blessings on the paperback publisher who makes it possible for you to write a sensible, informative reference:

36] B. H. Wardmoore.
   The Nightingale and the Lark.
   Vintage, 1973.
   Originally published as *Dualities in Keats and Shelley,*
   University of Tennessee Press, 1948.

All too often one or another of these pieces of information is missing. Fill in as much as you can.

Worse still are reprints of works from previous centuries. Copyright dates on these are useless—the copyright refers only to the front matter, not to the work. Relying on the information the reprint publisher provides would often produce such anomalous references as:

▷ Charles Dickens.
   Great Expectations.
   Ehrlich & Murphy, 1954.

You will probably want to plump out this scanty information for your own sake, to keep from feeling foolish, as well as for the sake of your naive reader, who might picture Charles Dickens as a figure from the time of Eisenhower's administration. At the least, insert the word "edition" into block III to give your reader a clue about what's going on:

Charles Dickens.
Great Expectations.
Ehrlich & Murphy edition, 1954.

Better yet, supply the author's dates:

Charles Dickens (1812–70).
Great Expectations.
Ehrlich & Murphy edition, 1954.

Never let a reference go without a date. Here is how to indicate an exact date established from external evidence:

> 18] Elizabeth (pseudonym).
> *The Tale of a Girl.*
> Birmingham, England [1833].

Here is how to indicate a good guess:

> 9] R. V. Hailor.
> *The Hygienic Instructor.*
> William Manor & Sons, Boston, approximately 1910.

("Ca." is justified here in place of "approximately" if you prefer.)

> 6] Albert Edwardi.
> *The Universal Parent.*
> Edinburgh, early 19th century.

Use your knowledge of the source to date it as best you can.

Library of Congress: Many books published recently in the United States have Library of Congress cataloging information on the page behind the title page; some reproduce the whole cataloging-in-publication card. This information looks impressive, bristling as it does with multi-digit numbers and secret code. It is, however, of no use in writing a reference.

Compilations

By "compilation" I mean the work of several authors gathered together by an editor into a book. In a reference to the whole compilation, the editor takes block I and the authors are not mentioned:

13] N. C. Grafton, editor.
   Recent Results in Analysis.
   Addison-Wesley, 1968.

In a reference to one of the articles or stories or poems in the compilation, the author takes block I:

29] C. H. Varick-Weiss.
   Slow patching routines with very small error bounds.
   In N. C. Grafton, editor, *Recent Results in Analysis*,
   pages 40–49. Addison-Wesley, 1968.

If you're referring to more than one piece from the compilation, you'll certainly want to mention the whole work as well in order to make cross-reference possible:

4] G. N. Fontana.
   Needlepoint and bargello.
   In McNeill [16], pages 320–342.
   . . .

16] A. R. McNeill, editor.
   Renaissance Handiwork.
   Thames and Hudson, 1959.
   . . .

24] F. S. Sibbett, Jr.
   Secular gold.
   In McNeill [16], pages 41–63.

Collections

By "collection" I mean the work of one author gathered into a book. (In reality, of course, there's no difference between a compilation and a collection; the artificial distinction is for the sake of convenience.) The reference to a whole collection looks like any other book reference:

8] Glenda Batson.
   Thoughts and Afterthoughts.
   Crown, 1971.

If you're referring to only one piece from a collection, the whole work gets no separate entry; push it down to block III:

8] Glenda Batson.
   Castro at fifty.
   In *Thoughts and Afterthoughts*, pages 288–320. Crown,
   1971.

If you're referring to several pieces from the same collection, do not use a cross-reference. It looks quite strange, and there's no advantage to it:

▷ C. R. Ridgeway.
   Preventive detention.
   In Ridgeway [27], pages 239–248.

Construct a compound reference instead:

C. R. Ridgeway.
Currents in Criminal Law.
Eerdmans, 1966.
   [27] The Miranda decision, pages 13–40.
   [28] Preventive detention, pages 239–248.

Editions with Editors

Sometimes an author does a substantial revision of his own work; the new version is called a new edition:

22] D. F. Stockham.
   Land Values in Parma, 1400–1700.
   Louisiana University Press, second edition 1958.

Sometimes a publisher reprints work that's no longer under copyright with no editing or none to speak of; that too is called an edition:

17] John Ruskin (1819–1900).
The Seven Lamps of Architecture.
The Ridge Press edition, 1968.
Originally published in 1849.

But in the sort of edition that this section is about, an editor prepares the work of an author for publication, and the editor's contribution is acknowledged. Except in comparing two or more editions of one author, the editor takes block III:

11] K. M. Hofmann.
The Collected Correspondence.
Edited by G. V. Larch. Random House, 1958.

When a book is both a collection (several pieces by one author) and an edition (with an editor), it's possible to refer to a piece of the work. Block III gets a little crowded, and the editor's name must follow the name of the whole collection:

39] Chaim Muybridge.
Uncontrolled chain reactions.
In *The Posthumous Papers*, pages 560–596. Edited by Kevin Costabel. Cambridge University Press, 1969.

In referring to several pieces from one collection-edition, construct a compound reference.

Translations

Here again the work you're referring to has a midwife. Except in comparing two or more translations, the translator of a single author takes block III:

29] Cosimo Varda.
A New Classification System for the Succulents.
Translated from the Italian by R. Wyllie. New Horizons Press, 1975.

The translator of a single author's work may also edit it:

14] J-M. Gaudel.
The Vest-pocket Park. [*Un Coin de Verdure.*]
Edited and translated by H. L. Prior. Schenkman, 1971.

What with translated collections and translated compilations and translated multivolume works and translated articles, there are hundreds of kinds of references in which the name of a translator might appear. When you encounter one of these situations, you must combine the format for the work with the format for the translation. A compilation-translation, for instance, would look like this:

28] H. E. Harton, editor and translator.
Readings from Modern Arabic.
University of Georgia Press, 1970.

Just be sure that no information gets lost in the combination.

Multivolume Works

A multivolume work, unlike a series, contains a definite number of volumes. One author may write a work of several volumes, or several authors may write a volume or two apiece under the guidance of an editor.

The key to writing good references to multivolume works is never to mention the name of more than one volume in any one reference. In referring to a multivolume work by a single author, the names of the individual volumes are suppressed:

▷ Georges Branaque.
The Decline of Manners. Volume I: *The Jacksonian Age.*
Volume II: *The Plutocrats.* Volume III: *The Modern
Barbarians.*
Schocken, 1961, 1964, and 1969.

Georges Branaque.
The Decline of Manners.
Three volumes. Schocken, 1961–69.

Notice that only the first and last dates are mentioned in the correct version. In referring to a multivolume work by several authors, both the names of the individual volumes and the names of the authors are suppressed:

▷ Alma MacRae, editor.
Natural-language Processing. Volume I: *Machine Translation,* by R. Wilensky. Volume II: *Artificial Intelligence,*
by J. R. Meehan.
Yale University Press, 1974–75.

Alma MacRae, editor.
Natural-language Processing.
Two volumes. Yale University Press, 1974–75.

That's how you would refer to a multivolume set as a whole. But such references are uncommon; usually you want to refer to the individual volumes. For a work by a single author, drop the reference to the whole set:

4] Georges Branaque.
The Decline of Manners. Volume I: *The Jacksonian
Age.*
Schocken, 1961.

For a work by several authors, retain the reference to the whole set to make cross-reference possible:

15] Alma MacRae, editor.
Natural-language processing.
Two volumes. Yale University Press, 1974–75.

. . .

38] R. Wilensky.
Machine Translation.
Volume I in MacRae [15], 1974.

If you refer to several volumes in a set by several authors, the references will be scattered around your list in alphabetical order. If you refer to several volumes in a set by a single author, ignore alphabetical order for those references and put them in volume order instead.

4] Georges Branaque.
The Decline of Manners. Volume I. *The Jacksonian Age.*
Schocken, 1961.

5] Georges Branaque.
The Decline of Manners. Volume II: *The Plutocrats.*
Schocken, 1964.

6] Georges Branaque.
The Decline of Manners. Volume III: *The Modern Barbarians.*
Schocken, 1969.

Volume order, I, II, III, not alphabetical order, Jacksonian, Modern, Plutocrats. It is not reasonable to ask authors to name their works in alphabetical sequence just for the sake of reference lists.

It is important to get the pattern straight at the start, because multivolume works are subject to many a change between conception and completion. They can be unfinished:

39] D. N. B. Preston.
Paths to Socialism.
Six volumes planned. Volumes 1–4, Scribner's, 1963–74.

Editors can quit or die:

13] E. van der Leigh, editor.
Economics, Armament, and Foreign Policy. Volumes
II–VI.
University of Wisconsin Press, 1957–64.
Eight volumes in all. Martin Handsore edited volume I
[6]; Catherine Shotte edited volumes VII and VIII,
1966–67.

Publishers can change:

29] Diane Halas, general editor.
The Medieval Town.
Four volumes. Volumes 1 and 2, Princeton University
Press, 1956–58. Volumes 3 and 4, Simon and Schuster,
1960–64.

Projects can be abandoned:

8] J. Sachs, editor.
Vernacular Gothic.
Four volumes. Livermore, London, 1922–28.
Of the fifteen volumes originally planned, only those on
Northumberland, Durham, Lincoln, and Chester were
completed.

In numbering volumes, follow the style of the original unless the
original uses a mixture of Arabic and Roman numerals, which
happens surprisingly often; use all Roman if there is a mixture.

Span Dates: I tend to give span dates in elided form (1750–82)
although I write span pages out in full (pages 1750–1782). My
reasoning is that dates have come in fours for almost a thousand
years now and will continue to do so for another eight thousand.
We automatically supply the missing "17" in the elided form
"–82." Page numbers, on the other hand, have no automatic

shape; they come in a jumble of ones, twos, threes, and fours. It takes only a fraction of the reader's time to think, "Pages 1750–82, must be 1750–1782," but I see no point in troubling him at all. If this rationale seems specious to you (and I admit that it's not watertight), give both dates and pages in full. You must not, of course, impose your preference on someone else. If the author calls his book *Vienna 1858–1861*, you may not change it to *Vienna 1858–61* to suit your style.

Journal Articles

In the best of all possible worlds, you would refer only to English-language pieces in thriving major publications, and all your references would look like these:

112] Richard P. Schaedel.
   The native ethic of Latin American cities: Hope or illusion?
   Journal of Urban Studies LV(7):246–287, 1968.

7] Cynthia Benton.
   Upper and lower bounds on the solution to Bay's problem.
   Readings in Analysis and Theory 19(3):146–151, 1954.

19] Simon Hamish.
   Collective psychology in the "era of crowds."
   The Positivist XXXIV (12):9–58, 1972.

Here is what the parts of block III stand for:

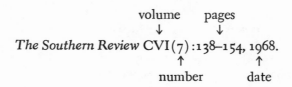

Every journal reference is an elaboration on this simple format.

Abbreviations: Old-fashioned references to journal articles were marvels of abbreviation, harder to crack than the Purple Code. Having eliminated bibliographic footnotes and all the duplication they entailed, we can spend a little of that space on avoiding abbreviations.

▷ *J. Amer. Ass. Mech. Eng.*

The Journal of the American Association of Mechanical Engineers.

▷ *Q. Soc. Res. Psych. Psych.*

Quarterly of the Society for Research in Psychology and Psychiatry.

If the name of a journal incorporates an abbreviation your reader may not recognize, spell it out for him:

▷ *SIAM Journal of Numerical Analysis* XVII(8):212–214, 1968.

SIAM Journal of Numerical Analysis (Society of Industrial and Applied Mathematics) XVII(8):212–214, 1968.

Missing elements and extended dates: Some journals number their issues but do not collect them into volumes:

Civil Disobedience Newsletter 43:18–26, 1972.

Some number the volumes and call the numbers by months or seasons:

Journal of East Asian Studies IX:349–362, Autumn 1936.

The American Anthropologist 46:231–235, February 1961.

Some number both volumes and issues but are easier to identify by date:

Vogue XXXIII(7):47, April 1923.

Newsweek XXIX(35):19, 17 March 1968.

Some carry only a date:

The Pathfinder 36–51, July 1947.

Notice that extended dates are written:

month (no comma) year

or day (no comma) month (no comma) year.

Notice too that you must write out the name of the month; if you were to represent it numerically, it would be difficult to read and subject to ambiguity.

▷ 9 11 1969.
9 November 1969.

Whole number: Sometimes an entire issue of a journal is devoted to one article. It makes no difference; it's still an article:

12] M. Clemens.
Datives of purpose and intent.
The Classical Philologist CIII(3):1–128, 1971.

If you feel that you must stress the importance given the article by devoting a whole number to it, here is how you show it:

9] A. L. Heppel.
The census in Massachusetts 1880–1920.
Social History Quarterly XIV(whole number 2):156–213, 1975.

I am unable to think of an occasion that requires this form.

New series: Have you ever seen a journal issue marked something like "Volume 2 n.s., number 3"? "N.s." means new series, and the story behind it is usually that the old volume and number system got so mixed up and behindhand that the editor gave up on it and started over. There is no need to indicate the new series in your reference to such an issue; the date will serve to distinguish the new 2(3) from the old one.

Combined numbers: Have you ever seen a journal issue marked something like "Volume XXXI, combined numbers 5 and 6"? Here again, the journal has fallen further and further behind its publication schedule and the editor has decided to catch up by a piece of legerdemain, numbering one issue as two. Follow his lead with bland acceptance in your reference—XXXI(5–6)—and with compassion in your heart. Most journals are understaffed and underfunded, and any little tricks their editors need to use should be forgiven them.

Broken pagination: Rarely in scholarly journals but frequently in magazines, articles are split into small pieces and strewn through an issue to fit layout and advertising requirements. Use the first page number and a plus sign to indicate broken pagination.

▷ Garry Wills.
   A primer of state and local politics.
   The Atlantic Monthly CVII(8):186–188, 191, 194, 200–
   214, 228–230, August 1968.

   Garry Wills.
   A primer of state and local politics.
   The Atlantic Monthly CVII(8):186+, August 1968.

Serial publication: Sometimes an article is split into several parts and published in several issues. Compress this information as neatly as you can.

▷ R. Proffer.
Requirements in translation.
Part 1, *Russian Literature Triquarterly* VIII(2):38–65,
1967. Part 2, *Russian Literature Triquarterly* VIII(3):
12–55, 1967. Part 3, *Russian Literature Triquarterly* IX
(1):31–60, 1968.

R. Proffer.
Requirements in translation.
Three parts. *Russian Literature Triquarterly* VIII(2):38–
65, VIII(3):12–55, IX(1):31–60, 1967 and 1968.

Obscure and ephemeral journals: Periodical publication is so precarious an enterprise that it makes dowsing for water look secure by comparison. Share with your reader whatever information you have about sources that are hard to find:

12] S. L. Mouli.
Aspects of Wagner's harmonies.
Agrippa III(2):49–61, 1956.
The library at the Boston Conservatory of Music has a
complete set of this journal.

25] Martine l'Hereux.
Downward-sloping demand curves and Markham's observation.
The Economists' Monthly, Paxmore House, Raile Place,
Cambridge, England. XXI(4):27–38, 1972.

Reviews

If the title of a review does not indicate what work is under consideration, supply the information:

29] R. A. Russo.
Plaything of the gods. Review of Anatos Teriekes, *The
Forgotten Prophet.*
The Literary Review VIII(4):28–31, 1957.

Use cross-reference when you can:

12] Daniel Gomez.
Review of Trenton [26].
Pharmacology Notes and Abstracts 15(6):95, 1971.

In a reference to an omnibus review, you may mention all the works reviewed or just the ones you're interested in.

Pamphlets

Pamphlet, report, memorandum, broadside, leaflet, brochure, tract, folder, booklet—something thin, bound by itself. Block II of the reference to a pamphlet is punctuated as a non-book:

29] Frank Tergon.
Handlist of Negro playwrights in the American theater.
English Department, Tulane University, 1962.

Pamphlets are often published in series, and the number in the series may be an important piece of identification:

52] M. L. Zabibian.
The gittern (with notes on the guitar, cithara, and cither).
Juilliard Stringed Instruments Series #74–23, 1974.

Pamphlets are seldom issued by the standard publishing houses, and describing non-standard publishers requires some thought. The middle road is the one to seek, neither so little information that your reader will have trouble finding the source nor so much that your reference will be a cluttered mess.

▷ Michael A. Harrison.
Miosinic coagulation in rigor mortis.
Washington University, 1958.

▷ Michael A. Harrison.
  Miosinic coagulation in rigor mortis.
  Department of Pathology, Room 404-B Thalier Memorial
  Building, Washington University Medical School, 2382
  Flora Avenue, St. Louis, Missouri 67228. 1958.

  Michael A. Harrison.
  Miosinic coagulation in rigor mortis.
  Department of Pathology, Washington University Medical
  School, 1958.

Works Not Yet Published

In most fields, scholars know about each other's work before it
is published. If you refer to such a piece of work, it will be because
you know the author; check with him at the latest possible
moment to see what state his work is in. It may have been accepted
by a journal and assigned to an upcoming issue but not yet
paginated:

  30] Leonard H. Gordon.
      Effectiveness under stress: The Chinese Communist
      army in Korea.
      To appear in the *Washington Newsletter* XXII(8), 2
      March 1978.

It may have been accepted but not yet assigned a publication date:

  12] Janet F. O. Moyle.
      High-speed printers in word-processing shops.
      To appear in *The Journal of the Association for Com-
      puting Machinery.*
  5] A. T. Embree, editor.
      Muslim Civilization in India.
      To be published by E. P. Dutton.

If it hasn't yet found a publisher, give the author's work address:

> 18] J. E. B. Linkman, Department of Chemistry, State University of New York at Binghamton.
> Lineoleic-acid treatment of oil paints with vegetable pigments.
> In preparation, May 1976.

"In preparation" may be a bit of a fiction, and you may have to invent your own name for an article the author seems disinclined to finish. Many a scholar finally settles down to work only because so many references have been made to an article he's talked about that he finally feels obliged to write it. If all you have to go on is a letter, a memo, a telephone call, or a conversation over coffee, you may have to write your reference:

> 38] Martin Henner, the Wellcombe Unit, Cambridge University.
> Private communication, 15 June 1975.

Reserve this form for results that will probably never be published independently because they are too small.

Theses and Dissertations

More confusion surrounds writing a reference to a thesis than any other common scholarly reference; what follows is arbitrary, but not capricious.

Let us say that a PhD thesis is a book and any paper short of a PhD thesis is an article:

> 92] Onora Nell.
> *Acting on Principle: The Application of Kantian Ethics to Real-life Choice.*
> PhD thesis, Marquette University, 1951.

8] J. N. Munson.
   Envelope solutions to sparse matrices.
   Master's thesis, University of Nebraska, 1964.

Degrees are granted by universities, not departments:

▷ G. H. von Wright.
   Parsee Refugees of the 7th and 8th Centuries.
   PhD dissertation, Department of Oriental Studies, University of Oklahoma, 1968.

   G. H. von Wright.
   Parsee Refugees of the 7th and 8th Centuries.
   PhD dissertation, University of Oklahoma, 1968.

If you're writing a reference to a thesis that you know was subsequently published, share whatever information you have with your reader:

42] Christine Tyler.
   The audience as author.
   Master's thesis, Sudbury University, 1969.
   Published under the same title by Little, Brown, 1971.

"Thesis" applies to papers at all levels, "dissertation" only to the doctorate. You may follow the style of each original scrupulously, or call everything a thesis so as not to worry about the nomenclature.

Secondary Reference

A writes a reference to B. You learn about B by reading A. May you copy A's reference? Not without adding the information that it comes from A:

17] Kenneth Hudson.
The role of the museum in the urban cultural center.
American Architect LIII(3):138, 1963. Cited in Marshall Hohenburg, Toward a more realistic renewal.
Dimensions in Planning XXIX(9):14–28, 1971.

Only if you have the original Hudson article before you may you write:

17] Kenneth Hudson.
The role of the museum in the urban cultural center.
American Architect LIII(3):138, 1963.

Once it's in front of you, it makes no difference how you found out about it.

I've said it before, but it can't be overstressed: The principle of secondary reference is crucial to sound scholarship. Treating a secondary reference as if it were primary is a highly refined way of talking through your hat.

Hard References

Hard references (you may have wondered what was so easy about the easy ones) do not fall neatly into three blocks for author, title, and bibliographic information. Some can be squeezed and squashed into a fair approximation of the usual format; some resist.

Archival Sources

Sight unseen, you can predict a few things about almost any archive in the world. It's short on money, short on space, short on time, and short on manpower. It probably once started in on a system of classification that, although not yet complete, has proved inadequate, so that another system (and sometimes even a third) is also under way. You're safe in assuming that the physical size and shape and condition of the holdings have had an astounding influence on the way they're organized.

Aside from that, there's little that can be said about archives in general. Every archive is unique; no archive arranges, describes, and manages its holdings like any other archive. Before you start on a project of archival research, you might want to read

T. R. Schellenberg.
The Management of Archives.
Columbia University Press, 1965.

You can be more sensible and more appreciative if you have some idea what archivists are up against.

Write your references while the material is before you—and while the archivist is by your side. He has a vested interest in helping you, since he's the one who will have to suffer the weird, unintelligible queries from your readers if you write your references badly. Even if you understand the organization of your archive thoroughly, double-check with the archivist. Only he can predict the future of the holdings; that item you've come to think of as "Gathering 27-J" may be reclassified "19 Record Series 212" before the year is out.

The archival reference is no place for false dignity. Some small archives are very informally arranged. If your source is in the big red folder, you're going to have to designate it "Big red folder"; if it's in the green cardboard box, you're going to have to write out "Green cardboard box." I once knew a small private archive where the file drawers were called by saints' names as a pious gesture, having nothing to do with their contents. References to small archives make up in charm whatever they lack in formality.

If you have a group of references to one archive, you will probably want to give them a section of their own in your reference list and preface the section with a note about how they're arranged and how you're describing them. The address of the archive and the name of the archivist belong in this preface, along with any other information your reader will find useful. (You will certainly want to mention it, for instance, if your archive does not permit photocopying.)

A few examples, to give you the flavor of the archival reference:

9] Concordia Parish Courthouse, Vadalia, Louisiana.
   General mortgage books: Delinquent taxpayers.
   Volume HH, page 459. Mortgagees, 13 May 1870.

18] Richard Blackmere to Sir Andrew Maurice, undated,
    probably 15 or 16 September 1885.
    North Riding County Archive, Yorkshire, England.
    Maurice family codex, 1884–1888 gathering, number
    139.

69] James Lucas: "My mother give me to know . . ."
Longhand transcription of a slave narrative, apparently
done for the Leeder study [16] but never collected.
Dated 15 January 1939.
File RL, item 12 (4 pages).

The first and second examples are self-contained. The third is part
of a special section and depends on the explanatory preface of that
section in order to make sense.

What to say in the preface depends on the state of the materials
you have used. If you have the good fortune to use only cataloged
material, a heading may suffice:

Archivo general de Indios
Seville, Spain

If a published catalog is available, be sure to mention it to your
reader:

Archives Municipales
Chartres, France
There is a summary catalog through 1901 in Langlois [67],
pages 399–415.

If your notation is likely to seem odd to your reader, explain:

Braseman Family Archive
Warwick, Rhode Island

The archive contains about three thousand items relating
to the Braseman family in the 18th and 19th centuries.
Much of the material up to 1750 has been cataloged; whenever possible, I have used the archive's identification numbers (for example, series 9, item 22). For the uncataloged
materials, the name of the donor is the best identification
(for example, Rebecca).

In writing an archival reference, you're on your own about breaking the information up and punctuating and capitalizing it. Use

blocks and divisions within blocks to group related information and feed it to your reader in easy bites. Use one block or two or three or four, whatever you need to make your reference readable. Shun abbreviations. Punctuate no more heavily than you have to. Remember that uppers-and-lowers is harder to read than sentence capitalization and that italicized or underlined material is harder to read than plain roman. Spend a little time testing different formats before you settle on one.

Department of Things Nobody Ever Tells You: If you've done research in an archive that doesn't charge you for the privilege and that's not supported by your taxes (even if it is by someone else's), you may quite properly offer a small gift for the upkeep of the archive as you're leaving. The offer may be refused, but it will be appreciated.

Author Equals Publisher

Infrequently with books but very frequently with pamphlets, a corporate author publishes its own work. Furthermore, the title of such a pamphlet often incorporates the author's name yet again. Any attempt to use the three-block format produces laughable results:

▷ The Interseminarian Benevolent Association.
   Annual report of the Interseminarian Benevolent Association.
   The Interseminarian Benevolent Association, 1969.

Tidy all this up into two blocks with no repetition:

   The Interseminarian Benevolent Association.
   Annual report, 1969.

Bad examples are marked with an arrowhead (▷).

The address of an obscure author-publisher goes with its name:

> The Nash Circle, Bath, England.
> A report on the repair and restoration of the Haymarket Theatre, 1974.

If two references to an obscure author-publisher come together on your reference list, give the address only in the first:

> 7] The Association of Professional Historians of Music, Pennfield, Massachusetts 03277.
> A brief life of Marianna Bulgarelli, 1971.

> 8] The Association of Professional Historians of Music.
> Metastasio in Vienna, 1969.

Conference Proceedings

Occasionally conferences result in the publication of perfectly normal volumes:

> 39] Ruth E. Hartley, editor.
> *Understanding Children: Proceedings of the 16th Annual Convention of Child Psychiatrists and Psychotherapists.*
> Academic Press, 1969.

But mostly what you get is a program committee and private publication. The attempt to fit this information to the usual three-block format is not successful:

> ▷ Jane A. Krout, chairman; B. L. Forbush, Martha C. Reinert, and Peter Zeber, program committee.
> *Proceedings of the 2nd Annual AIID Meeting.*
> Association for the Investigation of Iatrogenic Diseases, 1926 Commonwealth Avenue, Boston, Massachusetts 02176. 1972.

The solution is to forget about the program committee and treat the organization as both author and publisher:

> Association for the Investigation of Iatrogenic Diseases, 1926 Commonwealth Avenue, Boston, Massachusetts 02176.
> *Proceedings of the 2nd Annual Meeting, 1972.*

Suppress needless repetition:

▷ The Society for International Law, Geneva, Switzerland.
218th Meeting of the Society for International Law, 1973.

The Society for International Law, Geneva, Switzerland.
218th Meeting, 1973.

Suppress needless repetition of dates too, but be aware that the conference date and the publication date may differ. When they do, use the world "published" with the publication date to keep your reference from stuttering. Here the conference date and the publication date are the same:

▷ American Management Associates.
19th Biennial Conference and Symposium Proceedings, 1965, 1965.

American Management Associates.
19th Biennial Conference and Symposium Proceedings, 1965.

Here they're different:

▷ The Franco-English Translators' League, Bristol, England.
Proceedings of the Annual Convention, 1962, 1964.

The Franco-English Translators' League, Bristol, England.
Proceedings of the Annual Convention, 1962, published 1964.

Where a conference was held is of no concern, and you can eliminate this information from the title of a proceedings. On the other hand, where an organization has its headquarters is of great concern, and you should include that information except when you're sure that your reader knows it.

▷ The National Association of Toxicologists.
    Seventh Annual Symposium on Agricultural Pesticides, San Francisco, California, 1968.

The National Association of Toxicologists, School of Agriculture, University of Oregon.
    Seventh Annual Symposium on Agricultural Pesticides, 1968.

When two or more references to an organization fall together, only the first needs the address.

31] The Scots Gaelic Society, Aberdeen, Scotland.
    22nd Meeting, 1949.
32] The Scots Gaelic Society.
    24th Meeting, 1951.

Organizations have a maddening way of changing the style of their proceedings titles from one time to another. Follow the style of each original, but arrange two or more proceedings in chronological order.

18] Friends of Asian Literature.
    Minutes of the 3rd Annual Meeting, 1969.
19] Friends of Asian Literature.
    Eighth Annual Meeting: Proceedings, 1974.

Ignore alphabetical order (Eighth, Minutes) and pursue chronological order (1969, 1974).

Correspondence

What your reader wants to know about a letter is who wrote to whom on what date and where he can find the letter. A simple reference to a published letter looks like this:

> 28] Edward Tinsley to G. A. Sala, 6 March 1862.
>   In Rebecca Waters, editor, *The Professional Publisher*, pages 313–315. Faber & Faber, 1968.

A compound reference to published letters from one person to several people looks like this:

> Sarah Bernhardt.
> In M. L. Evans, editor, *Selected Correspondence*. Pinnacle Books, 1961.
>   [4] To Walter Treach, 8 May 1921, page 308.
>   [5] To Alma Becker, 9 July 1922, page 340.

Choose chronological order (1921, 1922), page order (308, 340), or alphabetical order (Becker, Treach), whichever seems most useful to you.

A compound reference to published letters from one person to one other person looks like this:

> Herman Melville to Charles Trapp.
> In P. L. Quincy, editor, *The Moby Dick Letters*. University of South Carolina Press, 1951.
>   [39] 2 May 1850, pages 122–124.
>   [40] 14 August 1850, pages 156–161.

Chronological order (May, August) and page order (122, 156) usually coincide; when they don't, choose the one that seems more useful to you.

Finally, there's the reference to a published interchange. Do not put all the letters that A wrote to B in one reference and all the ones that B wrote to A in another. Which name should go first? Choose the one that you're more interested in, or flip a coin.

> Frederick Belding Power and Fred Hoffmann. In A. M. Maysles, editor, *The Correspondence of Frederick Belding Power: Scientist and Humanitarian.* Plenum, 1949.
> [51] FBP to FH, 13 August 1917, page 304.
> [52] FBP to FH, 19 November 1917, page 322.
> [53] FH to FBP, 2 December 1917, page 329.
> [54] FBP to FH, 4 January 1918, page 340.

Chronological order is usually the best one in this circumstance.

Play it by ear in dealing with unpublished correspondence. The different formats for published correspondence can serve as a rough guide, but you will also need to include archival information, which tends to be longer and less straightforward than information about publication.

Court Cases

If you are writing a legal paper, you shouldn't be following the system of citation and reference set out in this book. The Harvard Law Review Association publishes a guide called *A Uniform System of Citation* designed especially for the uses that lawyers make of court cases. Every lawyer should know it and follow it.

Now. If all the lawyers have left the room, we can speak frankly. The forms described in *A Uniform System* are slick, sophisticated, clean as a whistle—and utterly unsuited to lay use. I can attest (having tried it) that walking into a law library and asking for an English translation of "30 Ala. 49 (1847)" or "9 Mo. 690 (1846)" is a rattling experience. One might almost entertain the uncharitable thought that lawyers don't want other people to look at court cases.

But the courts belong to us all, and the records of court cases are a rich source in social history, for instance, or in situation ethics. So it behooves the rest of us to work out our own way of writing references to court cases, a way that will permit us to march boldly up to the desk in a law library and look the librarian in the eye.

Start a reference to a court case by giving its short name. The court reports usually suggest a short name by using full caps amidst ordinary uppers and lowers: "Arthur L. SMITHY v. Melissa MANDERS." That becomes:

Smithy v. Manders.

You needn't follow the suggestions rigidly; they are informal designations. One report, for instance, suggested calling a case "United States v. Florida," when "United States v. Richard Florida" seems a more revealing name. Regardless of the style of the original, do not underline or italicize the expressions "ex parte," "in re," and "ex rel."; lawyers sometimes italicize these expressions and sometimes do not, so we might as well do it the easier way uniformly.

Then give the name of the court and the date:

Supreme Court of Arkansas, 18 September 1972.

Colorado Court of Appeals, Division I, 29 August 1970.

Then write the reference to the report:

Volume 484 South Western Reporter (second series), page 517.

Volume 252 Federal Supplement, page 806.

Some reports have two names, one for the jurisdiction, one for the reporter. Give both names, with the reporter in parentheses:

Volume 211 Tennessee Reports (McCanless), page 599.

Here are a few examples:

6] Green v. State.
Supreme Court of Arkansas, 18 September 1972.
Volume 484 South Western Reporter (second series),
page 517.

111] Muller v. Daws.
Supreme Court of the United States, October 1876.
Volume 94 United States Reports, page 444.

38] Sedalia Land Company v. Robinson Brick and Tile.
Colorado Court of Appeals, Division I, 29 September 1970.
Volume 475 Pacific Reporter (second series), page 351.

12] Ex parte Hartman.
Circuit Court of Appeals, Fifth Circuit, 11 April 1911.
Volume 186 Federal Reporter, page 434.

81] United States v. Mudge et al.
United States District Court, 10 December 1965.
Volume 252 Federal Supplement, page 806.

37] Mid-State Baptist Hospital v. City of Nashville.
Supreme Court of Tennessee, 3 April 1963.
Volume 211 Tennessee Reports (McCanless), page 599.

78] State v. Fouts.
Court of Appeals of Ohio, 25 January 1947.
Volume 79 Ohio Appellate Reports (Henney), page 255.

Government Documents

Sometimes in doing research you may suddenly find yourself in a strange world where none of your ordinary patterns of thinking apply any more. Government documents represent such a world; in every country and at every level, governments publish their papers in ways that bear no relation to ordinary publishing practices.

To write a first-rate reference to a government document, you would have to understand the whole system of publication behind it. Appendix 2, for instance, spells out the main features of one such system, United States federal documents. As you can see from glancing at this appendix, a great deal of background information is necessary. If you deal extensively with the documents of a government, you will have to master its publication system. But it would be madness to expect such mastery if all you have is one or two references to write. Do the best you can. Ask yourself, as you would with any source, "How did I find this? What would I need to know to find it again? How do I help someone else find it?"

Start by identifying what government you're talking about:

Illinois.

West Riding, Yorkshire, England.

Brandenburg, Germany.

Portugal.

Call foreign countries and cities by their conventional English names—Mexico, not los Estados Unidos de México; Moscow, not Moskva.

Next name the governmental body (if you can) and give a date. Then copy out every piece of identification you can from the document. Some of what you copy may be significant and some may be completely useless, but since you have no way of knowing you should not let embarrassment stand in your way.

Finally, tell the reader where your copy is. In other words, treat it as archival even though it is a publication. That way, if all else fails, your reader can get a photocopy or an interlibrary loan.

References written under these constraints look horrible. Don't feel shy; everyone else's will look just as bad as yours.

18] Montana. The Governor's Commission on Alternative Uses for State Lands, 22–29, March 1968.
Hearings on JL114, known as Barton's Park. C-114. MPC 1,841. 99138-R. #541, series F.
There is a copy at the Widener Library of Harvard University cataloged M 13994.381, 3966.278.

See? Horrible, but it has a chance of serving its purpose, which is to help your reader get a copy.

If it's at all feasible, consider the possibility of reproducing the document in question as an appendix to your work.

Microfilm and Microfiche

Microphotographic archives: Some archival material exists only in microfilm or microfiche; some archival material is so fragile that scholars must use microphotographic copies rather than the originals, which may be sitting no more than six feet away in glass cases or evacuated containers. Don't let the technology spook you—there's nothing special about references to microphotographed archives. Like all other references, their job is to answer the question "How do I put my hands on these sources?" Like all other archival references, they are likely to give the question idiosyncratic answers:

> 8] Carey County Records Office, Freestone, Kansas.
> Register of title, Northeast Quadrant.
> Reel RT-69/6: Mary Blandish, widow of K. Blandish, 30 June 1869.

> 71] C. to Dear father. (Charles Blice to his father, Rudolph Blice, or Plice.) 18 February; probably 1914.
> Alton Group, reel 13.

The first example could stand on its own in a reference list; the second would have to appear as part of a special section with a preface explaining how the archive is organized.

Microphotographic reprints: It's usually a matter of complete indifference to your reader whether you happen to be working with the paper original of a publication or a microphotographed copy. Take this as an example:

47] Martin Traub.
The guest word: Reanimated corpses.
The New York Times Book Review, page 39. 13 June
1976.

Your reader has no reason to care whether you're sitting with the
Book Review spread out across your lap or squinting into the
fishy light of a microfilm reader. Make mention of the mode of
reproduction only to help your reader get hold of elusive sources:

16] Simon Ankers.
A History of the Ankers Family in North Carolina.
Privately printed, 1948.
Available on microfilm from the Family History Project,
University of North Carolina.

Here again it makes no difference to your reader whether you're
working with the original or a copy, but he does want to know how
to get a copy for himself.

Microphotographic publications: Publication directly in microfilm or microfiche is still rare, but it may become more common.
I started to say alas, but I suppose a medieval monk would have
said alas at the distortions and deformities of early printing, and
that worked out well enough. Microphotographed publications
may present other difficulties, but there's nothing hard about writing references to them:

5] Timothy C. Diller.
*Proceedings of the 13th Annual Meeting of the Associa-
tion for Computational Linguistics* (microfilm).
Sperry-Univac, St. Paul, Minnesota 55101. 1975.

38] James R. Meehan.
Frames and planboxes for narratives about machines.
*The Journal of the International Association for Arti-
ficial Intelligence*, fiche 33, 1974.

12] Joan Wells.
Hypertension in confined adult male primates.
University of Washington Medical School Report
11R3219 (microfiche), 1976.

The time may come when even such laconic reference to micro-publication will be unnecessary. We'll all have film/fiche readers in our living rooms, our shelves will hold nothing but bric-a-brac and statuary, and the quaint old habit of reading in buses and restaurants will be replaced by scrimshaw, perhaps, or contemplation.

Newspapers

Unsigned items: References to unsigned articles and editorials in newspapers fall into two blocks:

7] *The New Haven Register* 164(80):1, 21 March 1976.
All-state hoop squads.

44] *The World* (Newcastle-on-Tyne, England) CXII(128):
26, 19 September 1939.
Remonetisation crisis.

Volume, number, and page are given in the same way as they are for journals:

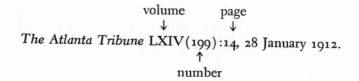

When it's not clear from context where a paper is published, put the information in parentheses after the name of the paper. Do not interpolate into the name.

▷ *The Chelmsford [Massachusetts] Tribune* 26(17):39, 18
February 1958.

The Chelmsford Tribune (Chelmsford, Massachusetts)
26(17):39, 18 February 1958.

Show broken pagination with the plus sign:

▷ *The Wyler News* XXXII(3):14,16,17–19,22, 8 March 1971.

The Wyler News XXXII(3):14+, 8 March 1971.

Always give a fully extended date for a newspaper reference; the
date is your reader's best hope of finding the original.

▷ *The Trumpet* XLVI(8):27, 1968.

▷ *The Trumpet* XLVI(8):27, December 1968.

The Trumpet XLVI(8):27, 23 December 1968.

You may if you like leave off the volume-number information,
since the fully extended date is sufficient to specify an issue.

The Daily News 26(7):13–14, 30 April 1961.

or   *The Daily News*, pages 13–14, 30 April 1961.

You may want to indicate which edition of a newspaper you're
referring to. Sometimes a story appears in full only in one edition
and is subsequently cut to make room for other news. Some newspapers have colorful designations for their editions, and it's up to
you whether to repeat them or to translate them into ordinary
language.

The Star 76(22):33+, sundowner edition 5 May 1958.

or   *The Star* 76(22):33+, evening edition 5 May 1958.

Use the headline of an article as the title:

8] *The Sun* 31(2):16–18, 7 July 1934.
Panel find abuses in deferral of pay rises.

Suppress subheads unless they clarify obscure headlines. But stick with headlines, even the very long ones, through to the bitter end.

47] *The Advocate* CCXIV(17):15+, 17 December 1972.
South Vietnam, after 30 years of war, is land of widespread disease, U.N. group says.

You may sometimes want to indicate the place of origin of a story, called (confusingly) the dateline:

9] *The Tribune* LV(344):1+, 14 October 1933.
Rice crisis continues: Thousands swarm Delhi ministry.
Dateline London, England.

And you may sometimes want to mark off an item as an editorial, rather than a news story:

15] *The Crier-Dispatch* 42(76):18, 15 July 1922.
A fig for progress (editorial).

Signed items: The reference to an item with a by-line starts with the name of the author, not the newspaper:

▷ *The Reporter* XLIII(26):16+, 21 August 1964.
State legislature flip-flops, by Martha Hamlin.

Martha Hamlin.
State legislature flip-flops.
The Reporter XLIII(26):16+, 21 August 1964.

Consider the wire services corporate authors:

▷ *The Post-Times* XXXI(86):17+, 15 July 1944.
Iaban Atoll falls (UPI).

United Press International.
Iaban Atoll falls.
The Post-Times XXXI(86):17+, 15 July 1944.

Reference Works

References to reference works (that sounds like something from Gilbert and Sullivan) fall into a two-block format much like the one for unsigned newspaper articles. The first block gives all of the publication information; the second gives the title, or catchword, of the item.

8] *The Concise Oxford Dictionary of Current English.*
Oxford University Press, fifth edition 1964.
Maffick.

23] *The Encyclopaedia Britannica.* 11th edition 1910.
Aberration.

If the work is arranged alphabetically and you're referring to a main entry, no more information is necessary. Otherwise, give enough information with the catchword so that your reader can find it easily. No universal format is possible; use your knowledge of the work to supply your reader with clues.

4] *The Encyclopedia Americana.* Americana Corporation,
1949.
Texas: population. Volume 17, page 382.

56] *Roget's International Thesaurus.* Crowell, third edition
1962.
Nonobservance. Item 767.

Signed articles in reference works fit the standard three-block format.

▷ *The Encyclopedia of Psychology.* Prentice-Hall, 1974.
Memory, by Joanna Gutas.

Joanna Gutas.
Memory.
In *The Encyclopedia of Psychology.* Prentice-Hall, 1974.

Speaking of signatures, many modern reference works acknowledge editors and compilers who would have remained anonymous fifty or a hundred years ago. The tradition of the scholarly mole, scraping away at underground passages, invisible and silent, ill suits today's temperament. We like to see our names in print. For the scholar at work on a reference list, this trend poses a problem. He has no wish to slight honest toil, but the authority of many a reference work rests on the enterprise rather than on the collection of people around the current edition. What weight should you give these considerations?

If only one person's name appears on the title page of a reference work, you need have no hesitation about fitting the reference to the familiar three-block format:

76] Eric Partridge.
   Origins: A Short Etymological Dictionary of Modern English.
   Macmillan, second edition 1959.

At the other extreme, if the names of half a dozen people appear, each with his own job title, you're safe in using the standard reference-work format:

▷ M. G. Heany, editor-in-chief. R. Collins Broom, general editor, with the assistance of Helen Ailesworth, E. L. Chioffi, and Randall Means. F. X. Malcolm and Sheila M. Jones, associate editors.
   The Dictionary of Saints. Mary the Egyptian.
   Little, Brown, 1962.

   The Dictionary of Saints. Little, Brown, 1962.
   Mary the Egyptian.

Short of either extreme, you may have to flip a coin.

A word of caution: Some reference works stand at one remove from scholarship. This is no disparagement—what would the general reader do without them?—but it does mean that the young scholar must eye them suspiciously as references. To give a far-fetched example, the agronomist who finds himself referring to *The Oxford Book of Food Plants* has probably gone awry, but the work is perfectly suitable for explaining a pastoral image in a poem or a play. Getting to know what constitutes an authority is one of the most important parts of learning the ropes of scholarship. When in doubt, ask an old hand in your field for advice.

Shoes and Ships and Sealing Wax

Besides the written word, scholars also deal with music, paintings, buildings, and artifacts of all kinds—nothing squeaks by the analytic mind. Often the explanation and description you give in your text obviates any need for a reference to such a work. But if you should ever need them, here are a few hints.

Architecture: A minimal description of a building contains the name of the architect, the name of the building or a brief description, the date, and the location. Frequently you will mention all of these naturally in your text and have no need to write a reference. If, for instance, your text says, "The construction of Durham Cathedral [8] proceeded at a remarkable pace from 1093 to its completion in 1133," you add nothing to your reader's knowledge by writing a reference that says:

▷ Anonymous.
   Durham Cathedral, 1093–1133.
   Durham, England.

If he doesn't already know that Durham is in England, there's something wrong with your text. Similarly, the anonymity of medieval architects should not be news to him. Don't clutter up your reference list with self-evident information.
   On the other hand, street addresses for all buildings short of

the monumental are a blessing to the reader. Addresses generally do not fit easily into your text, so references are a good idea:

38] Dwight H. Perkins.
Grover Cleveland Elementary School, 1910.
3850 North Albany, Chicago, Illinois.

Expand the format when you have more information to share by adding a double-indented paragraph:

38] Dwight H. Perkins.
Grover Cleveland Elementary School, 1910.
3850 North Albany, Chicago, Illinois.
The left wing was damaged by fire in the 1940's and the reconstruction (by an unknown contractor) does not match the rest. A gymnasium (1954) now abuts the right wing.

Refer to buildings you haven't seen yourself by using a variation on the format for secondary references.

Art works: The name of the artist, the name and date of the work, and the current location constitute a minimal description of a work of art. When they don't fit naturally into your text, write a reference:

19] Pietro Lorenzetti.
The birth of the Virgin, 1342.
Cathedral Museum, Siena.

For purposes of punctuation, the names of works of art are non-books; use sentence capitalization and don't underline them.

References to ancient works will usually require brief descriptions in place of the name of the artist and the name of the work:

13] Anonymous Susa artisan.
Painted beaker, approximately 4500 B.C.
The Louvre, item #371009.

All works of art are archival; that is to say, they all require descriptions of location. For major works, the name of the repository is sufficient:

    41] Henri Rousseau.
       The dream, 1910.
       The Museum of Modern Art, New York.

Minor works require more explanation:

    56] Paul Klee.
       Drawing, 1922.
       The Art Institute of Chicago, Prints and Drawings Collection, catalog #6/21.133.

Many works of art are in private hands:

    20] Anonymous Choctaw artisan.
       Mortar and pestle, approximately 1800.
       Collection of Sylvia Choate, 2619 Parker Lane, Philadelphia, Pennsylvania 16069.

Some collectors prefer to remain anonymous, to the detriment of scholarship. Never broach the subject; discuss anonymity only if the collector brings it up, and then do your best to dissuade him. If you must, write the reference like this:

    48] Robert Motherwell.
       Homage to the fathers, 1968.
       Private collection.

You can expect letters from readers asking for more information and decide what to do then on the basis of your conscience and your relationship with the collector.

These references contain only the bare necessities and should usually be enlarged on. Start with the minimum reference and then double-indent a paragraph of explanation.

48] Robert Motherwell.
Homage to the fathers, 1968.
Private collection.
Acrylic on canvas, 5'8"×13'. Sold by the Sabarsky
Gallery, 1969; the gallery has black-and-white photo-
graphs of the painting.

Refer to works of art you haven't seen yourself by using a variation on the format for secondary references.

Computer programs: Write a reference to a description of a computer program or its documentation like any other reference, in
the format for a pamphlet, a journal article, an item in a conference proceedings, or whatever it happens to be. For the program
itself, the only sensible information you can give is the name of
the program and where it is. If the information does not fit
smoothly into your text, write a reference:

61] TRU-CHAMP.
Electronic Equipment Corporation, 1483 Meller Road,
Cambridge, Massachusetts 02138.

7] CLINGER.
Computer Science Department, University of Texas at
Austin.

To say anything more than this is a waste of time. Your reader
can't read the program himself. He needs to find out whether his
machine can read it or, more often, whether there is a machine
that can translate it from the version that the source machine can
read to a version that his machine can read. The whole thing is
better handled with a letter or a telephone call.

As a rule of thumb, do not reproduce more than fifty lines of
program code in your text or an appendix. That's at or above the
upper limit of human comprehension. Beyond it, your reader wants
his machine to do the reading, and you are in a loop back to the
sentence that begins, "For the program itself . . ."

Movies: A minimal description of a movie contains the name of the director, the name of the movie, the name of the production company or the distributor or the country of origin (whichever best establishes the provenance of the film), and the release date. Often the information fits smoothly into your text: "Douglas Sirk's *The First Legion* (United Artists, 1951) took Boyer out of his usual pretty-boy role." No entry on your reference list is necessary unless you need to say more. But often you do need to say more.

The prime example is the need to write a secondary reference. The disgraceful practice of talking about movies that they have never seen makes most film buffs' pretensions to scholarship a farce. If you want to write for a fan magazine in this style, fine. But if you want to do film scholarship, you have to play by the scholarly rules. If I sound like a Dutch uncle, it's because there are now a number of wholly imaginary film titles floating around. So if you haven't seen a movie, reveal the source that leads you to believe it exists:

> 41] Douglas Sirk.
> *The First Legion.*
> United Artists, 1951. Described in R. A. Blackmer, Sirk's middle years. *Films in Transition* XII(3):41–56, 1969.

If you've read about a movie in several places, give the secondary reference that your reader will find most useful, or give more than one secondary reference:

> 41] Douglas Sirk.
> *The First Legion.*
> United Artists, 1951. Described in R. A. Blackmer, Sirk's middle years. *Films in Transition* XII(3): 41–56, 1969. Also in Chalmers Coop, *The Director's Eye.* New American Library, 1961.

If you work mostly with plot and theme, exact running times will not be important to you. If you work mostly with the visual side of movies, with camera work and editing, go out and buy a stopwatch. You will want to add to your reference the running time you've clocked yourself:

21] John Huston.
The African Queen, 86 minutes.
Great Britain, 1951.

Never accept the distributor's word; never, never go by something you've read about the film. It is better to give no running time than to give one you didn't clock yourself. Only your own measure can give your reader some indication of what version you've seen. A literary scholar would recoil in horror at the thought of referring to the Classic Comic of *Great Expectations* or the Reader's Digest condensed version of *Too Late the Phalarope.* But film scholars have to do the equivalent every day; they have no choice. They are at the mercy of producers and distributors who feel free to hack away at movies, their lackwittedness held in check only by their venality. Giving the running time doesn't solve the problem, but it does advance the cause of serious film scholarship by specifying what the dimensions of the problem are.

Do not tack on endless lists of credits to your film references. If you're interested in the screenplay, list the scriptwriter; if you're interested in the editing, list the editor; and so on. All such information should, of course, be taken from the movie itself. If you know about it from some other source, use a variation on the format for secondary reference.

If you set off a section of your reference list for references to films, "Films" is a good title for the section. "Movies" is a good title; "Cinema" is not so good, but acceptable. "Filmography" is a grotesque mutant and will undermine your reader's confidence in your good taste and common sense.

Music: Start a reference to a piece of music by giving the composer. Then give the title. For purposes of punctuation, operas and cantatas and albums and masses are books, arias and songs and cuts and kyries are not.

So far, so good. Now, for a published piece of music you proceed as you would for any other publication:

83] Flor Peeters.
 Missa in Honorem Sanctae Lutgardis (opus 15).
 McLaughlin & Reilly, 1950.

36] Robert Schumann.
 Faschingsschwank aus Wien (Viennese carnival, opus 26), 1838.
 Edited by Harold Bauer. G. Schirmer, 1946.

19] Wolfgang Amadeus Mozart.
 Ah! fuggi il traditor!
 In *Don Giovanni* (1787), page 69. C. F. Peters, 1965.

A reference to a recorded performance should include the performer's name and the recording company's identification number:

12] Johann Sebastian Bach.
 Von Himmel hoch, da komm' ich her (BWV 769, 1738).
 Played by Helmut Walcha. Archive ARC 3030, 14553 APM. Undated, approximately 1960.

The date of the recording is frequently impossible to discover; use your knowledge of the source to make the best guess you can.

In most cases, jazz musicians should be treated as the "composers" of pieces of music they use for improvisation, even though the basic melodies are someone else's.

53] Sonny Rollins Quartet, featuring Thelonious Monk.
 The way you look tonight.
 On *Work*, Prestige 7169, 25 October 1954.

These are minimal references. Frequently you will want to add a good deal more information. A good format for this is to start with the minimal reference and then double-indent a paragraph of explanation.

53] Sonny Rollins Quartet, featuring Thelonious Monk. The way you look tonight. On *Work*, Prestige 7169, 25 October 1954. Sonny Rollins, tenor sax; Thelonious Monk, piano; Tommy Potter, bass; Arthur Taylor, drums. Recording by Van Gelder, supervised by Bob Weinstock. Re-recording by Matt Baines. Compare this version to Rollins [58].

References to music in manuscript or in non-commercial recordings must be treated as archival; you must tell your reader how he can see it or hear it for himself.

Radio and television programs: Begin your reference by giving the call letters of the station or the abbreviated name of the network; say whether it's radio or TV you're talking about; and for local stations give the location:

WAVZ radio, New Haven, Connecticut.

WTTW–TV, Hartford, Connecticut.

WFCR radio, Amherst, Massachusetts.

NBC–TV.

Then give the name of the show and the air date. It's usually but not always necessary to add a brief description.

Nova: The language of genes, 28 March 1976.

Face the Nation, 15 August 1960. Interview with Richard Goodwin.

Harry O, 6 January 1974. Trench is kidnaped.

Morning Pro Musica, 12 February 1968. Interview with Alfred Deller.

Eyewitness News, 9 July 1969. Hurricane Connie.

Series are books (uppers-and-lowers, underlined); episodes are not (sentence capitalization, no underline).

For network shows since roughly 1960, this is sufficient. For local shows and for older footage and recordings, it is a joke. Writing a reference implies that the reader can get his hands on the source unless you tell him otherwise. Since many local stations destroy or tape over their footage within forty-eight hours of broadcasting it, you'd better investigate your material before you send your reader off on a wild-goose chase. Very often, your reference will have to read:

> 59] KXLM radio, Kansas City, Missouri.
> *Fiddling Around*, 10 April 1971. Interview with Blind
>   Joe Crockett.
> The station has no copy.

If on the other hand there is a copy, give your reader whatever additional information you've found that will help him trace it:

> 17] WRYE–TV, Macon, Georgia.
> 11 *O'Clock News*, 30 May 1971. George Wallace on the
>   food-stamp program.
> Dope #328.

The responsibility for doing this investigation is yours, not your reader's. If your source is not the original broadcasting station, let your reader know:

> 36] KXXM radio, Fargo, North Dakota.
> *The Ready Ear*, 26 April 1944. Leo Haines reading
>   Dickens.
> Audio-Visual Workshop, University of North Dakota.

Unpublished interviews and studies: Sometimes in the course of your research you may conduct an interview or a study that is too slight to merit independent publication but can be incorporated into a larger work.

The reference to an interview should give the name of the person you talked to, a description of him if that's necessary, the date of the interview, and any other relevant information:

28] Robert Lowell.
   15–19 June 1956, interviews during the Alton Grove
   Writers' Conference.

12] Ida Barrett, District 69 member.
   29 October 1955, interview after the resolution of the
   May Company warehouse strike.

Be prepared to respond to requests for your notes or tapes.

The reference to a study should at the barest minimum indicate
the date, the population, the sample, and the procedure or the tool.
No one format will suit all cases:

61] Merchants' and Mechanics' Bank, Haverhill, Massa-
   chusetts.
   Interviews with 25 of the Bank's 34,000 depositors,
   May–July 1965.

36] MMPI and TAT on all 36 children with hearing dys-
   function in the Alice Lovett School, San Diego, California. 12 January 1976.

Be prepared to respond to requests for your data. Or better yet,
forestall requests by forgetting about the reference and working
your material up into an appendix.

References to unpublished interviews and studies by other people follow the usual format for works not yet published.

THE
REFERENCE
LIST

It's hard to think of your reference list as a communication. Young scholars sometimes call it, with more disrespect than affection, the grocery list and throw the items together no more thoughtfully than they would "two lbs. boiling potatoes, 1 fish, what kind?, for Saturday, six lemons if not disgusting, ½ gal. skim milk."

But if you've worked hard, as I hope you have, at making each of your individual references useful and helpful for your reader, this is not the time to abandon him. Yes, it's true that your reader can make his own way through whatever you provide him, but why discard the chance to help him one last time? Wouldn't a cross-reference from item [14] to item [46] show him a connection he might not otherwise make? Wouldn't collapsing that compound reference into a simple one reflect more accurately the use you want him to make of the source? Wouldn't a special section, arranged chronologically, help him to follow the historical background of your subject? You've gone the first mile with him, and the second; don't leave him to finish the journey alone.

Reference List versus Bibliography

Reference lists are sometimes called bibliographies, but a useful distinction can be made. A reference list need be neither exhaustive nor normative; a bibliography should be either one or the other. If you have put together a list of all the works of such-and-such a description, all of Woodrow Wilson's published papers, for instance, or all the books and articles on color vision in human neonates, then you may call that a bibliography. If you have put together a list of works you recommend, the best English grammars in each of the several schools, for instance, or the most useful analyses of East Coast immigrant patterns, call that a bibliography. But if your list contains nothing more than the sources you've used in working on a piece of research, call that a reference list. Most research produces a reference list, not a bibliography. The bibliography is usually a project in its own right.

Dissertations are the major exception to this rule. By and large, the dissertation writer is expected to produce a genuine bibliography, a list of all the works that have some direct bearing on his topic. The requirement is an outgrowth of the requirement that a dissertation be an original piece of research, not just a mosaic of previous results. Some dissertation bibliographies are nothing but a polite acknowledgment of the tradition; others make a real contribution by identifying obscure sources or organizing and classifying sources or both.

Some of the items on a bibliography may lack citations in the text. Does this present a problem? Not a bit of it—simply number the items that have matching citations in the text and leave the others unnumbered:

81] Margaret Tobin.
Wordsworth and the image of the daemonic.
19th Century Studies CIV(11):38–69, 1971.

Herman Toole.
A Life at Odds: Wordsworth in the Lake District.
University of Illinois Press, 1955.
Pages 30–55.
Pages 155–168.

82] F. G. Tynan.
Mystery and brightness in Wordsworth.
In William D. Church, editor, *Visions of Light: The English Romantics*, pages 213–265. Harvard University Press, 1969.

C. M. Upham.
Wordsworth's last decade, pages 308–314.
Poetry Review XIII(1):288–340, 1959.

This dissertation is not, of course, about Wordsworth—that bibliography would run to several volumes—but about Wordsworth's light imagery, or religious sentiment in Wordsworth, or some other manageable topic.

Compound References

If you haven't already constructed compound references in your notes, this is the time to do it. If you have, this is the time to check them over and improve them.

Suppose, for instance, that you have the three references:

Charles Miner.
A Chronicle of the Provincial American Theater, page 414.
University of Oklahoma Press, 1971.

Charles Miner.
A Chronicle of the Provincial American Theater, pages 167–172.
University of Oklahoma Press, 1971.

Charles Miner.
A Chronicle of the Provincial American Theater, pages 232–238.
University of Oklahoma Press, 1971.

These get combined into one big reference, with the points of reference arranged in order, the heading unnumbered, and the points of reference numbered:

Charles Miner.
A *Chronicle of the Provincial American Theater.*
University of Oklahoma Press, 1971.
  [36] Pages 167–172.
  [37] Pages 232–238.
  [38] Page 414.

Sometimes, on the other hand, you may find that your notes indicate a compound reference where a simple one would be better. Suppose that you have the two references:

Bridget Riley.
Atomic Thermometry, pages 212–215.
Crane, Russak, 1975.

Bridget Riley.
Atomic Thermometry, pages 216–224.
Crane, Russak, 1975.

Do not blindly combine these into a compound reference:

▷ Bridget Riley.
Atomic Thermometry.
Crane, Russak, 1975.
  [56] Pages 212–215.
  [57] Pages 216–224.

Now, it is possible that a compound reference might be the right thing here, if for instance there's a chapter break at page 216 in the source. But probably what you want your reader to do is read the passage through from one end to the other; probably your reference should read:

56] Bridget Riley.
Atomic Thermometry, pages 212–224.
Crane, Russak, 1975.

Both citations in the text get the bracketed number [56].

Bad examples are marked with an arrowhead (▷).

Compound references to sources like articles and pamphlets are seldom justified. Keep a sharp eye out for needless compound references:

▷ Robert Wagenknecht.
The empty sea.
American Geophysical Journal XXII(3):130–142, 1961.
[126] Page 130.   [129] Pages 136–139.
[127] Pages 132–135.   [130] Pages 138–141.
[128] Page 136.

This is a hangover from the worst of the old footnote style; it is almost inconceivable that the author really intends for his reader to use the source as he has indicated. The whole mess should be collapsed into one simple reference:

126] Robert Wagenknecht.
The empty sea.
American Geophysical Journal XXII(3):130–142, 1961.

All the citations in the text get the plain bracketed number [126]:

▷ The areas of deep blue water are the deserts of the sea [126, page 130].
The areas of deep blue water are the deserts of the sea [126].

Excessive pinpointing is characteristic of pseudo-scholarship. All those nitty little page numbers look impressive to the uninformed. When a real scholar wants his reader to make use of a whole article, he refers to it whole, not in bits and pieces.

As you have probably already noticed, you may run your points of reference in double or triple columns:

J. D. Fiore.
Music at the Court of Frederick the Great.
University of Missouri Press, 1937.
[9] Pages 38–41.   [12] Page 343.
[10] Page 115.   [13] Pages 412–414.
[11] Pages 166–168.

Choose a format, whether single, double, or triple columns, and stick to it through any one reference list.

The points of reference are usually page numbers, but they might just as easily be other kinds:

Ralph Batriban.
Chemical gasification of solids and liquids.
Journal of the American Engineering Association XXXIV (2):1248–1267, 1965.
[8] Figure 3.
[9] Figure 14.

If your points of reference are of several kinds, don't jumble them all together:

▷ Gaylord Fite.
Fissure and jointure in hyperplanes.
In Wanda Farnham, editor, A *Symposium on Hyperplane Geometry*, pages 303–379. Plenum Press, 1972.
[28] Page 318.   [31] Page 366.
[29] Theorem 2.5.   [32] Theorem 5.7.
[30] Theorem 3.1.

Gaylord Fite.
Fissure and jointure in hyperplanes.
In Wanda Farnham, editor, A *Symposium on Hyperplane Geometry*, pages 303–379. Plenum Press, 1972.
[28] Page 318.   [31] Theorem 3.1.
[29] Page 366.   [32] Theorem 5.7.
[30] Theorem 2.5.

Some kinds of research produce massive compound references. Although you should try to avoid it, you may sometimes need to carry a compound reference over a page break. Repeat just enough of the heading to remind your reader of what's going on:

Steinman, continued.
[95] Page 315.   [99] Page 531.
[96] Pages 344–346. [100] Pages 560–564.
[97] Page 412.   [101] Page 654.
[98] Pages 441–450. [102] Pages 730–735.

Special Sections

The next step is to decide on the over-all organization of your reference list. Most lists will simply run from beginning to end in alphabetical order by author, but you should keep in mind the possibility of setting aside special sections for special sources.

For example, a study of Orson Welles might have a special section set aside for films; a study of working conditions in the Pennsylvania mines might have a special section set aside for the legislative history; a study of the efforts to canonize John of Kanti might have two special sections for archival references, one for the archive in Poland, the other for the archive in the Vatican. A study of local charities in Grenoble from 1500 to 1800 might have a very long reference list divided into the following sections:

> The 16th Century
>   Primary Sources
>   Secondary Sources
> The 17th Century
>   Primary Sources
>   Secondary Sources
> The 18th Century
>   Primary Sources
>   Secondary Sources

You must use your knowledge of your sources and your topic to decide whether special sections are appropriate for your reference list. Never set aside a special section with fewer than, say, half a dozen references.

The heading of a special section may make it possible for you to shorten the references that fall under it. For instance, all the references under the heading "Works by E. M. Forster" can omit block I. All the references under the heading "United States Government Documents" can omit the words "United States" from block I.

Center your section headings or lay them out flush left, so that they stand out from the references; you may also want to underline or italicize them.

26] Valerie Zetman.
The printing trades in Brussels.
Modern European Letters 26(3):122–203, 1972.

Antwerp

27] M. H. R. Carruthers.
The House of Plantin.
University of Michigan Press, 1968.

28] R. V. Dantzig.
The French "colony" in Antwerp, 1535–1585.
Journal of the Netherlands Historical Association CIX
(2):13–55, 1969.

Cross-reference

Already in working on your notes you have probably used some cross-references. This is the time to polish them up and add any others your reader may find useful. Cross-references may fall in any of the blocks except, I think, block II. They may also stand alone, in which case they are not numbered. The following example is constructed to illustrate all the different placements; on any real reference list, it's most unlikely for cross-references to come so thick and fast.

7] Charlotte Baile (later Charlotte Baile Wyatt [56–59]).
The Fragile Compact.
Matthews & Sommerville, New York, 1893.
This book so closely resembles Norcross [35] that I sus-
pect it was plagiarized.

8] Henry Baile.
The gothic heroine as feminist.
Short Fiction Studies IX(4):39–123, 1974.
Also in Vennit [54], pages 412–490.

9] J. C. Ballard.
The Stranger Within.
Volume II in Plachette [42], 1969.

A. M. Barnard (pseudonym of Louisa May Alcott [2–4]).

10] A. M. Barnard.
Twice Again, or The Revenge of the Egyptian.
Gasset & Mayes Brothers, 1868.

11] A. M. Barnard.
The Vampire Beau.
Gasset & Mayes Brothers, 1866.
Badly abridged in Roth [48].

The Barnard cross-reference to Alcott could also appear in block I of Barnard [10]. There is no strong reason for preferring one placement to the other, and both kinds may appear on one list.
Be sure in doing cross-references never to write:

▷ See [12].

The bracketed reference numbers are not words. You must always write:

See Coleman [12].

Whenever you can, say why you want the reader to look at the other reference:

Coleman [12] gives more elegant proofs for several of the central lemmas.

Alphabetical Order

Believe it or not, alphabetizing is a controversial topic. I mention this because you may at some time in your life have occasion to work with an editor who follows a different alphabetizing scheme from the one recommended here. You must decide for yourself whether the matter is worth arguing over.

The rule for alphabetizing is nothing before something; to put it another way, think of the alphabet as starting space–A–B–C rather than A–B–C.

Begin alphabetizing by the authors' family names:

Nider.

Nissen.

Nye.

Overton.

Ignore internal punctuation except for hyphens:

▷ O'Hara.

Oberly. .

Oberly.

O'Hara.

Treat hyphens ˙as spaces; remember that your alphabet starts *space*–A–B–C:

▷ Bateson.

Bates-Simpson.

Bates-Simpson.

Bateson.

If you have two or more authors with the same family name, alphabetize them by given name:

A. Vitale.

R. L. Vitale.

T. Vitale.

Again, nothing goes before something:

> W. R. Bernstein.
> William Bernstein.
> William Bernstein, editor.

Following the rule nothing before something yet again, sole authorship precedes first authorship:

> M. R. Kain.
> M. R. Kain, G. Downes, and E. Riefstahl.

For joint authors, alphabetize first by the first, then by the second, and then if necessary by the third and so on:

> P. Linders, C. R. Matthew, and L. Carey.
> P. Linders, C. R. Matthew, and B. F. Taine.
> P. Linders and A. H. Seton.

If you have two or more items with the same author or the same joint authors, alphabetize them by title. Ignore the words "a," "an," and "the" and their foreign equivalents. Book and non-book titles are alphabetized together.

> S. J. Ezell.
> *The Conquest of the Plains.*
> Yale University Press, 1975.

> S. J. Ezell.
> Southerners forever: A chronicle of the Georgia settlers in Oklahoma.
> *The Journal of the Association for Historical Research* LXIV(7):12–41, 1971.

> S. J. Ezell.
> States' rights as reflected in the Nebraska Constitution.
> *Southwest Studies* XXVII(3):113–164, 1973.

When a person's name appears in a title, it's alphabetized first name first, not family name first—Maria, Methods in the example below, not Methods, Montessori:

L. H. Wren.
Maria Montessori and the tactile sense.
In Bronfman [6], pages 165–204.

L. H. Wren.
Methods and procedures in encouraging group play.
Classrooms: The Journal of Primary Education IX(1): 17–48, 1976.

Alphabetize numerals and symbols as if they were spelled out:

B. I. Singeman.
Backsearch routines.
Math Notes for Programmers 14(5):32, 1969.

B. I. Singeman.
The β^2 searching algorithm: A reconsideration.
Computation Quarterly XV(2):56–71, 1968.

B. I. Singeman.
Blanket search in dense data bases.
Math Notes for Programmers 13(7):55, 1968.

B. I. Singeman.
☐ ☐ queries in quick searching.
In Frankel [6], pages 134–151.

The symbolic expressions are alphabetized as if they were spelled out "beta squared" and "block-block." Sometimes there's more than one way to spell out an expression. Many people would spell out Stanley Kubrick's *2001* as "two thousand and one"; some would do it "twenty ought one." On a reference list, where the entries are grouped first by author, it makes no particular difference. If you were doing an index, you might want a cross-reference from one version to the other.

Hard names: You will sometimes see the advice to alphabetize family names by the rules of their mother tongues, French names by French rules, Italian names by Italian rules, and so on. The trouble with this advice is that scholarship is a gloriously mongrel calling, and even the simplest reference list is likely to include names from a dozen backgrounds. If you find the mother-tongue rule attractive, test yourself on the following list:

C. O. Gofter.

Helmut af Tunderhatz.

Michele Del Rio.

Antoine Ste. Fauvelle.

Raymond V. Scandolo.

H. L. von Bülow.

Erin M'Naughton.

Michael X. MacPatton.

A. K. da Tandera.

Sheila McOrdry.

M-J. de La Fontaine.

Alfred Göltel.

Ready? Here's the list in order by the mother-tongue rule:

H. L. von Bülow.

Michele Del Rio.

Alfred Göltel.

C. O. Gofter.

M-J. de La Fontaine.

Erin M'Naughton.

Sheila McOrdry.

Michael X. MacPatton.

Antoine Ste. Fauvelle.

Raymond V. Scandolo.

A. K. da Tandera.

Helmut af Tunderhatz.

Only if you scored 100 percent should you even consider alphabetizing by mother tongue. Even then, you should ask yourself whether you want to be the sort of person who parades small knowledge. And be warned that you must go on making perfect scores forever; there's nothing funnier than a failed finick.

The safer and seemlier way is to forget about language of origin and alphabetize with bald literalism:

Helmut af Tunderhatz.

A. K. da Tandera.

M-J. de La Fontaine.

Michele Del Rio.

C. O. Gofter.

Alfred Göltel.

Michael X. MacPatton.

Sheila McOrdry.

Erin M'Naughton.

Raymond V. Scandolo.

Antoine Ste. Fauvelle.

H. L. von Bülow.

With some names, the naive reader has no way of telling whether the middle section represents a given name or the first part of an unhyphenated family name. If your list has thirty or more items, use a cross-reference to give your reader a hand. Suppose, for instance, that you alphabetize Arthur Wicklowe Townes under W on a long list; a cross-reference under T will do a service to your reader without compromising your erudition.

The same reasoning applies to names that put the family name first and the given name after. By all means alphabetize Lee Chin under L, but on a long list you should also have a cross-reference under C.

Some people are known by only one name; use that for alphabetizing and remember the rule "Nothing before something":

H. V. Batton.

Bede.

Alicia Bede.

R. L. Bedford.

Count honorifics and designations only in ordering two or more people who use single names; ignore them otherwise:

Gregory of Nazianzus.

Gregory of Tours.

Michael Gregorylich.

Monarchs and popes and such have alphanumeric designations; order two or more of them with the same name numerically, not alphabetically:

▷ Charles Fourth.

Charles Third.

Charles Third.

Charles Fourth.

Tidying: Some authors simply cannot decide what to call themselves. And, in all fairness, it must also be said that some authors have to work with high-handed editors who impose a house style on every name they get into their clutches. So you may from time to time be faced with alphabetizing two or more different versions of the same name. Use bracketed information to bring all the versions into conformity and then alphabetize by title:

J[udith] R[illington] Farme.
The Arab minorities in Israel.
Diffusion IV(2):31–62, 1975.

Judith Rillington Farme.
Israeli policy in the Galilee.
The Journal of Mid-East Studies XXIII(3):23–37, 1976.

Judith R[illington] Farme.
Separatist Palestinian nationalism: Its origins and its future.
In M. R. Allyn, editor, *Tomorrow's Battles*, pages 364–389.
    Anchor Press, 1970.

Unfortunately, the longest version always wins, regardless of the author's preference, but at least your reader knows that all three items are by the same person. You must, of course, be absolutely certain that they are by the same person. If there's the slightest doubt in your mind, add no extra information and alphabetize by the usual rules:

J. R. Farme.
The Arab minorities in Israel.
Diffusion IV(2):31–62, 1975.

Judith R. Farme.
Separatist Palestinian nationalism: Its origins and its future.
In M. R. Allyn, editor, *Tomorrow's Battles*, pages 364–389.
    Anchor Press, 1970.

Judith Rillington Farme.
Israeli policy in the Galilee.
The Journal of Mid-East Studies XXIII(3):23–37, 1976.

Mixed lists: Not all references have authors by which to alphabetize. Alphabetize ones without authors' names right along with the authored ones, first word first, ignoring "a," "an," and "the," and their foreign equivalents:

Edith Nance.

The New York Times.

Morris Newton.

The Noncooperation League.

L. G. O'Keefe.

When the name of a person is part of the name of an organization or a group, alphabetize it first name first, not family name
first. The Robert Browning Society, for example, goes under R,
not B. But on a long list a cross-reference under B certainly can't
hurt anything:

5] M. R. Bascombe.
   Uplift and enlightenment in the workers' study circle.
   19th Century Studies XXXII(1):28–74, 1971.

   The Robert Browning Society [71].

6] Rebecca Byrman.
   A *History of the Popular Lecture in England and
   America.*
   University of Louisiana Press, 1968.

Breaks in alpha order: There are a few cases where strict alphabetical order is relaxed in order to make your reference list more
readable. Regardless of what the alphabetical order would be, the
books of a multivolume work by one author are listed in volume
order, the proceedings of conferences of an organization are listed
in chronological order, and popes or monarchs of the same name
are listed in numerical order.

Chronological Order

Although there's seldom any reason for arranging a whole reference
list in chronological order, some special sections lend themselves

to this organization, and it's a happy way around the alphabetical chaos of some sources. Feel free to use chronological order wherever it seems suitable to you; just be sure to let your reader know what you're doing:

123] Laura Shires Wooten.
Themes of change in Ozark Mountain stories after the Great War.
Studies in American Ethnology VII(6):41–60, 1971.

124] C. H. Ying.
Tellers of Tall Tales, pages 235–246.
Princeton University Press, 1958.

The Ozark Mountain Archive
St. Louis University
(in chronological order)

125] Harry Weeks. ("Blind Harry.")
One day six bear rose up . . . (26 stanzas, apparently fragmentary.)
Gathering LL-134, 1850.

126] "Little Zeb."
Fishing-bear story.
Gathering RO-916, postdated 1855.

127] Anonymous Missouri tale-teller.
Honey-bear story.
Gathering RO-901, 1868.

Order of Mention

Sometimes the best way to arrange your references is by the order in which you mentioned them in your text. Suppose that the first citation in your text comes on page 3:

Johnson and Boone [1], however, argue against using lithotripsy to crush calculi so that they can be passed.

You explain Johnson and Boone's point of view, continue your own exposition, and reach the second and third citations on page 5:

In 1971, Abramsen [2] and Mellors et al. [3] almost simultaneously discovered the possibility of inducing autotripsy by chemical means.

The matching references read:

1] R. E. Johnson and C. F. Boone.
  Cystorrhexic incidents following lithotripsy.
  The Journal of Renopathic Medicine XXII(1):144–198, 1966.

2] N. W. Abramsen.
  Inducing autotripsy and ectasis by chemotherapy.
  The Journal of Renopathic Medicine XXVII(3):12–47, 1971.

3] T. A. Mellors, G. N. Marsh, P. I. Donati, and T. L. Champion.
  The dread stone: A quassia-picrotoxin technique for the inducement of autotripsis.
  Asclepius XXXIX(7):602–647, 1971.

When is this method preferable to alphabetical order or chronological order? It depends on the style of exposition characteristic of your own work and of work in your discipline. In medicine, for instance, as you may have guessed from the example, the tendency is for each source to be introduced, sucked dry, and set aside. There is none of the complicated interweaving of sources that you find in, say, literary criticism or historiography.

The advantage to arranging your reference list by order of mention is that it permits your reader to go backwards, list to text, as well as forwards, text to list. Suppose, for instance, that your reader has very little interest in crushing kidney stones but a great deal of interest in picrotoxin therapies. If in skimming through your reference list his eye lights on item [3], it is very handy for him to be able to go back to your text and find the citation after [2] and before [4]. If your list were in alphabetical or chronological order, he might have to leaf through your whole article looking for Mellors et al.

If you choose this arrangement for your reference list, you should have very few compound references, and the citations for them should all come together:

> P. L. Corbett.
> Hepatic transposition in drill operators.
> In F. V. Ormans, editor, *Occupational Hazards*, pages 220–271. University of Idaho Press, 1973.
> [19] Pages 255–262.
> [20] Pages 230–238.

Notice that in this method the points of reference as well as the main entries come in order of mention—pages 255–262 first because they were mentioned first.

Every now and then you may return to a source that you cited before. Do not abandon your over-all scheme:

> ▷ Barnes [38], Abramsen [2], and Stametz [39] all report cases of caudal aerocelism.

Number the late citation in order:

> Barnes [38], Abramsen [39], and Stametz [40] all report cases of caudal aerocelism.

On your reference list, use cross-reference both at the main entry and at the late entry:

> 2] N. W. Abramsen (also reference [39]).
> Inducing autotripsy and ectasis by chemotherapy.
> *The Journal of Renopathic Medicine* XXVII(3):12–47, 1971.
>
> . . .
>
> 39] Abramsen [2], page 44.

These late mentions should be rare; if you have many of them, you've chosen the wrong arrangement for your reference list. Wait to number your citations and your references till you're on your final draft; the order of mention in your first draft bears no necessary resemblance to the final order.

Last-minute Changes

It does sometimes happen that you need to change your reference list at the last minute, and it isn't necessarily your fault. Some blasted graduate student has just written a dissertation that supports one of your shakier conclusions; you've got to refer to him. Or some infernal colleague has written months after you asked him to read your manuscript, telling you that your use of a source is in error; you've got to pull the reference. The article is already in page proofs and the journal's been on the phone to you twice asking where they are. And of course, the change is always in the worst possible position—if you're using alphabetical order, the author's name is Aademsen; if you're using order of mention, the topic is the very first thing you discuss; and if you're using chronological order, the date is practically prehistoric.

Contain yourself. Form is never more important than sense. If you must add a reference at the last minute, tack it onto the end of your list:

83] C. R. Zeisman.
Lee's Tactics.
Dutton, 1971.

84] Violet Aademsen.
Popular Views of Robert E. Lee: 1870–1885.
PhD thesis, Marquette University, 1978.

If you must delete a reference at the last minute, mention the gap in your list so that your reader won't be confused:

3] Chalmers V. Asmond.
The case for Panamanian sovereignty.
Time and Tide 39(15):43–48, 1975.
No reference [4].

5] Ricardo Barrio.
Torrijos at the crossroads.
Latin American Studies XX(2):103–124, 1976.

These eleventh-hour changes are distressingly unbeautiful, but beauty is a secondary consideration. Informing your reader comes first.

Now be honest. Weren't you really working a bit close to the wire?

Compression

Almost all of the examples in this book use the open reference format:

15] A. R. Montley.
The preparation of malachite green by petroleum substitution.
The Journal of the Royal Chemical Association XVIII (3):14–21, 1938.

16] Frances Simms.
Benzine ring formation and modification in the production of malachite green.
Proceedings of the 9th Annual Meeting of the United Petrochemical Association, pages 231–236. 1941.

But another possibility exists. Exactly the same information in exactly the same order can be given in the compressed format:

15] A. R. Montley. The preparation of malachite green by petroleum substitution. *The Journal of the Royal Chemical Association* XVIII(3):14–21, 1938.

16] Frances Simms. Benzine ring formation and modification in the production of malachite green. *Proceedings of the 9th Annual Meeting of the United Petrochemical Association*, pages 231–236. 1941.

The sole advantage of the compressed format is that it saves space, but that can be a prime consideration. If, for instance, you find yourself editing a professional journal, you can be sure that your budget will be as tight as a steel corset. You will be in no position to overlook any opportunity for holding down your paper costs, and over many articles in many issues in many copies the savings that result from using the compressed format will mount up.

Even when you're not worried about cutting costs, you should still give a thought to saving paper, and the trees that must be felled to make it. If your reference list is simple and straightforward, with few annotations and comments, consider using the compressed format.

Just remember that mistakes are much harder to catch in the compressed format than in the open one. The typographical errors most likely to occur and most difficult to see are in the numerical information—volume number, issue number, page number, and date. Even a minor error is an irritation to the conscientious reader, and a major one may render the whole reference useless. Don't trust your eyes. If you must do your checking alone, check numbers by reading them aloud. It's better to read aloud from your original notes while a friend checks the final version.

The Finishing Touch

All that remains is to number your reference list and go back through your text inserting the reference numbers into the brackets that wait for them. The task seems so mechanical that you might almost be tempted to ask a friendly six-year-old to do it for you. But don't.

Any chance to look at your text in a fresh light is precious. There are a thousand tricks for fooling yourself into seeing with fresh eyes. Read the carbon; photocopy the text onto yellow paper; read it backwards (page by page, not word by word); read it aloud; have a friend read it to you; diagram every tenth sentence; make a list of your most common faults and search for them; get the text typed on a strange typewriter; search every sentence for two words you can delete; circle all conjunctions and prepositions and relative pronouns; take at least one word on every page and look it up in the dictionary—in other words, use any device, however silly it feels, to wrench the reality of expression away from the context of intention. Improving what you've said is not the hardest part; it's seeing what needs improvement. All of us read in our own words not what we've said but what we meant to say, what we hoped to say. Any gimmick that checks this tendency is a godsend to the careful writer.

So, as you enter the bracketed numbers in your text, let your eye stray over the page, taking advantage of the queer context in which you can now see what you've written. Is that word really spelled with an "e"? Haven't you used that turn of phrase elsewhere? Is that transition as fluent as it might be? What's that flab doing there in the middle of the paragraph? Have you done the best you can?

Special Schemes

You will by now have realized that the form in which you do your documentation is considerably less important than the content. Complete and thoughtful instruction on how to get hold of your sources—that's what your reader needs, and as long as he gets it almost any vehicle will do. Given a bent for innovation in small things, you may decide to invent your own format, some unique combination of sidenotes, footnotes, endnotes, and interpolation. Well, there's probably no harm in it, but there are better uses for your ingenuity.

With that warning in mind, I have some hesitation about presenting the two special schemes in this chapter. They are not meant as an invitation to proliferate new systems of documentation. They should, in fact, be ignored in ninety-nine cases out of a hundred and eyed, even in the hundredth, with suspicion.

Short Names

Both the white-copy system and the super-quick system require that you assign short names to your sources. The simplest short names are the last names of authors. Suppose, for instance, that your reference list includes R. J. Weston's *The Evolution of English Syntax*, that he's the only Weston on your list, and that this book is the only work of his that you use. Then you may call it simply:

Weston.

If your reference list includes two or more authors with the same last name, use their initials or their given names to differentiate them. Suppose that you list both R. J. Weston's *The Evolution of English Syntax* and Susan Weston's "Notes on the Pluperfect" but no other works by either author. Then the short names for the two works are:

> R. J. Weston.
>
> Susan Weston.

If you have two or more works by the same author, use abbreviated titles along with his name. Suppose that you list one work for R. J. Weston, his *The Evolution of English Syntax*, and two for Susan Weston, "Notes on the Pluperfect" and *Tense and Mode in Middle English*. Then the short names for the three works are:

> R. J. Weston.
>
> Susan Weston, Pluperfect.
>
> Susan Weston, Tense and Mode.

There's a knack to doing these abbreviated titles. Try to suck the pith out of the full title. Take, for instance, Simon Chaney's "An Interpretation of Vandalism as the Expression of Loss of Ego":

> ▷ Chaney, Interpretation.
>
> Chaney, Vandalism.

Good abbreviated titles depend on context. In an article on computation, the best short title for Stephanie Maysles's "Fast Algorithms with Floating-Point Numbers" might be:

> Maysles, Floating Points.

In an article on floating-point numbers, the best short name for the same work might be:

> Maysles, Fast Algorithms.

Using initials for abbreviated titles seldom works well. Take for instance Krishnan Alkamir's *An Account of the Development of the Wool Trade in the Early Period of the Republic:*

▷ Alkamir, ADWTEPR.

Alkamir, Wool.

Don't go overboard in abbreviating titles, especially when you're dealing with well-known works:

▷ James, Portrait.

James, Portrait of a Lady.

There are no underlines, italics, or quotation marks in short names, even for titles like the one in the example above, which has not been abbreviated. No distinction is made between books and non-books.

Editors and compilers are treated just like authors when you're assigning short names:

▷ Mayhew (ed.), Energy.

Mayhew, Energy.

Give the names of both authors when there are two, but only the first of three or more. H. M. Kronenberger and B. G. Katz's *Immaterial Expectations* becomes:

Kronenberger and Katz.

T. L. Sale, V. Brazier, and G. Colter's "An Etiology of the Falling Sickness" becomes:

Sale et al.

Notice that "et al." can make different sets of joint authors look the same. Sale, Brazier, and Colter and Sale, Harkness, and

---

Bad examples are marked with an arrowhead (▷).

O'Hare both collapse to "Sale et al." Restore the names of the second and following authors or use abbreviated titles to make the distinction.

> Sale, Brazier, and Colter.
>
> Sale, Harkness, and O'Hare.
>
> or Sale et al., Etiology.
>
> Sale et al., Symptomatology and Spread.

In some contexts, a title or an abbreviated title may be enough of a short name without the author:

> Shaw, The Devil's Disciple.
>
> or The Devil's Disciple.

Sources without authors use titles or abbreviated titles alone as short names:

> NY Times.
>
> Commerce Handbook.
>
> Panjika.

For both the systems that follow, short names are used to tie the text and the reference list together; the reference list therefore needs no numbers. Pinpointing accompanies the short names; the reference list therefore needs no pinpointing, and there are no compound references. Otherwise, the reference list is just like the one in the standard system. Short names never appear on reference lists.

White Copy

This is the most beautiful of all the systems of documentation. The text is completely unmarred with the apparatus of scholarship; there are no bells and whistles, just smooth, unbroken copy. Between the text and the reference list comes a section of notes keyed backwards to the text by means of page and line numbers and forward to the reference list by means of short names. The notes section can't be done until the text is finished and paginated; that means you have to do a demanding, picky task at the last minute, under pressure.

Here's how it works. The beginning of page 56 in the text reads:

> their origins. These children are fearful about any small alteration in their routine. If juice appears at break for four days and soup for the fifth, the change will trouble them. Rage and tantrum among the outspoken ones may be difficult to deal with, but even more upsetting is the nausea the quiet child experiences, the wary, shamed expression you

The corresponding section of the notes reads:

> Page 56, lines 1–2. Wykoff, pages 366–401; Zeeman, pages 38–67.
> Page 56, line 4, tantrum. Seefer, Reaction Formation, pages 22–35; Zeeman, page 47.

And the corresponding section of the reference list reads:

> Marla Seefer.
> Reaction formation among child schizophrenics.
> *The Journal of Abnormal Child Psychology* XI(3):20–46, 1971.
>
> Marla Seefer.
> Trauma in infant schizophrenics: Three case studies.
> In Barnard Wilkinson, editor, *The Troubled Child*, pages 368–440. St. Louis University Press, 1966.
>
> H. L. Wykoff.
> *The Mark of Cain: Child Schizophrenics and Their Families.*
> Basic Books, 1972.

Martin O. Zeeman.
Schizophrenic children in pseudo-classroom situations.
The Journal of Abnormal Child Psychology XII(2):38-80,
1972.

Why would anyone go to all this trouble? For the scholarly reader there's no advantage to this system; on the contrary, he may find the absence of visible documentation in the text an irritation. But for the lay reader it's a blessing. The layman is likely to classify any work studded with notes and numbers and the paraphernalia of scholarship as heavy stuff and set it aside till he has more time. In other words, he never reads it. So the white-copy method is worth considering when you hope to reach both a scholarly and a popular audience. Reserve it for times when there is real hope—when your topic is broadly attractive, when you're being published for general distribution, and when you've tried twice as hard as usual to make your writing open, clear, and graceful.

Super-quick

Of course you should never do anything at the last minute. No one should ever run behind schedule, approach or pass a deadline, no one should ever be late. Of course. But somehow, mysteriously, all of us have found ourselves at seven-fifteen working on page 6 of a twenty-page paper due at nine o'clock. Turn in such an emergency to this method; the little time you have should be spent on composition, not on technical details of bibliographic style.

The lightning method of doing documentation simply encloses short names in parentheses and drops them directly into the text:

under the influence of his advisors (Kappel, page 541). He was reluctant to call out the army, as he indicated in his diary (pages 322–329), but Manders, Fulsome, and Lord Barley convinced him that he had no choice (Raymond, The Little War, pages 211–215). By the beginning of June,

The reference list has no numbers for the items and no pinpointing, but otherwise it looks just like a standard reference list.

As you can see, for elegance and grace this system is strictly Rube Goldberg, but it works. It is suitable only for informal presentations, for student papers, say, or manuscripts to be circulated in draft. I hope you'll never have to use it.

MANUSCRIPT PREPARATION

Late at night, as the wind makes unearthly music outside, as a cloud passes over the face of the moon and the fire dies down to embers, scholars begin to tell weird and terrible tales. The protagonists of these horror stories are not ghosts and ghouls, not monsters and zombies, but typists, editors, and printers. "The whole thing had to be retyped, you know. There wasn't so much as a single page that was usable. I had to get a bank loan for it." "The galleys come and it's 'badly,' not 'baldly.' So I change it to 'baldly.' The page proofs come and it's still 'badly.' So I change it to 'baldly' again. Then the thing comes out and there it is, you know it has to be. 'Badly.' Now I'm waiting for the second edition." "You should have seen the tables. I mean, as abstract designs for wallpaper they were probably quite chic, but you couldn't make out the figures for love or money. They were, like, engraved on the head of a pin."

Meanwhile, on the other side of town, gathered around a similar fire, there sits a group of typists, editors, and printers. They too are telling horror stories. "Do you know, there were six different colors of ink on the blasted thing, including yellow? There was yellow writing on it, I swear to you." "I thought the galleys were incredible. The whole thing was practically rewritten word for word, and the sheets looked like somebody had used them for wrapping sandwiches, or maybe garbage. I thought they were the worst thing I had ever seen. But of course that was before I saw the page proofs." "They seem to have the idea type is made of rubber or something. The only way you could get these tables on one page was in a compressed agate and they looked, I'm telling you, like they were engraved on the head of a pin." Would the scholars recognize the protagonists of these stories?

If it were true, and I don't believe it for a minute, but if it were true that all typists, editors, and printers are maniacal vandals, your task would be to thwart them. If, as is much more likely, they want to do their jobs well, your task is to cooperate with them. Whatever your motives are, you need to look at copy from their point of view.

What follows is a description of four different kinds of typescript: final draft, classroom copy, photo-ready copy, and perfect copy. Who gets what?

Final draft is the necessary predecessor to photo-ready copy and perfect copy; without final draft to work from, no typist in the world can produce the disciplined, immaculate pages that are characteristic of photo-ready copy and perfect copy.

Final draft is also the form in which you should submit a manuscript that's to be set in type. Your editor and the printer he works with must be able to read your draft without any confusion or difficulty, but aside from that they don't care what it looks like.

Classroom copy is the form in which you should submit student papers. Once you're no longer a student, you'll have no more use for it. If you do your own typing, you can probably do classroom copy from rough draft; if someone else does it for you, he needs final draft to work from.

Photo-ready copy, or camera copy, is the form in which you should submit a manuscript to be shot directly from the pages you provide. Many journals and some books are no longer typeset but photographed from manuscripts that authors provide. If what's

wanted is photo-ready copy, you'll be asked for it. Your responsi-
bilities here are very heavy. Even when the over-all design is set
for you, the layout of each page is still in your hands. Clarity, balance, and beauty are the criteria for photo-ready copy.

Perfect copy is really an anachronism, and I hope that no one
will ever ask you for it. But typically, dissertation requirements are
for perfect copy, not photo-ready copy. I suppose it's even conceiv-
able that some martinet of a teacher should ask his students for
perfect copy, not classroom copy.

Final Draft

The best way to explain the difference between rough draft and
final draft is to show an example of each. Here is a passage in
rough draft:

```
      will
    shall mean the sort of valid step by step,
  ?  (syntacticly) xjp checkable deduction as
     maybe carried out witzhin a logical
...which  calculus like Zermelo-Freenkel set theory
     or Peano arithmetic. formatl, consistant,
```

It doesn't matter whether your rough draft looks as bad as this or
worse; no eyes but yours are ever meant to see it. Final draft, on
the other hand, is meant for other people. Here is the same passage in final draft:

```
    mean the sort of valid, xtas step-by-step,
                                       that
    syntactically checkable deduction which
    can be carried out within a consistent,
    formal, logical calculus like Zermi Zeri
    Zermelo-Fraenkel set theory or Peano arith
```

The criterion for final draft is that a stranger find it immediately,
easily readable. It doesn't have to be beautiful, it just has to be
accessible to someone who has no idea of what you're trying to

say, and accessible without pause or hesitation. No puzzling; no pondering; no late-night telephone calls to ask what that word is in the upper left-hand corner of page 178.

Cut, tape, and copy: The best way to make corrections on final draft is with a scissors, a roll of cellophane tape, and a photocopying machine. Say that in checking over a page you find the line:

    had laerned that teh Moscow Embassy was

You take a piece of paper big enough so that it won't wobble around in your carriage (this is an excellent use for the margins of discarded pages), and you type:

    learned that the

You cut it out with your scissors, trimming it close, lay it against a piece of tape a little longer than the scrap, position the tape above the errors, and flatten it out with your thumbs. Presto, you now have:

    had learned that the Moscow Embassy was

For final draft to go to a typist, that's enough. For final draft to go to editors, printers, and most teachers, the copying machine now comes into play. As long as the tape is clean and the scrap is pressed down so that it can't throw a shadow, a photocopy of the page looks flawless.

For larger mistakes or revisions—and this method works for changes of every size—position the correct copy on top of the incorrect copy first. Then anchor it with four little bits of tape, one at each corner. Then tape down the top and the bottom edge with ten-inch pieces of tape, folding the tape over onto the back of the page. Again, remember that tape does not copy if it's clean; shadows do.

But now for the real beauty of the system: Suppose that, in

looking back over the line that you corrected, you decide it's still not exactly right. "Learned" is a little too strong; what you really want to say is "thought." So you type on another piece of paper the word:

```
thought
```

You cut it out, lay it against a piece of tape, press the tape down in place, and you have:

```
had thought that the Moscow Embassy was
```

There may be an upper limit on this process, where there are so many layers of tape that they start to obscure the original typing, but I have photocopied pages that were five or six layers thick in some spots and the results still looked perfect.

In final draft, the error and the correction needn't be exactly the same length. You could, for instance, substitute "heard" for "learned" in the example above, centering it so that it would look like this:

```
had   heard   that the Moscow Embassy was
```

Also in final draft, the correction needn't be perfectly aligned. It shouldn't be cockeyed, but a degree or two off the true horizon will do no harm.

White out: Use correction fluid to white out no more than one or two extra characters. The effect may be to correct the spacing or to leave it a character or two short. Suppose you have the line:

```
larger programs or routines in the library
```

If you decide to change from the plural to the singular, whiting out produces a line that's still easily readable:

```
larger program  or routine  in the library
```

But whiting out more than an extra character or two makes your copy difficult to read. Suppose that you decide to say just "routine" in the line above. Do not white out the extra words:

▷ `larger               routine   in the library`

Cut and tape the correct version:

`larger routine in the library`

Don't worry about the shortness of the line; you have no obligation to maintain your margins in final draft. Cutting and taping the correction is best, but exing out or crossing out is better than whiting out extra words:

`larger xxxxxxxxxxxx routine   in the library`

`larger program—or routine   in the library`

White out and type over: Just be patient and wait till the correction fluid is dry. On final draft, perfect alignment is not necessary.

Correction tape: For the amateur typist, correction tape works only on mistakes caught while the page is still in the carriage. Once it's out, it will never go back in the same way again. With that exception, correction tape is very useful for making final drafts.

Ex out: Ex out no more than, say, a dozen characters. For more than that, cut and tape.

Bad examples are marked with an arrowhead (▷). In this chapter, "bad" often means not lines with mistakes in them, but lines in which the mistakes have been badly corrected.

Ex out with one string of lower-case letters; the object is just to indicate omission, not to blast your errors off the face of the earth.

▷ proposal he ⬛⬛⬛⬛⬛⬛⬛⬛⬛ soon wished he had

   proposal he ẍäẍẍẍẍẍẍ soon wished he had

Punctuation should not be left at the end of a string of x's:

▷ for future research ẍẍẍẍẍẍ. The

Ex out the punctuation too, back-space, and put it in where it now belongs:

   for future research. ẍẍẍẍẍẍẍ The

Ex out and type above: Do not ex out a character and type another above it:

                 e
▷ no consistant approach to the epiphenomenal

Ex out the whole word and type above it:

         consistent
   no ẍẍẍẍẍẍẍ approach to the epiphenomenal

Better yet, cut and tape the correct version.

Strikeovers: Never correct an error by back-spacing and typing the correct version on top of it. Even when there's no mistaking what word you intend, strikeovers slow down the stranger for whom you're doing final draft:

▷ sounds that thḇ patient feels are related

And when the word is unfamiliar or, worst of all, a proper name, the stranger can only guess what's in your mind:

▷ some home truths that Feeldman doesn't want

Cut and tape the correction.

Cross out: Now we begin the hand corrections, which should always be done in non-smearing black ink. Not in pencil; not in colored ink, not even blue, let alone red or green or violet; not in the beady, syrupy ink of cheap ballpoints. A black felt-tip pen is a good choice so long as the felt is not worn down; a black hard-tip pen is even better. A fountain pen with a narrow nib is good, but a broad-nibbed pen is not.

Taking your pen in hand, you should cross out no more than roughly a dozen characters; for more than that, cut and tape. Cross out with one or two neat horizontal lines. Do not leave punctuation at the end of your crossing out; cross it out as well and put it in by hand, neatly, where it now belongs.

Cross out and print above: Never, never, never write corrections on final draft. Print. Print with ordinary sentence capitalization, not all in caps. Form your letters scrupulously, as if you were a diligent and unusually dextrous first-grader.

Do not cross out a character and print above it; cross out the whole word and print the whole word correctly above.

Insertions: Insert punctuation if there's space for it; if there's not, cut and tape.

Do not insert a single character; cross out the whole word and print the whole word correctly above.

It is acceptable to insert two or three words above the line, with a caret to show where. The words may be printed:

other
larger than any⌃tank they had ever seen.

If the words are typed, show the placement with a caret, not a slash:

```
                as
 ▷  as much/if not more than earlier models.

                as
    as much if not more than earlier models.
             ^
```

Do not attempt to make an insertion between a word and a mark of punctuation:

```
                    or disallowed
 ▷ subsequently contradicted  others are
                            ^
```

Cross out the mark and put it where it now belongs, at the end of the insertion:

```
                    or disallowed,
    subsequently contradicted  others are
                             / ^
```

For insertions longer than two or three words, either cut and tape or use a separate page. A separate-page insertion requires an instruction; to differentiate them from corrections, instructions should be printed (not typed) in full caps.

```
                              INSERT A
    toward normal relations.   China and Japan
                            ^
```

The insertion is typed with a matching label at the head:

```
    Insert A
    Normality amounted to undeclared border
    warfare, of course, but it was better than
    nothing.
```

It is a very wise idea to include paragraphing instructions with the insertion, just for safety's sake:

```
       Insert A
 No ¶  Normality amounted to undeclared border
       warfare, of course, but it was better than
       nothing. No ¶
```

At the end of a long insertion, one that goes on for three-quarters of a page or more, it is very wise to include return instructions:

> for every man he had lost.   The pension was small, but every widow and orphan in the territory knew his name. RETURN TO PAGE 156.
>   NEW ⁋

Cutting and taping is better than using separate pages for insertions because it is easier to follow.

Cumulate and retype: Corrections made by cutting and taping, by whiting out, and by using correction tape do not cumulate. You may have as many as you need on a page. But corrections made by exing out or crossing out, by printing or typing above the line, and by using a separate page for an insertion do add up. Set yourself a limit of, say, four to a page. If you have more than that, either retype the page or cut and tape over corrections that were first made by some other method.

Spacing: In general, everything in final draft should be double-spaced. Unless you are submitting to a journal that instructs you otherwise, type content footnotes in with your text, double-spaced, set off by bars, and marked "footnote":

> disagreement among the gods.* Euthyphro put
>
> _____
>
> FOOTNOTE { * They get off onto a side-track about the
>
> apple of discord, in which the language
>
> is much more elevated and poetic, but not
>
> poetic in the characteristic Platonic
>
> way.   There are many small images heaped

FOOTNOTE CONT'D

up one on top of the other, rather than

one commanding metaphor.   It seems

possible that the passage is by another

hand, although it may just represent

hasty writing.

---

forward another definition: Piety commands

Displayed quotations should be double-spaced on final draft, and so should your reference list. You need the double-spacing to make corrections and improvements on the draft.

The only exception is for diagrams or similar materials. It would be crazy to double-space a binary tree, for instance:

▷
```
                    A
                   / \
                  B   C
                 / \
                D   E
```

What you are doing here is not really typing but drawing with your typewriter; space whatever way makes the drawing come out right:

```
              A
             / \
            B   C
           / \
          D   E
```

Make corrections only by cutting and taping.

Count characters: If you are submitting final draft to a journal that uses three-inch columns, it is foolish to draft a display or a diagram or a table that comes out five inches wide in the journal's standard typeface. The editor is going to have to do something to your material to make it fit, and he may not know enough about your subject to make the best choice. Count the number of characters in ten lines of the journal, take the average, and work to that character count.

Suppose, for instance, that you want to display an equation that's 56 characters wide and that you're submitting to a journal with a column width of 48 characters. Displaying the equation full-length in your draft would leave to the editor the decision about where to break it, a decision that he cannot make as well as you can. In your draft, you should break the equation at the best possible point and type it on two lines.

Numbering citations: When the final draft of your reference list is done, go back to your text, fill the bracketed numbers in neatly by hand, and white out whatever marginal notes you made to yourself about what belongs there:

```
on the dark side of the moon [ 6 , 18]. Here
```

Syllabication: The only purpose for syllabicating a word at the end of a line is to maintain your margin. Since you have no obligation to maintain margins on final draft, do not syllabicate any words.

```
▷ annual contributions continued to grow pro-
  portionately but accomplished no more.

  annual contributions continued to grow
  proportionately but accomplished no more.
```

It's especially important not to break hyphenated words at the ends of lines:

▷ the role that the conspirators, heartstricken at the results of their actions,

If you give final draft with a break like this to a typist or a printer,
you're likely to get back "heartstricken," and it's your own fault.
Do it the safe way:

    the role that the conspirators,
    heart-stricken at the results of their

Instructions: As much as you can, try to show on your final draft,
not to tell. When you must give instructions, print them neatly in
full caps:

    convicted of behavior unbecoming to an
    officer.
                    ↑ SKIP TWO LINES
                    ↓
            The 57th Regiment } SINGLE-SPACE
    INDENT   SKIP   of Foot   AND CENTER
            A LINE ↘
         ↘ The 57th Regiment were the original

This is acceptable, but it's not in your best interests. A few minutes
more, a snip of the scissors, a dab of tape, and you have a much
safer version:

    convicted of behavior unbecoming to an
    officer.

            The 57th Regiment
                of Foot

    The 57th Regiment were the original

If you have instructions on final draft that's going to an editor,
explain them in a cover letter, not on the draft itself. It's the
editor's job to mark copy, and he can do it much better than you

can. If you have done a good job of showing what you want on your final draft, you should have little to tell.

Final means final: Your final draft should be perfect in everything but the typing. No sentence, no word, no comma should be anything but your very best. Once you have passed the stage of final draft, corrections are expensive, irritating, and dangerous to make. Do not rush to thrust your final draft into the hands of your typist or your editor. Linger a little; read it again; mull it over. This is your last chance to make corrections without causing yourself and other people a good deal of grief; grasp the opportunity.

Hiring a typist: Even a poor typist can do his own final draft with enough patience and cellophane tape, but if you're simply not able to type at all you may have to hire someone to turn your rough draft into final draft.

Explain what you're after. Carry this book along with you and go over the characteristics of final draft with the typist. It's very important, for instance, that he understand what kinds of corrections he can make. He needs to know about double-spacing everything and about setting up your content footnotes in draft form. If your handwriting is, like most people's, illegible in spots, tell him to leave space for words he can't read so that you can fill them in later, printing carefully. Be sure to mention that he should not syllabicate words at the ends of lines; most typists do it by second nature and need to be reminded when not to.

Since the quality of your rough draft is likely to vary considerably from one page to another, it's better to agree on an hourly rate than a page rate for typing final draft. A sensible rate for a good typist to charge is two to two and a half times minimum wage. Be suspicious of anything lower than that; you may end up with another rough draft.

The typist is of course responsible for correcting his own mistakes without charge. But since fifty of the mistakes are likely to be yours for every one of his, it would be mean-spirited and unbecoming to haggle over typographical errors. Correct them neatly by hand, along with your own mistakes. If you make so many mistakes on a page that it needs to be retyped even to achieve final-draft status, pay him again at the full rate. If he makes so many mistakes that a page must be retyped, get another typist.

Never give the only copy of your manuscript to anyone. Make a copy of your draft before you let it out of your hands.

Classroom Copy

In classroom copy, your footnotes and your reference list should be single-spaced. You may choose a display format with single, space-and-a-half, or double spacing. Everything else should be double-spaced.

Corrections: Make as many corrections as you like by cutting and taping, whiting out, and using correction tape. The spacing and the alignment need not be perfect. Set yourself a limit of four to a page for corrections made by exing out or crossing out, by printing or typing above the lines, and by using separate pages for insertions. Submit photocopies of your pages, not the originals, so that your cut-and-tape corrections won't show.

Margins: There's no need to maintain perfect margins on class-room copy, but it would be a pleasant courtesy to your instructor to make a stab at some kind of margins. For amateur typists, the bottom margin is the hard one. Try ruling your bottom margin onto a backing sheet in glaring red and purple. Tamp the backing sheet and the page you're typing down so that the tops are even with each other, slide the backing sheet over so that it laps out on the left side of the page, and roll the page and the backing sheet into your carriage together. If you get distracted and go beyond the bottom margin anyway, white out the extra line and type it on the next page.

Displays: Choose an indentation for your displays that's different from your paragraph indentation. A little extra space above and below each display also looks good. Aside from that, choose any layout that you like and stick to it. Several examples of display layout follow. The examples do not by any means exhaust the possibilities.

Examples of Display Layout

with greater plasticity.

    Stendhal's words on the subject [81] are worth repeating:

        Romanticism is the art of presenting people with
the literary works that are capable of giving them
the greatest possible pleasure in the present state
of their customs and beliefs. Classicism, on the
other hand, presents them with the literature that
gave the greatest possible pleasure to their
great-grandfathers.

These sentiments did not prevent him from turning to classical

---

with greater plasticity.

    Stendhal's words on the subject [81] are worth repeating:

  Romanticism is the art of presenting people with the literary
works that are capable of giving them the greatest possible
pleasure in the present state of their customs and beliefs.
Classicism, on the other hand, presents them with the
literature that gave the greatest possible pleasure to their
great-grandfathers.

These sentiments did not prevent him from turning to classical

---

with greater plasticity.

Stendhal's words on the subject [81] are worth repeating:

> Romanticism is the art of presenting people
> with the literary works that are capable of
> giving them the greatest possible pleasure
> in the present state of their customs and
> beliefs. Classicism, on the other hand,
> presents them with the literature that gave
> the greatest possible pleasure to their
> great-grandfathers.

These sentiments did not prevent him from turning to classical

---

with greater plasticity.

Stendhal's words on the subject [81] are worth repeating:

> Romanticism is the art of presenting people with
> the literary works that are capable of giving them
> the greatest possible pleasure in the present state
> of their customs and beliefs. Classicism, on the
> other hand, presents them with the literature that
> gave the greatest possible pleasure to their
> great-grandfathers.

These sentiments did not prevent him from turning to classical

Footnotes: In classroom copy, footnotes appear single-spaced, at the bottom of the page. Cutting and taping them into place works best; rolling down and rolling up and changing the spacing back and forth is too much of a headache for the amateur typist. Run a fifteen-character bar above the first note.

A page of classroom copy with footnotes follows. Notice that the footnotes are indented two spaces to make the signals stand out. Notice too the few visible corrections, neatly made.

Classroom Copy with Footnotes

a symbolic, formalistic way. Since symbols can be written and

moved about with negligible expenditure of energy, it is

tempting to leap to the conclusion that anything is possible

in the symbolic realm.* But it is no more possible to construct

symbolic structures without using energy than it is to construct

material structures for free. If symbols and material objects

are to be identified in ~~the~~ this way, then we should perhaps pay

special attention to the way material artifacts are engineered.

We might in principle expect that the same limitations apply to

symbolic artifacts.

Engineers have been remarkably adept at reconciling the

creation of reliable structures with two human failings: People

cannot create perfect mechanisms, and people tend to plunge into

activities before they understand them perfectly. This

reconciliation is accomplished by means of the same social

mechanisms that work to convert mathematical intuitions into

mathematical proofs.† First, in mature engineering disciplines,

---

* This is the feeling behind computability theory -- solvable
  versus unsolvable problems -- and also behind complexity
  theory -- solvable problems versus feasibly solvable problems.

† "One of the chief duties of the mathematician in acting as an
  adviser to scientists ... is to discourage them from expecting
  too much of mathematics." -- Norbert Weiner

Reference list: In classroom copy, the reference list is single-spaced. Cut and type, white out, or use correction tape for all corrections; a reference list is hard enough to read without visible corrections. Try not to carry an item over from one page to the next.

A page from a reference list follows.

Page from a Reference List

7] O. L. Etkind.
Late-type model atmospheres: A complete linearization.
Astrophysical Journal 15(8):641, 1969.

8] W. R. Fairbanks and E. P. Schwartz.
Multiline hydrogen-helium models for O- and early B-stars.
Astrophysical Journal 15(7):123-148, 1969.

9] Elizabeth Fishbein.
The Future of Celestial Mechanics.
Academic Press, 1972.

10] G. C. Freed.
Planetary distances according to general relativity.
The Journal of Astronomy XXXVIII(4):203-249, 1971.

11] G. C. Freed.
Toward a new celestial mechanics (editorial).
The Journal of Astronomy XXXVII(2):3-9, 1970.

L. R. Ginath.
Simultaneous Determinations.
Freeman, 1972.

[12] Pages 44-68.
[13] Pages 122-135.
[14] Page 366.

15] E. M. Hayward.
Helium and metal abundance in old open clusters.
Astrophysical Journal 16(10):711-721, 1970.

16] Gardner LaPalombra.
Red giants and the helium flash.
The Journal of Astronomy XXXIX(2):132-161, 1972.

17] M. D. Nims, C. H. Oparka, and D. Sealey.
     Advanced evolution of population II stars.
     Astrophysical Journal 16(12):891-913,1970.

18] G. O'Hearn.
     Spherical coordinate intermediaries for an artificial
       satellite.
     To appear in the Astrophysical Journal.

Photo-ready Copy

Corrections: You may have as many corrections as you like on photo-ready copy, but they must all be invisible to the camera.

Cut and tape remains the best method, and correction fluid is also good for small mistakes; but on photo-ready copy the correction must be exactly the same length as the original error and the alignment must be perfect. The white substance that correction tape deposits on the page usually muddies the letter typed over it, so don't use the tape on photo-ready copy. Exing out, crossing out, and all other visible corrections are forbidden; all insertions are forbidden.

Margins: There should be no problem about maintaining constant top margins and left margins, I trust.

The right margin on photo-ready copy should be maintained to about seven characters. Ten is too many; the copy looks chewed at. Five is too few; it requires too many syllabicated words, too many lines that end with hyphens. Seven is a good compromise. Suppose that the character grid on your typewriter reads:

```
0     5    10    15    20    25    30    35    40    45
|IIIII|IIIII|IIIII|IIIII|IIIII|IIIII|IIIII|IIIII|IIIII|
```

Suppose too that you choose position 45 as the outermost point of your right-margin range. That means that your range is from position 39 to position 45; any line that ends in that range is acceptable.

But typing photo-ready copy is not a mindless, mechanical task; taste and judgment come into it too, nowhere more than in the care and feeding of margins. Take the single most hated word in careful typing, "through." Suppose you have the line:

```
 0      5     10    15    20    25    30    35    40    45
|| | | | | | | | | | | | | | | | | | | | | | | | | | | | | | | | | | | | | | | | | | |
```

▷ the firm resolve to put the mine-owners through

If you stop at "mine-owners," the line's too short; if you add "through," it's too long. If the line above ends at or before position 41, you can move "the" around from the beginning of this line to the end of that one. But what if you can't do that? Stop at "mine-owners"; a line that's too short is better than one that's too long.

Take the case of the word that's already hyphenated. Suppose you have the line:

```
 0      5     10    15    20    25    30    35    40    45
|| | | | | | | | | | | | | | | | | | | | | | | | | | | | | | | | | | | | | | | | | | |
```

▷ that the poor invalid had been gregory-powdered

Again, if the line above ends at or before position 40, you can move "that" around. If you can't, the thing to do is to stop at "gregory-." The one thing that you must never do is double-hyphenate:

▷ that the poor invalid had been gregory-pow-

Take the case of successive syllabication. Suppose that you have the two lines:

```
 0      5     10    15    20    25    30    35    40    45
|| | | | | | | | | | | | | | | | | | | | | | | | | | | | | | | | | | | | | | | | | | |
```

▷ patient exhibits the classic signs, furfu-
  raceous scalp, sore, bleeding gums, hypo-

(The last word in full is "hypopituitarism.") Syllabication on two lines in a row is justified, forgive the pun, when the right margin is justified—that is to say, when it's straight, as it is when a printer sets it in type. When the right margin is ragged, as it is in typing, successive syllabication is bad form. If you're doing your own typing, you have an easy out:

```
patient exhibits the classic signs, sore,
bleeding gums, furfuraceous scalp, hypo-
```

If you're typing for someone else, you don't have that option. If the line above ends with a short word, like "the," you're in luck:

```
the patient exhibits the classic signs,
furfuraceous scalp, sore, bleeding gums,
```

If you have no other choice, stop the first line short:

```
patient exhibits the classic signs,
furfuraceous scalp, sore, bleeding gums,
```

It's easy to maintain bottom margins on pages that are all straight text; you just type the same number of lines on every page. Displays are the headaches here. If you have few displays, it's worth your while to adjust the space above and below each so that you maintain a constant bottom margin for your page. But if you have many displays, you'll waste too much time on the endeavor, and it's better to set a range for the bottom margin as you do for the right margin.

Buck teeth and widows: As you can see, your object in typing photo-ready copy should be to make it not only accurate but shapely, pleasing to the eye. Of the many little tricks that add up to an inviting page, avoiding buck teeth and correcting widows are among the most important.

A buck tooth is a line that ends with a word dangling out over the line below it:

> ▷ ways in the secret documents that Moulton and
> his assistant had prepared. There could

The dangling word should be moved down:

    ways in the secret documents that Moulton
    and his assistant had prepared. There could

Try to establish the habit of hitting the carriage return at the first word break within the right-margin range. It's trying to cram as many words as possible onto a line that results in buck teeth.

A widow is a word that stands alone on a line. Worse than a plain widow is a widow that's shorter than your paragraph indentation or one that's the second half of a syllabicated word. The worst widow of all is the one that starts a page. There's no cure for a widow but to move back up in the paragraph and fiddle around with the ends of the lines till you can move the widow up a line or move another word down beside it.

Footnotes, displays, reference lists: Footnotes, displays, and your reference list appear in photo-ready copy as they do in classroom copy. If you need reminders, look at the examples in that section (only remember that the footnote example shows visible errors, which are not allowed in photo-ready copy).

Look at the page: I wish that I could recommend a good book or pamphlet on typing layout, but I don't know of one. The final guide in any case must be your eye, and you must be strict with yourself. Look at the balance of the page. It should neither shrink in nor balloon out at any point. Look at the page before it and after it. One should not be thin and skimpy while the next is fat. Look hard. If what you see is ugly or awkward or disconcerting, try again.

Hiring a typist: You need to be able to type pretty well to do photo-ready copy, although a good eye, patience, and the willingness to start over are more important than speed or even accuracy, since you can make as many invisible corrections as you need. But supposing that you decide to get someone else to type for you, you have a problem.

Most professional typists are trained for the two things you care least about, speed and accuracy. They have sat for hours in class getting faster and faster and more and more accurate on material that's already laid out for them. To do a good job of typing photo-ready copy, a professional typist must in effect ignore 90 percent of his training and substitute a completely new skill. The crack typist who does a hundred words a minute on copy that's already laid out may be the least able to readjust; you might be better off with a smart, willing duffer.

The only way to find out whether a typist can do what you want is to try him. Get him to do a short manuscript or a part of a manuscript for you; ten or twelve pages should be enough to tell. If the pages look good, you're set. If they look awful, you're out a little money but you've learned what you need to know. Try another typist; try again till you find a good one.

Obviously, the time to do your experimenting is not two weeks before your dissertation is due or four days before the deadline on your big conference paper. Get a good typist and book him well in advance, allowing him plenty of time for all that juggling and playing with margins he will need to do.

How to pay? At a page rate of eighty cents, a very fast typist can make eight or ten dollars an hour for five or six hours, before he gets too tired. The copy that results looks a little slap-dash, but that's not his concern. If you want him to take his time and get better results, you have to make it worth his while. I think that an hourly wage with an agreed-on rate of production helps put the typist in the right frame of mind, although of course it works out the same as a page rate. Three times minimum wage and five or six pages an hour should give you a good starting point for negotiations.

By the way, take your friends' recommendations on this subject with a grain of salt. "Fabulous typist" all too often seems to mean "typist who is willing to put up with me."

The sine qua non: No one can type photo-ready copy from rough draft. Anyone who says he can is fooling himself or feeding you hogwash. You must provide your typist with good, clean final draft—final draft with all of the characteristics spelled out in this book under that heading. Anything less, and you have only yourself to blame.

Instruction sheet: Often in preparing photo-ready copy you must work to someone else's instructions, those of a dissertation secretary or a journal or a publisher you're submitting to. Pass the instruction sheet on to your typist, but not before you've read it yourself. Insofar as you can, you should follow these instructions in your final draft. If, for instance, all your main headings must be centered, it's a great waste of time to put them all at the left margin in your final draft. You'll just have to go back and mark all of them with centering instructions. Why not issue a blanket instruction to the typist at the beginning of the paper, "Center all headings now at left margin"? Because you'd like them all to be centered, that's why. The instruction sheet cannot take the place of good final draft.

I would like not even to consider such blanket instructions as "Every time you see 'glabela' please correct it to 'glabella.'" Any typist who undertakes to perform such a task needs his head examined; the less said about anyone who asks him to undertake it, the better.

If you have no instruction sheet to work from, you should prepare one for your typist. Leaving it all up to him is unwise; you may think you don't care and then find out that you do, very much, when he does something that looks all right to him and perfectly terrible to you. A sample instruction sheet follows; adapt it to your own needs and preferences.

Sample Instruction Sheet

paper	substance 20 opaque white bond, 8½x11″
top margin	1″ from top of page; line 1 contains page number, 1½″ from right side of page, line 2 is blank, line 3 starts text
bottom margin	approximately 1½″ from bottom of page, 26 double-spaced lines (including line 1, with page number, and line 2, blank)
left margin	1″ from left side of page
right margin	outermost character 1″ from right side of page, 7-character range
spacing	double-spaced except space-and-a-half for displays, single-spaced for footnotes and reference list
paragraphs	indent 7 spaces
main headings	start a new page; heading on line 5; heading centered, uppers-and-lowers, underlined; text starts line 7
sub-headings	do not start a new page; leave two lines blank between last line of text and sub-head; sub-head at left margin, uppers-and-lowers, underlined; leave one line blank after sub-head; start first paragraph after sub-head at left margin, with no indenting

sub-sub-headings	do not start a new page; leave one line blank between last line of text and ss-head; ss-head indented 7 spaces, sentence capitalization, underlined; followed by a colon with no underline; skip 2 spaces and start paragraph
displays	space-and-a-half (warning: displays are double-spaced in final draft); indent 12 spaces from left margin; maintain usual right margin; adjust space above and below display to maintain usual bottom margin on page, but leave at least a line and a half of the usual double-spaced lines blank
footnotes	single-space (warning: footnotes are double-spaced in final draft); mark text and note * for first note on page, † for second note, ‡ for third note, § for fourth note; note goes at the bottom of the page; maintain usual bottom and right margins; put a 15-character bar above first footnote; indent note 2 spaces to make symbol stand out
reference list	single-space (warning: list is double-spaced in final draft); adjust spacing between items to maintain usual bottom margin on page, but leave at least a line blank; maintain usual top and right margins; follow draft exactly for left margin and all details of style; notice that the numbers 1 to 9 must be indented one space to make them line up with 10 and so on; try not to carry an item over from one page to the next except for long compound references

Sit down and talk over with your typist what you have in mind. There's no point in treating a typist as if he were a back-alley numbers runner, to be greeted with a wink, a raised eyebrow, a shrug, and silence. You and he are collaborators in a difficult, complicated enterprise; you should talk to each other. Take this book with you and go over the requirements for photo-ready copy together. If you typed your own final draft, you may have noticed some tricky spots; tell him about them. You don't need to be buddies, but it's absolutely essential that you be on speaking terms.

Proofreading: Photo-ready copy should not just be checked over; it should be proofed. Get a friend or a colleague or hire someone if you must to go over the copy with you. You, the copyholder, read the final draft aloud, word for word, with all the tricky punctuation too. For instance, you would read the first sentence of this paragraph, "Photo-hyphen-ready copy should not just be checked over, semi, it should be proofed." Show the capital letter at the beginning of a sentence and the period at the end by letting your voice rise and fall naturally, but don't rely on vocal cues to communicate other marks of punctuation; give their names aloud. Your friend, the proofreader, reads silently through the photo-ready copy, noting on a separate piece of paper any errors that he finds. Do not let him write on the photo-ready copy unless you want your typist to shoot the pair of you. The location of an error must be specified by line as well as page; count down from the top for the top half of the page and up from the bottom for the bottom half. Mark each error with an assignment of blame, "ae" for author's error, "te" for typist's. If your final draft was as good as it should have been, you should find no more than one author's error every dozen pages; if your typist is as good as he should be, his errors should occur at about the same rate. You pay for correcting your mistakes, he corrects his free. Just in case there's any doubt in your mind, the faithful transcription of a typographical error on the final draft is an author's error, not a typist's error. If your draft reads "study teh question" and your typist renders it "study teh question," you pay for changing "teh" to "the."

Perfect Copy

Perfect copy is typed on rag bond. The only permissible way to make a correction is with correction fluid; the error may be no

longer than two characters, the correction must be exactly the
same length, and the alignment must be perfect. No more than
one such correction a page is allowed. Otherwise, in the mainte-
nance of margins and so on, perfect copy is just like photo-ready
copy.

An artful dodge: It is possible to fake perfect copy by photocopying photo-ready copy onto twenty-pound rag bond. The machine
can't handle this paper in continuous feed. You have to copy a
page, wait for the copy to come out, and copy the next page; you
can't make more than one copy of a page at once. From time to
time the machine may jam anyway; you have to open it up and
remove the mangled piece of paper. It's slow work, but it goes
much faster than trying to produce genuine perfect copy.

Galleys and Page Proofs

The other possible fate for your final draft is to be set in type.
Sometimes between what you thought was the final draft and the
typesetting there comes a reprieve, in which you and your editor
work on a manuscript together, but don't count on it. The final
draft that you submit should be so accurate a reflection of your
intentions that you could drop dead that night with a clear conscience. No whispered messages to your deathbed companions,
"There's something not quite right about the beginning of section
three, if I could just look at it again." Final means final.

Galleys and page proofs are not, repeat not, an invitation to
revise. Your task is to check them over for typographical errors.
Inevitably you will find mistakes of your own as well; be firm with
yourself. An error of spelling or punctuation must be set right; an
outright error of fact must also be corrected, at whatever cost is
necessary. But the time for improving your style has passed. It's
too late now. Unless you learn to accept that fact, you will never
do your utmost on final drafts, and every editor who deals with you
will hold your name in infamy.

In general, typeset copy is proofread by the printer and proofread or checked by your editor. Therefore, for much of the text, checking it by yourself is sufficient. But tables, diagrams, mathematical and statistical copy, and your reference list should get the full treatment; you copyhold while someone else proofreads. Have your companion note his corrections on a separate piece of paper; enter them on the galleys or the page proofs yourself, later on. Mark galleys and page proofs with a #2 pencil, neatly. If you don't know the proofreaders' marks, ask your editor for a list and learn to use them. If there's something wrong and you can't tell from the list which mark to use, don't guess; explain in words in the margin what's troubling you. Don't mark the copy till your mind is made up.

Many deadlines are indications, guesses, orders of magnitude. Press deadlines are deadlines. Don't try the old abducted-by-a-band-of-gypsies, escaped-only-with-your-life excuse; your editor has already heard it. Be on time.

Much less advice is necessary about galleys and page proofs than about typing because you have an editor to guide you. Don't be shy about asking for help when you need it. If you've already shown good faith by submitting clean, neat final draft, your editor will probably be delighted to assist you.

The End

I wish that I could end this book with the section at the end of the chapter on the reference list: "Have you done your best?" That would be good rhetoric, but bad sense. The time to ask the question is on your final draft. Once you get to photo-ready copy and galleys, all you can do by tinkering with your prose is injure and infuriate the people you have to work with.

That's a bitter pill to swallow if you have really tried. The harder you work at your writing, the more aware you become of its failings, its weaknesses, places where you're not quite up to the mark. There's a sadness about seeing your words when it's too late to change them. Good; sometimes very good; but not good enough. Store up the lessons you learn as you read your photo-ready copy or your galleys. Next time you can remember to beef up your examples, to spend a little longer on your opening paragraphs, to eliminate more wordiness, to put what you have to say more directly, to conquer hard transitions instead of finessing them. Next time, next time, you can do better.

APPENDIXES

ACKNOWLEDGMENTS

INDEX

Appendix 1
The Vita

The idea of a vita is perfectly straightforward—it presents your qualifications for a post. There are three names current for this document, "vita," "curriculum vitae," and "résumé." (It requires no acute psychological insight to observe that we set job-hunting off in its nomenclature as something foreign.) Of the three names, "vita" is the least common, but it has the most to recommend it; it's short, it forms an acceptable Englished plural, and it needs no accents. So vita is what we'll call it.

Many manuals have been published about writing vitas for jobs in business and industry, but this information is no help with academic vitas. The academic vita is much more highly stylized than its counterpart in the outside world, much narrower, and therefore much easier to prepare. A thousand minute, delicate decisions that face the writer of a business vita have already been settled for you by the rigid format of the academic vita.

This rigidity can cause great discomfort in young scholars putting together their first vitas. They feel themselves reduced to the level of name-rank-and-serial-number. Where in these bland and faceless phrases is the writer's essence, his person, his spirit? The answer is: Nowhere. You might (while chafing) think about what the restrictions of the vita format represent. Not only in pious theory but also frequently in fact, academic posts are awarded solely on qualifications. If the academic vita reflects a little game with rules and points and goals, the game is at least acknowledged, the rules are set out clearly. Academy has its own peculiar definition of merit, but at least it spells that definition out, and often sticks by it. Small consolation if you're a brilliant weirdo, a square peg in a round hole; but compared to the rest of the world, where the shapes of the holes are often kept secret, some consolation nonetheless. Here are the rules of the game.

Heading

There is no need to use a heading on a vita—vitas look like nothing else in the world and proclaim themselves instantly.

Name, Post, Address, and Telephone Number

Begin by giving the name you commonly use for your signature. Give your current academic post, address, and telephone number below and your home address and telephone number at the right:

Dwayne L. Marchant
Assistant Professor of
   Music Theory
University of Maine
   Music School
Storrs, Maine 06112
203–983–1166

home:
1315 Ridge Road
Woodly, Maine 06519
203–477–9431

If you're still in graduate school, you'll need to check whether your department will accept mail and telephone calls for you. If so, give both your academic and your home address (your own residence, not your parents'):

Adele Vionnet
Department of Near Eastern
   Languages
Iowa State University
Missoula, Iowa 77188
851–234–1550 x366

home:
RFD Route 7
Bindale, Iowa 77189
851–229–8437

Otherwise, give only your home address:

```
Martin Wyler
2297 Flora Avenue
St. Louis, Missouri 51674
510-484-9075
```

If you're currently working in a non-academic job, probably you'll list only your home address and telephone number. To do otherwise would require that your job be academically prestigious, that your employer know about your job search, and that he be willing for you to conduct it on company time—an unlikely combination of circumstances.

Simple though this section looks, there are several pitfalls to avoid. Do not, for instance, attach to your name any titles or designations of degrees; they make you look very small-time:

▷ Philip Itisaki, MA, MFAT, PhD

   Philip Itisaki

Pare down your academic address to the minimum that will permit mail to reach you:

```
▷ Weak Force Group, Physics Department
  University of Wisconsin -- Milwaukee Campus
  Sherrill Memorial Hall, Room 39
  1536 Maple Avenue
  Milwaukee, Wisconsin 65998

  Physics Department
  University of Wisconsin
  Milwaukee, Wisconsin 65998
```

If you have no phone, say so:

```
home:
3314 East 57th Street
Chicago, Illinois 60615
no phone
```

Bad examples are marked with an arrowhead (▷).

Degrees

Under this heading, list your degrees with dates and granting institutions:

> BA 1963, Antioch College
> MA 1965, PhD 1968, State University of New
> York at Rochester

Abbreviate the names of your degrees unless they will be unfamiliar to your reader:

▷ Doctorate of Philosophy 1955, Brown
  University

PhD 1955, Brown University

▷ LTS 1964, Uppsala University

Licentiate in Sacred Theology 1964, Uppsala
University

Two styles of abbreviation are current, one with periods, one without. The one with the periods looks statelier, the one without, snappier. Use either as long as you're consistent.

> B.A., B.S., M.A., M.A.T., LL.D., Ph.D.
> or BA, BS, MA, MAT, LLD, PhD

List commencement honors with your degrees:

> BS magna cum laude with departmental honors
> 1969, Webster College

To indicate the breadth of your background, you may want to append informal designations to your degrees:

```
BS (microbiology) 1967, Coe College
MS (microbiology and biophysics) 1969,
   Arizona State University
PhD (history of science) 1974, Harvard
   University
```

There is no point, however, in adding such designations if your career has followed an undeviating path:

```
▷ BA (history) 1961, University of Michigan
  MA (history) 1964, PhD (history) 1966, Yale
```

Nor are you obliged to volunteer the information that one or more of your earlier degrees is in a field inappropriate to the post that you're applying for:

```
▷ BA (political science) 1962, Rosary College
  PhD (history of art) 1967, Ohio State
```

The presumption is that your highest degree is appropriate; if it's not, explain in your cover letter why you think you're qualified anyway. For a post in the history of art, this candidate should write:

```
BA 1962, Rosary College
PhD 1967, Ohio State
```

In using these designations, remember that they are informal; you need not adopt any awkward or misleading nomenclature your particular school happens to use. Suppose, for instance, that you do work in ethics at a school that calls the field moral philosophy for historical reasons:

```
▷ PhD (moral philosophy) 1961, Berkeley
    Divinity School

  PhD (ethics) 1961, Berkeley Divinity School
```

Don't be excessively specific:

▷ PhD (analysis of small-business failures)
   1974, McGill University.

   PhD (microeconomics) 1974, McGill University

The title of your dissertation, which appears later in the vita, will
reveal your precise area of specialization.

If you are right on the verge of receiving a degree, you may
list it:

   PhD 1978 (expected), Vanderbilt University

All the old saws about counting chickens before they're hatched
apply here. Nothing chills a prospective employer faster than learning that a degree a candidate lists as expected is, according to his
department, more accurately classed as an aspiration.

Some schools need place designations:

▷ BA 1955, Trinity College

   BA 1955, Trinity College, Burlington,
   Vermont

Some do not:

▷ PhD 1971, Johns Hopkins University,
   Baltimore, Maryland

   PhD 1971, Johns Hopkins University

For schools with several campuses, indicate succinctly which one
you attended:

   BA 1969, University of California at Irvine

Additional Education

This is an optional section even early in your career, and later it will tend to disappear altogether. The object is to describe schooling that did not lead to a degree but that is relevant to the post you're seeking. A lesser goal, but one that crops up occasionally, is to explain what would otherwise appear as large gaps in your history. Probably the best way to discuss these possibilities is to invent several examples.

Case A, for instance, is a young historian of the Edwardian period in England who does a special program on methods for social history. She enters the information on her vita thus:

> The Family and Community History Summer
> Training Institute, Newberry Library,
> 1976

Both because the Institute is very prestigious and because it has a formative influence on her work, this same item will continue to appear on her vita till the day she dies.

Case B is a small-group sociologist who does an immersion course in German so as to be able to read the many important materials in that language. Early in his career he lists this training:

> Marquette University Summer Language
> Program (German), 1967

Later on, by the time that he's an associate professor, it no longer seems so significant to him that he's able to slog his way through a German text with the aid of a dictionary, and the item disappears from his vita.

Case C is a psychologist who has participated in countless numbers of training sessions and workshops. Rather than list them all, he weeds them out severely and mentions only five, the four best ones and the one most recent. Five is a large enough number to indicate that he has a lively interest in this kind of activity, but not so many as to give his vita a frantic, excessive appearance.

Case D is a botanist who planned originally to go into math. After two years of graduate school, she changed her mind and switched fields. Although the mathematics has no direct bearing on her present work, she feels that it gives her a greater sophistication than some of her colleagues have, and the change of fields explains why she didn't get her PhD until nine years after her BS. So she enters the information on her vita:

> `University of Indiana, graduate work in`
> `mathematics, 1961–63`

Once she's done some research that makes use of her mathematical background and published several articles that demonstrate it, she will no longer feel the need to mention the false start she made years ago.

Case E is a late bloomer. As an undergraduate, he did a major in English and a minor in chemistry. He started doing graduate work in American literature, changed schools, dropped out, started in again in political science, dropped out again, and took several years off, working as a carpenter and taking night courses in philosophy, anthropology, and linguistics. Eventually he decided that what he wanted to do was linguistics, entered graduate school once again, and settled down very nicely. Despite the extensive additional education Case E has, he lists none of it on his vita; it's too tangled a trail to ask anyone else to follow.

Taken together, these cases illustrate three important points about the vita: It's a summary, not a recapitulation; stick to the high points. It's a construction, not a cumulation; updating requires the elimination of old material as well as the addition of new. And it's a presentation, not a confession; don't burden your reader with confidences.

Experience

Every part of your vita requires steady reexamination and reevaluation as your career progresses, but none more than this section. In looking for your first post, you will list rafts of information that disappear as soon as you have been hired. From then on, no single transformation will be so great, but you should strive constantly to compress this information, to paint in bold strokes.

Experience for your first job: At this point you should drag out whatever relevant experience you can—any teaching you've done and any work that bears some relationship to your field. Some items that might typically appear are teaching assistantships (with topics, not titles, for courses):

▷ Carnegie–Mellon University.   Teaching
     assistant in Engineering 101, 1971–72;
     in Engineering 226, 1974.

  Carnegie–Mellon University.   Teaching
     assistant in introductory engineering,
     1971–72; in materials and stress
     analysis, 1974.

Research assistantships:

  Ohio Wesleyan University.   Research
     assistant in human physiology, 1971–74.

Teaching below the university level:

  Francis Scott Key Consolidated School,
     Amundsen, Minnesota.   High–school math
     and English, 1968–70.

Tutoring (notice that volunteer work appears here along with paid employment):

  The Strick Street Project, East Orange,
     New Jersey.   Tutoring in remedial reading
     and business English, summers 1972–75.

Relevant employment in business and industry, whether full-time or part-time—but be sure that it is relevant to the post you're seeking:

```
IBM Watson Research Center, Yorktown
     Heights, New York.  Systems programming,
     summer 1975.
```

Gather all the items you can think of, arrange them in chronological order (by opening date), and then check over the list to see whether it needs consolidation and trimming. The following list, for instance, is too long and spotty to let stand:

```
▷ Blackstone Public Library, Chicago,
     Illinois.  Part-time library aide,
     summers 1966–67.
  First Baptist Church of Hyde Park Book
     Fair, Chicago, Illinois.  Volunteer,
     1966–69; chairman, 1970.
  Stephen Slaman Publishers, Madison,
     Wisconsin.  Proofreader and copyholder,
     evenings 1967–70.
  The Beeman Press, Chicago, Illinois.
     Proofreader and copyholder, summers
     1968–70.
  University of Wisconsin.  Senior grader in
     English, 1969–70.
  United Methodist Bookmobile, Urbana,
     Illinois.  Volunteer, 1970.
  Henry Regnery Company, Chicago, Illinois.
     Proofreader, summers 1971–72; copy
     editor, summers 1972–76.
  University of Illinois.  Teaching assistant
     in freshman composition, fall 1971,
     spring 1973, spring 1974; in various
     English literature courses, 1973–76
     (four semesters).
```

Chalmers House Outreach, Urbana, Illinois.
Hospital reading program supervisor,
1972–74; youth group leader, 1975.

The point is not that any one of these items is bad. It's just that lumped together they're too difficult for the reader to sort out. The author's task is now to look over the whole list with a cold eye and produce a better version:

University of Wisconsin. Senior grader in
   English, 1969–70.
Henry Regnery Company, Chicago, Illinois.
   Proofreader and copy editor, summers
   1971–76.
University of Illinois. Teaching assistant
   in freshman composition, 1971–74; in
   Victorian literature, 1973–75; in the
   modern American novel, 1975; in the
   short story, 1976.

Notice the alterations in the University of Illinois item—specifics about the courses are significant; specifics about the semesters aren't.

You may be aware that on business vitas experience is listed in reverse chronological order; that's because you're expected to account for every waking moment, practically from birth onward. On an academic vita, where you give only the highlights of your experience, plain chronological order, unreversed, is better.

Don't expect to be able to put a good vita together in an afternoon. What you're doing is presenting yourself in a highly artificial capsule form, and you shouldn't be surprised that it takes a good deal of discipline and humility. It's hard to get help with a vita because you're the only person in possession of all the necessary information. But you might ask a teacher or an older colleague to look over your best effort and then tell you what it says. His unconscious omissions are likely to suggest items you can profitably cut. If he forgets an item you consider crucial, perhaps you've buried it among too many other things.

Remember that your reader is going to have to sort you out from many other applicants, perhaps hundreds. You want to be memorable as "Oh yes, the one from Illinois who's done so much TA-ing," not as "Oh yes, the one with all those thousands of little jobs."

Experience thereafter: You got the job. It probably won't be your first thought, but you may immediately revise your vita so that the "Experience" section begins with your first full-time faculty post and forget about everything that came before. There are some few exceptions to this amnesiac rule; if, for instance, your first appointment is solely in research, as a post-doc or a research associate, you might want to continue to list previous teaching experience.

Give the closing as well as the opening date for a term appointment:

```
MIT.   Assistant Professor of Comparative
       Linguistics, 1976–79.
```

Use the magic word "since" in dating a tenured or open-ended appointment that you hold currently:

```
▷ Kent State University.   Professor of
       Sinology, 1968–  .

▷ Kent State University.   Professor of
       Sinology, 1968–now.

  Kent State University.   Professor of
       Sinology, since 1968.
```

A tenured appointment that you've left obviously gets a closing date:

```
Harvard Divinity School.   Professor of
       Christian Ethics, 1961–68.
```

Cluster appointments at the same school:

> Duke University. Assistant Professor of
> Economics, 1959-61. Associate Professor
> of Economics, 1961-65. Professor of
> Economics, since 1965. Reginald Heald
> Professor of Economics, since 1971.

Don't break open an item with a sabbatical appointment; drop it below:

> ▷ Gonzaga University. Associate Professor of
>   History, 1971–72.
> Catholic University of America. Visiting
>   Associate Professor of History, 1972.
> Gonzaga University. Associate Professor of
>   History, 1973–75.
>
> Gonzaga University. Associate Professor of
>   History, 1971–75.
> Catholic University of America. Visiting
>   Associate Professor of History, 1972.

Unless you're applying for an administrative post, ignore all administrative and committee assignments below the level of department chairman:

> ▷ University of Arizona. Assistant Professor
>   of Romance Languages, 1972–75. Member,
>   Committee on Joint Degrees, 1974.

Departmental chairs, deanships, and such do get mentioned—as a rule of thumb, list any administrative appointment that carries with it a reduction in teaching load:

> Princeton University. Associate Professor
>   of Physics, 1951–55. Professor of
>   Physics, since 1955. Chairman of the

> Physics Department, 1958–61; 1967–68.
> Dean of the Faculty of Arts and
> Sciences, since 1971.

Moonlighting, even in the exalted form known as consultant-ship, gets listed on an academic vita only when it's very prestigious:

> W. H. Freeman Company.   Consulting editor,
> biology series, since 1971.

Being the editor of a journal or a member of the editorial board is always listed:

> <u>Bulletin of the American Anthropological
> Association</u>.   Member, review board,
> since 1969; editor, 1974–76.

It's possible to have so many editorships and reviewerships that you will want to set aside another section of your vita, headed "Journals," and group this information there.

Applications from outside: Not everyone is transformed imme-diately from a graduate student to a faculty member, and not everyone goes directly from one faculty to another. There are some special problems about applying for an academic job from outside. For instance, there's no uniform system of nomenclature in the business world. An assistant professor is an assistant pro-fessor—your reader knows what that means. But what's an assis-tant line supervisor? Try to describe what you've done rather than give a vacuous formal title:

> ▷ Encyclopaedia Britannica, Inc.   Section
> manager, since 1971.

> Encyclopaedia Britannica, Inc.   Supervised
> six social-science editors, since 1971.

Don't, on the other hand, go into the sort of long description typical of business vitas; you'd better face the fact that no one in academy is going to take your outside experience very seriously unless it's both highly prestigious and highly relevant to your academic field.

If you've been doing a completely unserious job, driving a taxi or cooking in a hash house or panning for gold, forget about it on your vita. You might want to mention it in your cover letter if you can find a way to seem colorful but not flippant.

Honors

This section is likely to appear on your first vita, disappear for a long time, and return only toward the end of your career.

When you're just getting out of graduate school, you should list all your scholarships and fellowships from college on:

```
University of Rhode Island.   College
    scholarship, 1969—72.   Laura May
    Fellowes Memorial Scholarship, 1972—73.
University of Connecticut.   University
    fellowship, 1973—76.
```

Many schools blur the distinctions among fellowships, teaching assistantships, and research assistantships. If you must choose one or the other, it's better to list an appointment under "Experience"; but often you can justify a listing both here and there without the appearance of padding. Mention all your prizes, awards, and distinctions here as long as they're both academic and reasonably relevant. Undergraduate essay awards for applicants in English or history, yes; for applicants in biology or physics, maybe; Scout badges and ROTC awards, no. Honors societies get listed here, with explanations for all but the most famous of them:

```
Phi Beta Kappa, 1971.
Alpha Beta Tau (history honors society),
    1971.
```

Some groups straddle the line between honors societies and professional societies; give a listing here or under "Memberships," but not both. There's no reason to prefer one place or the other. Flip a coin.

Just as with your work experience, once you've gotten your first full-time faculty position you can drink the water of forgetfulness and stop listing all but the highest honors of your former life. There may be a long period when this section disappears from your vita altogether. Late in life, you can use it for honorary doctorates and National Book Awards and such.

Grants

Under this heading you should list all your grants, contracts, faculty fellowships, and similar awards with opening and closing dates:

> Office of Naval Research grant
>   GJ—331479—0—96 for the investigation
>   of numerical methods, 1964—66.

If a grant that you now hold is renewable, mention it:

> National Institutes of Mental Health grant
>   39956—V—CDOC—1228 for investigating
>   speech acquisition patterns in the
>   children of the deaf, 1977—79
>   (renewable).

If you held a renewable grant that wasn't renewed, mention only the grant.

If it's the custom in your field, list the amount—but be sure that it is the custom, since it will look tasteless otherwise. In general, people who work in areas that require heavy laboratory and equipment expenses disclose the amounts of their grants freely. Any technicalities about transfer from one school to another can be worked out when you're a serious candidate for a job; don't jump the gun by mentioning the matter on your vita or in your covering letter.

Memberships

This section is optional, and you should check to see whether it's customary in your field. If so, list only professional memberships relevant to the post you're seeking, not the Kiwanis or the Knights of Columbus. Give no dates except for offices. List only current memberships.

```
National Association of Art Historians.
The Ford Madox Brown Society; chairman,
     1971-73.
```

Personal Information

Under this heading tell when and where you were born. Give your visa status if you're not a citizen. Give your Social Security number.

```
Born 26 April 1938, Fargo, North Dakota
Social Security #458-40-9888
```

You may if you like add an item about your family, but you don't have to:

```
Married Sailor Tynes 1968, two children
```

It is not the custom on academic vitas to list your height and weight and condition of your health. If you're blind or in a wheelchair, you might want to mention it in your covering letter, but you needn't. The people who write your letters of recommendation are likely to discuss your impairment in the context of its effect on your work, and it's much less awkward for them than for you to be reassuring. There's nothing about being a faculty member that will require any more physical effort from you than graduate school did, so you can let your record speak for itself.

References

Never give anyone's name as a reference without asking his permission first. Your dissertation director has already agreed by implication to write letters of recommendation for you, but that's not true of anyone else. Two or three references are usual, certainly no more than four. Give the names and addresses just as they would appear on envelopes:

```
Professor Andrea J. Popoff
Department of Sociology
University of Montreal
Montreal, Quebec
```

Don't be afraid to repeat; it looks tacky to say something like "Same address for all." Don't explain your relationships with these people—it's up to them to do so in their letters.

If your school has a placement office that will hold blanket letters of recommendation on file and send copies out to prospective employers, by all means make use of the service in looking for your first job. (Recommendations for later jobs should be individually written.) Give the address of the office and, just for safety's sake, mention what letters should be there:

```
Letters of recommendation from A. E. Keyman,
Raymond S. van Dyne, and Harriet Bowman are
available from:
    Office of Student Placement
    Stanford University
    Drawer D, University Station
    Stanford, California 98834
```

A placement service may offer you the opportunity to look at your letters of recommendation. Don't do it. The service will then have to annotate them with the fact that you've seen them, no employer will take them seriously, and the whole exercise will be a waste of everyone's time.

This is not to say that you won't know what's in your letters. You wouldn't ask for a recommendation that you knew was going to be rotten. And one of your reference writers might himself offer to show you his letter; whether you should then look or not depends entirely on your relationship with him. You just want to avoid getting yourself down on public record as someone who's so insecure that he had to peek.

Publications

Everywhere else on your vita you may, within the limits of honesty, expand or contract information, trim it down or plump it up, but your publications list must be complete and uncensored. Not one publication from your professional career may be omitted—not even if you've changed your interpretation of the material, not even if your exposition now seems juvenile and vacant, not even if your results have been proved false. (Think about that before you rush into print with an ill-considered piece.)

Only what you've written outside your academic field should be ignored. If you write mysteries or cookbooks in the evening, leave them off your list and use the heading "Professional Publications" to account for the omission. An academic vita is no place to reveal your secret life as Agatha Christie or Julia Child.

The format for listing a publication on your vita is a little different from the one used on reference lists and bibliographies. If you wrote an item by yourself, there's no need to mention authorship:

The guru and enlightenment in the novels of Ruth Prawer Jhabvala. Carolina Quarterly LVI(2):37–91, 1975.

If you have co-authors, their names go after the title:

L-differentiates of the "coagulating"
sets, with H. N. Avrakian and D.
Monsart. American Association of
Applied Mathematicians Newsletter
VII(5):64–65, 1971.

People who work in fields where first authorship is a big deal will notice that this format knocks precedence into a cocked hat—no one can tell whether you were first author or last. If you insist, use "by" instead of "with" and insert your name in its proper order:

L-differentiates of the "coagulating"
sets, by H. N. Avrakian, C. L. Thomas,
and D. Monsart. American Association of
Applied Mathematicians Newsletter VII
(5):64–65, 1971.

I think of my Aunt Mary's three children, who always used to shove and push each other and pull each other's hair in order to be first. Finally one day Aunt Mary said, "You know, children, being last is not only last, it's also *third*." I would like to report that the children profited from this insight, but of course they only began to shove and push each other for the privilege of being third.

For works you've edited, the format is:

Pattern Recognition (editor). Oxford
University Press, 1965.

It's assumed that editing will include writing some front matter, which merits no special mention. If you edit a compilation that includes one of your own articles, use the format:

Pattern Recognition (editor). Heuristic
search techniques that learn, pages
69–74. Oxford University Press, 1965.

Co-editorship follows the same pattern as co-authorship:

> **Wilson Follett: The Correspondence** (editor,
> with Simon Teale). Crowell, 1968.

Never list the same item more than once:

- **Nesting and territory among the warblers.**
  Scientific American CXIV(9):71–93,1959.
  Nesting and territory among the warblers.
  In G. V. Simms and A. Trachtenberg,
  editors, **Notes Toward a North American**
  Ornithology, pages 240–259. Seamans
  Press, 1960.

  Nesting and territory among the warblers.
  Scientific American CXIV(9):71–93, 1959.
  Reprinted in G. V. Simms and A.
  Trachtenberg, editors, **Notes Toward a**
  North American Ornithology, pages
  240–259. Seamans Press, 1960.

The rule against double-listing carries through a change of title if
the work is essentially the same:

> **An Analysis of Masculine Stereotypes in**
> **American Detective Fiction 1920–1950.**
> PhD thesis, University of New Hampshire,
> 1972. Published as **Tough Guys.** Harvard
> University Press, 1973.

But if you carve your thesis up into several chops and joints and
publish them separately or publish a series of articles and essays
later collected as a book, each gets a separate listing.

Notice that items on your publications list are always in the
compressed format, not in the open format:

- **Distribution and frequency of the double**
  genitive in American speech.
  Lingua 8(1):37–64, 1968.

> Distribution and frequency of the double
> genitive in American speech. Lingua
> 8(1):37–64, 1968.

Do not number the items on your publications list.

Otherwise, these items are pretty much like references, and the chapters on references can help you if you're in difficulty.

The list is arranged in chronological order by year of first publication, and then alphabetically by title within each year. It is a good idea to close the list by indicating what you're working on now:

> The idea of the natural knowledge of good
> in the Lutheran Symbolical Books.   In
> preparation.

If you don't yet have a title, choose something sensible and descriptive; you're not under oath to stick by it. You may list two or three works in preparation, but never more than that, lest you look like a great dreamer. If you're really working on eight things at once, choose the three best.

Mechanics

If possible, your vita should be typed on an elite machine—the little type, twelve characters to the inch. But for almost every other purpose in the world, pica is better—the big type, ten characters to the inch—and you're under no obligation to buy a new typewriter just for doing vitas.

A plain, clean photocopy of plain, ordinary typing is the only acceptable medium for a vita. No composing and typesetting machines, no computer output, no hand lettering, no illuminated capitals, please. The effect to aim for is sobriety, even severity; you're supposed to be a scholar, not a set designer.

If at some point you're using the shotgun technique to search for a job, get a large batch of vitas photo-offset all at once. Otherwise, photocopy no more than ten or twelve at a time and wait till you're mailing one out to staple the pages together, so that you needn't have any qualms about discarding outdated pages.

Do not update simply by adding on; rethink and revise the material each time you have an addition to make.

If your vita is more than one page long, put your staple diagonally through the upper left corner; do not staple the cover letter to the vita.

The sample vitas that follow are to give you a reasonable pattern for the layout, not a rigid formula. What you're after is the maximum compression compatible with clarity. Again, don't expect to be able to type your vita in one pass. Play around with different arrangements and different layouts till you get one that pleases your eye. Don't feel that you have to stick to that format next time around; as the information changes, the way you choose to present it may also change.

Arthur Siddons
Department of Engineering and
   Applied Science
University of Arizona
Tucson, Arizona 76045
690-594-7785

home:
7236 Rowley Boulevard
Tucson, Arizona 76001
690-459-8667

Degrees: BS 1971, Illinois Institute of Technology
          PhD 1976 (expected), University of Arizona

Experience: University of Arizona. Teaching assistant in
            introductory calculus, 1972; in engineering
            for humanities majors, 1973; in physical
            oceanography, 1974-76.
          Stratton Brothers, Inc., Tampa, Florida. Diver
            and mechanic, summer 1969; assistant engineer,
            summers 1970-75.

Honors: National Merit Scholarship, 1967-71.
       University of Arizona, departmental fellowship,
         1971-76.
       Sigma Xi (national science honors society), 1972.

Personal
information: Born 15 March 1941, Athens, Greece (US citizen)
          Social Security #557-40-7896
          Married Helen D'Amato 26 April 1975

References:
Professor Simone Lashky
Department of Engineering
   and Applied Science
University of Arizona
Tucson, Arizona 76045

Assistant Professor Charles
   Welch
Department of Engineering
   and Applied Science
University of Arizona
Tucson, Arizona 76045

Publications
<u>Lesser Saline Distributions in the Florida Keys</u>. PhD thesis,
   University of Arizona. In preparation.

Lynn Marcus
Assistant Professor of
    Modern European History
Rutgers University
New Brunswick, New Jersey
    06620
413-976-4459

home:
8862 Oak Ridge Terrace
New Brunswick, New Jersey
    06615
413-388-1293

Degrees: BA (economics) 1966, Radcliffe College
          MA 1970, PhD 1974, Brown University
Additional education: London School of Economics summer
                       course in quantitative history, 1969.
Experience: Rutgers University. Assistant Professor of
             Modern European History, 1974-78.
Personal information: Born 5 July 1945, Boulder, Colorado
                       Social Security #299-30-7368

References:
Professor Townsend J. Warner
History Department
Rutgers University
New Brunswick, New Jersey
    06620

Professor A. N. McGillis
Department of History
Brown University
Providence, Rhode Island
    14459

Publications:
The cotton manufacturers of the Ruhr Valley, 1848-1860.
    Bulletin of the Economic History Association XII(4):
    311-369, 1972.
Hendke's pamphlets and the labor theory of value. Minutes of
    the Third Annual Meeting of the Caucus for Modern Economic
    History, pages 141-167. Association of American Historians,
    1973.
The Effects of Wage and Price Controls on German Manufacture,
    1848-1860. PhD thesis, Brown University, 1974.
Bismarck's economic advisors. Modern European Notes VIII(2):
    31-56, 1975.
The Koesterwerke: A case study in wage and price controls.
    Modern European Notes VIII(1):122-146, 1975.
The Iron Chancellor and the thirst for steel. Bulletin of the
    Association of American Historians 41(3):48-81, 1976.
An inquiry into the use of child labor in German cotton
    manufacture. In preparation.
The impact of technological innocation on labor practices in
    German cotton manufacture. In preparation.

The Cover Letter

For all the good your cover letter will do you, you might as well not write one. It would in fact be more rational just to mail your vita off by itself, but for some reason that's not done. There's no such thing as a good cover letter, only one that avoids being bad. Here are a few things to avoid:

Don't be too long about it. Take a hundred words as your outside limit and try to stay well within it. Nothing you can say will balance off your reader's irritation at your saying too much.

Don't apologize. "Although my background appears not to suit me for this position . . ." "I realize that I may not seem . . ." "While my formal course work does not . . ." "I wish that it were possible for me to say . . ." Your reader will have no trouble noting your defects without any assistance from you.

Don't be cute. "If there's anything a weary chairman needs less than another applicant, it's one who . . ." "Rising from my bed this morning, I was struck by the thought . . ." Don't be breezy, don't be slick, don't try to sound like an advertising brochure.

Don't be hyperspecific. "I could teach an advanced seminar on recent findings in the treatment of postnatal depression . . ." Wait to dicker about your assignment till someone's offered to hire you.

Don't be emotional. That includes the phrase "I would be interested . . ." Your reader has at this point no reason to care what interests you; the only issue is what interests him.

Don't grovel. "Almost any sort of opening . . ." "I realize that you may be in no position . . ." "I would be willing . . " Don't invite your reader to sell you short.

Don't mention money.

What's left? Very little. Tell what position you're applying for; if no post has been advertised, tell what you're looking for. Say when you'll be available. If you have outstanding qualifications to bring to the job, mention them briefly, but remember that you needn't repeat anything covered in your vita. Sincerely yours, the end. Save your warm, expansive nature, your wit and whimsy, for somewhere else; in this context they would be as out of place as ruby-heeled tap shoes on a funeral director. Let your vita, over which you've labored long and hard, speak for itself.

Appendix 2
Federal Documents
of the United States

A glance at the organization of our government documents may
suggest that the United States is neither a democracy nor a republic, but an anarchy. Writing a good reference to a federal document would be simple if only one of those brainy forefathers of
ours had thought to write at the bottom of the Declaration of
Independence, "Serial #1," but it's too late now.

Congressional Documents

This book is about how to write references to sources, not about
the sources, but you need a little background information on Congressional publication in order to write a good reference to a
Congressional document. Congress publishes four major series:

(a) The *Congressional Record*.
(b) House and Senate Reports and Documents.
(c) Bills, resolutions, acts, statutes, laws.
(d) Hearings and Committee Prints.

Here is how these series reflect Congressional activity:
(a) The proceedings of the two houses in plenary session appear
in the *Congressional Record*. That is to say, the House in plenary

session and the Senate in plenary session—they don't meet together. The *Record* is like the minutes of the houses. A member of Congress may read into the *Record* almost anything he likes, including prayers, poems, newspaper articles, letters from his constituents, what have you. Bills are introduced, labeled, numbered, named, and debated in plenary session, and all this is recorded in the *Record*; but the full texts of bills appear elsewhere (c). The *Record* appears in a daily version and then, eventually, in a bound version.

(b) Each house publishes a Reports and Documents series. Again, almost anything can appear in these series; for instance, Congress usually publishes the annual reports of the Boy Scouts and the Girl Scouts and the Daughters of the American Revolution in the Reports and Documents series. The various commissions such as Securities and Exchange and the Federal Communications Commission provide Congress with reports that appear in the Reports and Documents series. The houses may commission or adopt treatises, articles, studies, and disquisitions of all kinds and publish them as Reports and Documents. Items in these series appear first in slip form (that means as pamphlets) and then bound together.

(c) The complete text of every draft of every bill and resolution appears in slip form. Even depository libraries receive only the first draft, and intermediate drafts are printed in so few copies that they are quite rare—not rare and valuable, just hard to come by. At enactment, a law appears first in slip form, and then later it's bound into *U.S. Statutes at Large*.

(d) The Congressional committees have their own series of publications, the Hearings and Committee Prints series. Hearings —that's what they're called, not "Recorded Hearings" or "Minutes of Hearings"—are just what you would expect, the recorded testimony of witnesses called before the committees; a committee may hold a hearing on a specific bill or a group of bills or on any topic that might lead to legislation. Every hearing results in a Hearing, the publication of its minutes. Committee Prints are anything else the committees want to publish—monographs, canvasses, reports, or chronicles, their own or others'.

Now we can go through each of these series.

(a) **The Congressional Record:** Most references will be to the bound version of the *Record;* if you have a choice, that should be your preference. Begin by specifying the Congress, the session, and the date:

United States, 94th Congress, second session, 2 June 1976.

Then give the reference to the *Record:*

volume   page

↓   ↓

Congressional Record 114(17):22455.

↑

part

If you must refer to the daily version, be aware that your reader is more likely by far to be using the bound version; most libraries throw out the daily when the bound arrives. The date of the material you're referring to will be the same, but a great deal happens in Congress on any one day, so the page reference is crucial. And—wouldn't you know it?—the two versions are paged differently, with no automatic correspondence between them and no index from one version to the other. Pages in the daily have letter prefixes, while pages in the bound do not, but it's a little stiff to expect your reader to notice such a fine distinction. Spell it out for him:

▷ *Congressional Record* 122(83): H 5193.

Congressional Record (daily) 122(83): H 5193.

Finding the page in the bound copy that corresponds to H 5193 is no easy task, but at least you've warned your reader what lies before him.

Fine points: The number within the parentheses refers to the part in the bound version, to the issue in the daily; once your reader has the materials before him, he should have no trouble

---

Bad examples are marked with an arrowhead (▷).

making this out. Sometimes beneath the date of an issue of the *Record* there appears the legend "Legislative day of . . ." with a different date; ignore this legend and give only the large date in your reference.

Now give a brief description of what it is that you're referring to. Sometimes there will be a handy subhead you can copy:

> 97] United States, 94th Congress, second session, 2 June 1976.
> *Congressional Record* (daily) 122(83): H 5193.
> Laws applicable to the outer continental shelf.

Sometimes you will want to quote the first few words of a speech:

> 76] United States, 90th Congress, second session, 20 July 1968.
> *Congressional Record* 114(7):22455.
> Mr. Holland of Florida: "We have felt, since hearings . . ."

(As you can see, a disadvantage to this method is that the first few words of a speech often make no particular sense.) Usually you will want to describe the speaker and the topic:

> 29] United States, 91st Congress, first session, 22 May 1969.
> *Congressional Record* 115(10):13528–13529.
> Mr. Rooney of Pennsylvania on the Boys' Club of America.

> 58] United States, 89th Congress, second session, 27 May 1966.
> *Congressional Record* 112(9):11710.
> Mr. Reuss of Wisconsin on the Selective Service System.

(b) **Reports and Documents:** Most references will be to the bound versions. Start by specifying the Congress, the session, and the date; the year is usually sufficient.

United States, 85th Congress, second session, 1957.

Then give the name of the house (call the House of Representatives "House"), the name of the item (Report or Document), the number, the serial set number, and the title:

house   item   number   serial set   title
   ↓   ↓   ↓   ↓   ↓
House Document 85-384 (serial 12106): 2nd annual report
on trade agreements program.

Notice that the item number repeats the number of the Congress —85-384 was published by the 85th Congress. The serial set is sometimes called the Congressional set or the sheep set, for its once splendid binding; it is tempting to think of writing the reference to "(sheep 12106)." Notice that a report, the 2nd annual report, can be a Document, House Document 85-384. It's also possible for a document to be a Report.

Now here is a very nice point: If the version you're working with is in slip form, it won't have a serial set number. In the past, for reasons that no one can comprehend, some guides on government documents recommended against giving the serial set number in a reference to a bound Document or Report. Bound and slip forms looked just alike:

▷ House Document 85-384: 2nd annual report on trade agreements program.

▷ Senate Report 94-803: The Antitrust Improvements Act of 1976.

Since most libraries throw out the slip forms when the bound copies arrive and then catalog and shelve the bound copies by serial set number, documents librarians were puzzled and infuriated by the recommendation. So if the version that you're working with has not yet been bound, use the word "slip" in parentheses in place of the serial set number:

Senate Report 94-803 (slip): The Antitrust Improvements Act of 1976.

There is an index that links Reports and Documents numbers to serial set numbers, and the librarian will have to look it up. But your saying "slip" will let him know that you did not suppress the information, and he will feel cheered up.

Many publications in the Reports and Documents series have acknowledged authors, but they're almost never cataloged by author, so there's no point in leading your reader astray:

▷ Allen J. Ellender.
Senate Document 85-78 (serial 12088): A review of United States foreign policy and operations.
United States, 85th Congress, second session, 1957.

United States, 85th Congress, second session, 1957.
Senate Document 85-78 (serial 12088): A review of United States foreign policy and operations, by Allen J. Ellender.

Many items in the Reports and Documents series mention the Congressional committees in their titles. Again, most libraries catalog and keep this material by Congress, not by committee; putting your reader on the right track here is especially important because of the possibility of confusion with Committee Prints:

▷ United States, House Special Committee to Investigate Campaign Expenditures.
House Report 83-2685 (serial 11750): Report of the Committee.
United States, 83rd Congress, second session, 1955.

United States, 83rd Congress, second session, 1955.
House Report 83-2685 (serial 11750): Report of the Special Committee to Investigate Campaign Expenditures.

Usually an item in the Reports and Documents series has a handy slip title at the top of its title page, above the formal title; if you have a choice, the slip title is always the one to use. If you're dealing with an item that has only a formal title, you may want to invent an informal title:

House Report 81-2263 (serial 11381): Report of the Committee on the Judiciary on HR-6709, for the relief of Ed Howard Russell.

or   House Report 81-2263 (serial 11381): On the relief of Ed
      Howard Russell.

(c) **Bills and statutes:** For a bill, start by specifying the Congress,
the session, and the extended date (day-month-year).

United States, 89th Congress, second session, 27 May 1966.

Then give the bill's label, its number, and its name. Bills are
labeled S or HR, not plain H as the pages of the daily *Record* are.

S-644: Consumer Product Safety Commission Improvements Act of 1976.

Most bills specify their own short names. Use the short name, not
the formal one:

▷ An Act To Amend the Consumer Product Safety Act, To
  Improve the Consumer Product Safety Commission, To
  Authorize New Appropriations, and for Other Purposes.

  Consumer Product Safety Commission Improvements Act
  of 1976.

If necessary, invent a short name:

▷ An Act To Clarify the Application of Section 507 of the
  Classification Act of 1949 with respect to the Preserva-
  tion of the Rates of Basic Compensation of Certain Offi-
  cers or Employees in Cases Involving Downgrading
  Actions.

  Amendment to the Classification Act of 1949.

Notice that bills and statutes have proper names but not titles;
in other words, they're capitalized but not underlined.

    If your research requires working with bills, you already know
how elusive and ephemeral they are. Don't suddenly forget about

that when you start to write a reference. Whenever you can, provide documentation from the more readily available sources like the *Congressional Record*, where the interesting points in a bill may be subjected to debate.

Few bills are ever enacted into law. In the 93rd Congress, for example, 17,688 bills were introduced in the House, 4,260 in the Senate. Only 649 became laws. But once a bill becomes a law, you can refer to it with confidence. If you come across it in slip form, your reference will look like this:

> 87] United States, 94th Congress, second session, 11 May 1976.
> Public Law 94-284: Consumer Product Safety Commission Improvements Act of 1976.

The public law number incorporates the number of the Congress —94-284 was enacted by the 94th Congress. Your reader will have no trouble finding this law when it's bound into *Statutes at Large*. If you're using the bound version yourself, you should of course give your reader all the information you have, even though he can easily find it elsewhere:

> 51] United States, 85th Congress, second session, 23 August 1958.
> U.S. *Statutes at Large* 72(1):767.
> Public Law 85-726: Federal Aviation Act of 1958.

The reference to the *Statutes* means:

$$\text{volume} \quad \text{page}$$
$$\downarrow \qquad \downarrow$$
$$U.S. \textit{ Statutes at Large } 72(1):767.$$
$$\uparrow$$
$$\text{part}$$

If a bill or a law has a nickname, be sure to give it:

121] United States, 76th Congress, first session, 15 April
1947.
U.S. Statutes at Large 61(1):156.
Public Law 76-43: Labor Management Relations Act.
(The Taft-Hartley Act.)

References to private acts and resolutions look just like references to public laws:

47] United States, 57th Congress, first session, 27 June 1902.
U.S. Statutes at Large 32(2): 1487.
Private Act 57-1113: An Act Granting a Pension to
Fannie Reardon.

Another source of information about legislation is the *United States Code*, which organizes the laws in force by subject. A reference to the *Code* looks like this:

36] *United States Code*, 1970 edition.
Title 16: Conservation. Section 512: Segregation of
land for homestead entry.

125] *United States Code*, 1970 edition, supplement IV.
Title 42: The public health and welfare. Section 4913:
Research, technical assistance, and public informa-
tion.

(d) **Hearings and Committee Prints:** A reference to an item in this series, unlike all other references to Congressional publications, starts with the name of the committee:

United States, House Committee on Interstate and Foreign
Commerce.

United States, Senate Committee on the Judiciary.

The name of the subcommittee is irrelevant to finding the source; include it only if it has some bearing on your work:

United States, House Committee on Appropriations, Subcommittee on the Departments of Labor and Health,
Education, and Welfare.

or   United States, House Committee on Appropriations.

It's all too easy to confuse this series with the Reports and Documents series, especially because the titles of many Committee
Prints include the word "report." Therefore start the second line
of your reference with "Hearing" or "Hearings" or "Committee
Print":

Hearings on Department of Labor and HEW appropriations for 1977.

Committee Print: Cumulative bibliography on water pol-
lution.

If a Committee Print or a Hearing has a slip title at the top of
its title page as well as a formal title in the center, the slip title
is always the one to use:

▷ Committee Print: A compilation of information relating to
agriculture made by direction of the Committee on Agriculture of the House of Representatives.

Committee Print: Food costs—farm prices.

Do not let yourself be lured into using the formal title because it
looks, superficially, more informative. It's not. Items in this series
are cataloged by slip title, not by formal title. If you like, you may
use a combination of the two, but the slip title is the essential piece
of information:

▷ Hearings on matters pursuant to H-155 and H-156.

Hearings on milk labeling.

or   Hearings on H-155 and H-156: Milk labeling.

Some Committee Prints have acknowledged authors, who get
their credits buried in the references, not displayed at the top:

▷ Elwin Hill.
 Committee Print: Projected effects of damming the upper
  Snake.

United States, Senate Committee on Public Works.
Committee Print: Projected effects of damming the upper
  Snake, by Elwin Hill.

Close the reference by specifying the Congress, the session, and
the year:

88] United States, House Committee on Interstate and
  Foreign Commerce.
  Hearings on cigarette labeling and advertising.
  89th Congress, first session, 1965.

39] United States, Senate Committee on the Judiciary.
  Hearings on psychological tests and constitutional
  rights.
  89th Congress, first session, 1965.

113] United States, House Committee on Interior and
  Insular Affairs.
  Committee Print: Accomplishments of the Committee during the 89th Congress.
  89th Congress, second session, 1966.

Judicial Documents

Federal court reports are exactly like regional and state reports, and
references to federal cases are covered in the section on court
cases. You will be delighted to hear that, other than cases, the
judiciary publishes nothing.

Executive Documents

Federal regulations: The sole glimmer of organization among the
executive documents comes from the federal regulations, which

are set out by subject from their first appearance in the *Federal Register*:

67] *Federal Register* 41(114):23685, 11 June 1976.
  Title 7: Agriculture. Part 70: Grading and inspection of poultry and edible products. Section 36: Withdrawal of application.

They are then bound together, still by subject, in the *Code of Federal Regulations*:

77] *Code of Federal Regulations*, 1 October 1975.
  Title 47: Telecommunications. Part 18: Industrial, scientific, and medical equipment. Section 21: When license is required.

81] *Code of Federal Regulations*, 1 January 1976.
  Title 7: Agriculture. Part 48: Regulations of the Secretary of Agriculture for the enforcement of the Produce Agency Act. Section 4: Destroying or dumping.

49] *Code of Federal Regulations*, 1 April 1975.
  Title 25: Indians. Part 42: Enrollment appeals. Section 5: Supporting evidence.

It's a simple, attractive system, with only one minor point to notice: Many of the titles are divided into chapters as well as parts; ignore the chapter divisions in writing references.

Departmental documents: Now the fog begins. There is no uniformity among the documents that the executive departments put out. Many of them don't even have decent title pages, and you must search the front cover, the back cover, the spine, the introduction, the text, and the last page to come up with a reference. There seems always to be too little information or too much. Series abound, with no pattern from one to the next. The documents arrive already cataloged at depository libraries, and even trained specialists in government documents sometimes have trouble figuring out whether a peculiar catalog number is an insight or an error. Size and shape vary wildly, to encourage shelving mistakes. So what's a poor scholar to do? Hold on to his sense of humor, and proceed as best he can.

Try to start every reference to a document of the executive by telling what body it comes from. The major agencies are much too large to suffice for identification; the lowest subdivisions are much too small. When in doubt, give all the information you have, listing the units from the largest to the smallest:

▷ United States Department of Health, Education and Welfare.

▷ United States Division of Local Statistics.

United States Department of Health, Education, and Welfare; Office of Education; Division of Local Statistics.

▷ United States Department of Agriculture.

▷ United States Plains States Section.

United States Department of Agriculture; Farm Security Administration; Plains States Section.

Next give the title. Give the author's name if there seems to be a genuine author acknowledged, but don't mention the secretaries and bureaucrats who strew their names and messages through the first few pages of so many of these documents.

▷ Triticale yields in six sites.

Triticale yields in six sites, by D. Unger.

▷ Technical assistance and related programs, prepared under the direction of Undersecretary Boynton M. Boynton, Jr.

Technical assistance and related programs.

Begin the next line of your reference by giving whatever identification numbers your source bears. Don't be embarrassed by oddities; remember that your reader's interests are better served by scraggly completeness than by orderly sterility. Close with the printer and the date. Most but not all of these documents are printed by the Government Printing Office.

The following examples hint at the range of possibilities:

54] United States Department of Health, Education, and Welfare; Office of Education.
Psychology and the handicapped child.
DHEW publication number (OE) 73-05000. Government Printing Office, 1974.

83] United States, National Science Foundation.
Grants and awards for fiscal year 1968.
NSF 69-2. Government Printing Office, 1968.

32] United States Department of Housing and Urban Development; Office of the Assistant Secretary for Policy Development and Research.
Residential energy consumption: Multifamily housing. Final report.
Stock number 2300-00282. Government Printing Office, 1974.

131] United States National Aeronautics and Space Administration; Lyndon B. Johnson Space Center.
Skylab earth resources data catalog.
JSC 09016. Stock number 3300-00586. Government Printing Office, 1974.

75] United States Department of the Interior; National Park Service.
The giant sequoia of the Sierra Nevada.
0-596-106. Government Printing Office, 1976.

44] United States Watergate Special Prosecution Force.
Report.
Serial number 027-000-00335-4. Government Printing Office, October 1975.

143] United States Department of the Interior; Census Office.
10th Census of the United States (1880). *The U.S. Mining Laws and Regulations Thereunder.*
Government Printing Office, 1885.

82] United States Department of Labor; Bureau of Labor
     Statistics.
     Industry wage survey: Men's and boys' shirts (except
     work shirts) and nightwear, October 1968.
     Bulletin 1659. Government Printing Office, 1970.

Presidential documents: Presidential documents are published in
a weekly compilation and then bound together, a year at a time.
A reference to the bound version looks like this:

95] United States President: Richard M. Nixon, 1 July
     1973.
     195. Statement on signing the Second Supplemental
     and Continuing Appropriations bills.
56] United States President: Harry S. Truman, 2 May 1950.
     99. Special message to the Senate transmitting treaty
     with Canada concerning uses of the water of the
     Niagara River.

All the documents in the bound version are numbered and titled.
    If you have occasion to refer to the weekly compilation, your
reference should look like this:

133] United States President: Gerald R. Ford, 4 June 1976
      (week ending 5 June 1976).
      Meeting with delegation of British parliamentarians.

Documents in the weekly version are titled but not numbered.
    References to presidential documents that appear in the *Con-
gressional Record* look like all other references to the *Record*:

87] United States, 89th Congress, second session, 28 May
     1966.
     Congressional Record 112(9):11798.
     Special message from the President.

References to publications of presidential commissions and such look like all other references to documents of the executive departments:

71] United States Executive Office of the President; Special Commission on Immigration.
The role of immigration in meeting skilled-labor needs, by F. M. Wassily.
Stock number 1993-00381. Government Printing Office, 1958.

You may by now have the feeling that presidential documents are not so hard as you expected. But most presidential papers (to say nothing of tapes) are not official government publications; official documents make up perhaps only 1 percent of the total. A few are available in other published sources and treated like ordinary publications. Most are archival.

The Constitution

While nothing could be harder than most references to government documents, nothing could be easier than references to the Constitution:

87] United States Constitution, Article I, section 4.

23] United States Constitution, 16th Amendment, section 2.

I can't help feeling that there's something significant about the contrast.

Where to Go for Help

Only the major kinds of current government publications have been touched on here. If you are going to work extensively with government documents, it would be a good idea to read:

Laurence F. Schmeckebier and Roy B. Eastin.
Government Publications and Their Use.
The Brookings Institution, Washington DC, second edition
1969.

Any librarian who specializes in government documents can
help you write a good reference to an obscure document you've
come across. Most librarians are delighted to give this kind of
help. They're the ones who have to cope with bad references; a
bad reference can cost a librarian hours and days of dreary, thank-
less work. Too many people think of going to a librarian for help
only in reading a bad reference, not in writing a good one.

Acknowledgments

My thanks to Murdo Dowds, who first said, "But what sort of horrible crank would write a style book on documentation, anyway?" To the faculties of the Harvard Divinity School and the Department of Computer Science at Yale, who let me use their manuscripts as testing grounds for my experiments. To Larry Snyder, who badgered me into writing the original four-page draft of this book, which has grown, alas, a little longer. To Dick Curtis, who pointed out that funny names are funny for four pages but not much longer than that. To Martin Schultz, who helped me distribute copies of the next draft and who also, years ago, was the first person to tell me about cut-and-tape corrections. To Polly Bobroff and Rosemary Browne, who are so good at their jobs that I was able to turn to mine with a clear conscience. To Peter Allison, who introduced me to Carol Parke, and to Carol, who spent hours explaining the mysteries of government documents to me. To Bob Handschumacher, who pointed out the usefulness of arranging a reference list by order of mention. To Richard Lipton, who suggested many fine points I hadn't thought of and who will undoubtedly take my gratitude as sarcasm.

I was blessed with a large and generous group of people who were willing to use the manuscript in draft, testing its suggestions and revealing its inadequacies as no other method could. My warm thanks to all of you, especially to my two indefatigable nit-pickers, Jim Meehan and Michael Gursky.

Having so often been unkind and irritable in editing, I richly deserved a nasty, vile-tempered editor when the roles reversed.

Instead, Chuck Elliott turned out to be a model of gentleness and good cheer—a model that I'll try to imitate from now on. Barbara Grossman, who suggested both the panorama and the chapter on manuscript preparation, is equally reassuring and helpful. Virginia Tan must have inside information on my fantasies, because she designed exactly the roly-poly book I dreamed of. And as for Jack Lynch and Sally Rogers—they hunted out information in every field of human knowledge, suggested excellent additions to the manuscript, and saved me from a thousand embarrassments, large and small. There is such a thing as brilliance in copy editing, believe me; theirs was brilliant. Many thanks.

Many thanks to Will White, Joan Hargrave, and Steven Hargrave, who read the galleys and page proofs and missed all the errors irate readers have since discovered. It's nice to have someone to share the blame with.

If I thank my mother, a typical reaction might be "Oh, isn't that sweet!" So let me thank Zippy Kuhl for her beady eye, her sharp tongue, and her infallible nose for flim-flam and hint at the relationship only by saying that it helps a lot to get born into the right family, if you can manage it.

Thanks are not enough to cover the debt I owe Bill Stubbs, my husband, who read and reread and criticized and carped and then started in again on the next version. I hope to find other ways than words to pay him back properly; over a lifetime together, there should be opportunities.

Index

A Note About the Author

A free-lance scholarly and technical editor since 1963, Mary-Claire van Leunen has been a writer of textbooks in English and mathematics, editor of the *Harvard Divinity Bulletin*, and, most recently, technical editor in the Department of Computer Science at Yale University.

A Note on the Type

The text of this book is set in Electra, a type-face designed by W. A. Dwiggins for the Mergenthaler Linotype Company and first made available in 1935. Electra cannot be classified as either "modern" or "old style." It is not based on any historical model, and hence does not echo any particular period or style of type design. It avoids the extreme contrast between "thick" and "thin" elements that marks most modern faces, and is without eccentricities that catch the eye and interfere with reading. In general, Electra is a simple, readable type-face that attempts to give a feeling of fluidity, power, and speed.

Composed by Maryland Linotype,
Baltimore, Maryland.
Printed and bound by
American Book–Stratford Press, Inc.,
Saddle Brook, New Jersey.
Typography and binding design by Virginia Tan.

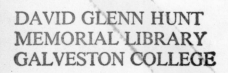
DAVID GLENN HUNT
MEMORIAL LIBRARY
GALVESTON COLLEGE